P9-DTQ-514

Baedeker's

LENINGRAD

Imprint

Cover picture: The Admiralty

111 colour photographs
26 plans and maps; 1 drawing; 1 plan of Metro; 1 large town plan

Editorial work: Baedeker Redaktion
English language edition: Alec Court

Text: Birgit Borowsky

English translation: Wendy Bell

General direction: Dr Peter Baumgarten, Baedeker Stuttgart

Cartography: Franz Kaiser, Singelfingen; Gert Oberländer, Munich; Falk Verlag, Hamburg (large town plan)

Source of illustrations: Borowsky (96); Historia-Photo (7); Kolb (1); Reetz (6); Sperber (1)

Following the tradition established by Karl Baedeker in 1844, sights of particular interest and hotels and restaurants of particular quality are distinguished by either one or two asterisks.

To make it easier to locate the various places listed in the "A to Z" section of the Guide, their coordinates on the large city map are shown at the head of each entry.

Only a selection of hotels, restaurants and shops can be given; no reflection is implied, therefore, on establishments not included.

In a time of rapid change it is difficult to ensure that all the information given is entirely accurate and up to date, and the possibility of error can never be entirely eliminated. Although the publishers can accept no responsibility for inaccuracies and omissions, they are always grateful for corrections and suggestions for improvement.

1st English edition

Licensed user
Mairs Geographischer Verlag GmbH & Co., Ostfildern-Kemnat bei Stuttgart

Reproductions: Gölz Repro-Service GmbH & Co., KG, Ludwigsburg

Printed in Great Britain by Jarrold Printing, Norwich

0 13 056921 6 US and Canada
0 86145 756 0 UK
3 87504–415–0 Germany

Contents

N.B. Russian names and terms used in the guide are given in the English transliteration.

Preface

This pocket guide to Leningrad is one of the new generation of Baedeker guides.

Baedeker pocket guides, illustrated throughout in colour, are designed to meet the needs of the modern traveller. They are quick and easy to consult, with the principal places of interest described in alphabetical order, and the information is presented in a format that is both attractive and easy to follow.

The guide is in three parts. The first part gives a general account of the city, its geography, population, transport and economy, notable personalities, history and architecture. In the second part the places and features of tourist interest are described; the third part contains a variety of practical information. Both the sights and the practical information are listed in alphabetical order.

The Baedeker pocket guides are noted for their concentration on essentials and their convenience of use. They contain numerous specially drawn plans and colour illustrations, and at the end of the book is a large map making it easy to locate the various places described in the "A to Z" section of the guide with the help of the coordinates given at the head of each entry.

Facts and Figures

Historic arms of St. Petersburg

General

Significance

Leningrad, formerly St. Petersburg and Petrograd, is the largest and most important city in the Soviet Union after Moscow. Within the Russian Soviet Federative Socialist Republic it is the chief town in the Leningrad area.
With its uniform Baroque and neo-Classical architecture the "Venice of the North", as the metropolis on the Neva is often called, is one of Europe's most beautiful cities.

Twinning

Since 1957 Leningrad has been twinned with the Hanseatic city of Hamburg. There have also been cultural and sporting links and, most recently, economic exchanges with Dresden, Gothenburg, Rotterdam, Bombay and numerous other European and non-European cities.

Geographical location

Leningrad is located in the Neva delta, 59°57'N 30°20'E, adjoining that part of the Baltic known as the Gulf of Finland. It is the most northern city in the world with over a million inhabitants.
The Neva, 74 km/46 miles long and up to 1300 m/4250 ft wide, flows out of Lake Ladoga, branching in the city into 3 main tributaries: the Great (Bolshaya) Neva, the Little (Malaya) Neva and the Great (Bolshaya) Nevka. Together with numerous smaller branches they form about 40 islands, some of which are only 1 m to 3 m/3ft 3ins to 9ft 10ins above sea-level. The city has always, therefore, lived under the threat of flooding – a threat which has been realised 250 times since it was founded – especially in autumn when the Neva can be transformed into a raging torrent. The Fontanka and the Moyka also flow through the centre of Leningrad; together with the Griboyedov Canal and the Obvodnyy Canal they create a system of waterways reminiscent of Amsterdam.

◀ *Tower of St. Nicholas's Cathedral*

A 25 km/16 mile long flood barrier is planned for the Neva bay. With work having already started on damming the western part of the bay, Leningrad's sewage is no longer able to flow freely away and the lovely Lisiy Nos beach near the city is heavily polluted. Scientists are now trying to remedy the disastrous effects using biological methods of purification.

Climate

Leningrad lies in the maritime, moderately cool west wind zone. The city's climate (see Climate Table in Practical Information: When to go) is controlled by the Baltic Sea, crossed almost unhindered by Atlantic air masses, and by the enormous Eurasian continent, which is hot in summer, cold in winter and has constant high and low pressure areas.
Rapid changes in weather are experienced in every season. Summers are relatively warm, with an average mean temperature in July of 12 °C/54 °F, and not too dry. Really hot days with a maximum of 30 °C/86 °F can occur as early as May, but daily temperature maxima of over 25 °C/77 °F degrees are recorded in September, too.
November to April is very cold, with the lowest temperatures (often below −30 °C/−22 °F) being recorded in midwinter. As a rule there is snow on the ground from December to March. Precipitation fluctuates between 400 mm/16 ins and 800 mm/32 ins, depending on pressure distribution over the Northern Hemisphere. Rainfall maxima are recorded during the thunderstorms which occur between June and September.

View from dome of St. Isaac Cathedral

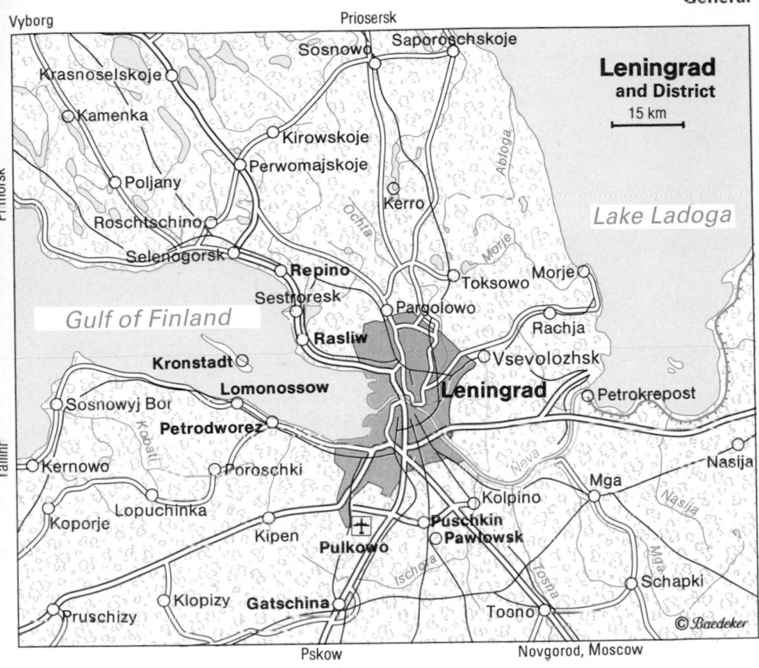

The "White Nights" about the summer solstice (11 June to 2 July), a new experience for people from middle latitudes, are a phenomenon of the northerly latitude on which the city lies. At this time of year it is dark for only about three-quarters of an hour, with bright daylight for the rest of the time. Conversely, about the winter solstice the dark nights are extremely long.

Area and population

There are currently about 4.9 million people living in the Leningrad area which extends over more than 600 sq km/232 sq miles, some 58 sq km/22 sq miles being covered by water. Leningrad has close economic and administrative links with a ring of smaller towns, most of which lie on the rail lines serving the city. The best known of these are the locations of the former imperial summer palaces at Gatchina, Lomonosov (Oranienbaum), Pavlovsk, Petrodvorets (Peterhof) and Pushkin (Tsarskoye Selo).

Administration

Leningrad, the capital of an *Oblast*, that is, an ethnically homogeneous administrative district, is divided into fifteen *rayons*, traditionally known as "sides". The city centre is on the Large or Moscow side, south of the Neva around the Admiralty. From the very earliest days the Vyborg and Petersburg side north of the Neva, and Vasil'yevskiy Island between the Great and the Little Neva were also built up.

Buildings

Leningrad city centre is composed almost entirely of Baroque and neo-Classical buildings. In and around the city

there are some 3000 protected monuments, and about 20% of the USSR's total budget for restoration work goes on their upkeep.
There is, however, another less splendid Leningrad which still resembles the one Dostoievsky described in his novels. Especially around Ploshchad Mira, the former Hay Market, the picture is one of gloomy 19th century tenements with murky backyards. Yet many Leningrad people prefer to live here rather than in the mononotous new housing in the outskirts and the suburbs.

Housing shortage

Although in recent decades huge satellite towns have appeared – and are still appearing – round the city, there is an acute housing shortage. In Leningrad at the moment the norm (the amount of living space per person, excluding kitchen and bathroom, which is calculated for each Soviet city) is 5.5 sq m/59 sq ft. In fact, many families have less than 4 sq m/43 sq ft living space for each member. More than 40% of the population live in community housing, sharing a kitchen and bathroom with other families. The Soviet government is trying to provide every family with a suitably large home, but it is uncertain when this target will be reached.

Population

Trends

The population of St. Petersburg grew dramatically from the time the city was founded: in 1725 the population was already 70,000, in 1784 the figure was 192,000 and in 1835 it was 515,000 (when Moscow only had 300,000 inhabitants). The First World War and the transfer of the capital to Moscow marked a clear turning-point in the population trend. Whereas Petrograd still had 2.4 million inhabitants in 1916, by 1920 the figure had fallen to 722,000. The losses of the First and Second World Wars were, however, soon made good, and by 1959 the population had increased to 3.4 million. In 1970 it stood at 4 million and in 1979 4.6 million; today the figure is 4.9 million and growing.

National groups

Russians make up the majority of Leningrad's population, but there are also Ukrainians, White Russians and people of many other nationalities.

Religion

The constitution of the Soviet Union guarantees its citizens freedom of conscience, i.e. "the right to profess any religion or none, to practise a faith or propagate atheism". Religious propaganda and pastoral activity outside the confines of the church are, however, prohibited.
Estimates of the number of Christians in the USSR belonging to the Russian Orthodox Church range from 20 to 40 millions, but in any case they are a social minority. In Leningrad some 15 Orthodox churches are still in use, Catholic Mass is celebrated in one church, and Baptist services are held in another. There is a mosque and also a synagogue.
The Russian Orthodox Church is financed by contributions from its parishioners, and by its own admission it does not lack funds. This will come as no surprise to anyone who takes part in a Russian Orthodox service and sees just how much is given, especially by elderly people who are themselves living in relative poverty.

Traffic

Streets and bridges

A dense network of roads has opened up the highly industrial Leningrad area.
In the city itself the original layout has been preserved with roads converging radially on the centre. The three main "Prospekts" (Nevsky Prospekt, Ulitsa Dzerzhinskovo and Prospekt Mayorova) were already made very broad when St. Petersburg was founded. Now at rush hours these have almost reached capacity, especially since bottlenecks build up at the many bridges.
In all there are about 300 bridges in the inner city, of which some 20 can be raised to let larger ships through.

Public transport

The most important form of public transport is the Metro, Leningrad's Underground. The first stations were opened in the fifties, and the network of lines is constantly being extended. The fact that Leningrad is built on marshy land created difficulties when tunnelling began, and still does. Only at a depth of 150 m/490 ft was it found to be firm enough to support an underground system. In some parts of the city, however, the nature of the ground made the laying of underground lines impossible and no Metro station could be built near the Hotel Pribaltiskaya for example. The Metro is supplemented by local trams and buses, but there are far too few of them and they are not very comfortable. At peak periods they are impossibly overcrowded.

Leningrad has more bridges than Venice

Shipping

There are regular hydrofoil and river boat services on the Neva throughout the summer half of the year. Ocean-going ships can only pass through the city at night and many of the bridges are raised between 1.30 and 5 a.m. Vasil'yevskiy Island, however, is not at present accessible to shipping. Leningrad's sea and river harbour is one of the most important in the USSR, with an annual turnover of approximately 16 million tonnes.

Rail

Altogether, 12 rail lines converge from all directions on Leningrad's 5 rail termini (see Practical Information).
The city can boast Russia's longest tradition of rail travel, the country's first stretch of line being opened between St. Petersburg, Tsarskoye Selo (now Pushkin) and Pavlovsk in 1837. The first station on the line was Vitebesk in St. Petersburg.

Airports

Leningrad has 3 airports. International flights come into Pulkova II airport, 17 km/11 miles south of the city.

Economy

General

Leningrad is the USSR's largest industrial centre after Moscow. This is, however, something of which most visitors are unaware, since almost all the industry is located outside the inner city. Some industrial installations in the Leningrad area have developed into little towns, such as Kolpino, Kirovsk, etc. However, Leningrad's industrial importance

Finland Station

used to lie – and still does lie – not only in industrial production, but also in passing on know-how. Particularly before and after the Second World War, manufacturing processes were developed in the city and then relocated in smaller, more favourably situated towns, together with machinery and trained personnel.

Branches of industry

Leningrad's industry is mainly labour intensive rather than requiring a heavy input of raw materials. The most important sections traditionally are iron working and electrical engineering. Shipbuilding has also retained its importance and there are several dockyards building tankers, ice-breakers, passenger ships and fishing vessels; the world's first nuclear-powered ice-breaker was launched in Leningrad. The Electrosila works, which employs over 10,000 workers in its main plant alone, produces turbines for the USSR's biggest thermal power and hydro-electric stations. The Kirov works in the south of the city turns out tractors, steam engines, ship's parts and cranes. Leningrad also has textile, leather and chemical industries, with the latter producing raw chemicals and artificial fertilisers, as well as plastics, man-made fibres and pharmaceuticals. Light industry and paper making also play their role.

Joint ventures

Glasnost and perestroika are now showing significant economic results and Leningrad has recently embarked on a number of joint ventures with companies and organisations from abroad.

Agriculture

Leningrad lies in the "podzol" soil zone and effective farming is limited. Recent costly agricultural development schemes (e.g. marshland drainage and forest clearance) have, however, resulted in rising yields, especially in cereals.
Fruit and vegetables are chiefly grown in the south of Leningrad in greenhouses extending over an area of 90 hectares/222 acres. The main crops are tomatoes, lettuce and cucumbers.

Availability of supplies

Leningrad ranks second in the USSR after Moscow so far as the supply of food and consumer goods is concerned. Even so there are long queues for fruit, vegetables and high quality foodstuffs, when these are to be had at all.

Tourism

Since almost every tourist visits at least one of the two historic capitals, Moscow or Leningrad, during a visit to Russia, tourism in the Soviet Union revolves round these two cities. Leningrad does not have nearly enough hotels and restaurants but after 1989 its current total of 6000 beds should be boosted considerably by the renovation work and new building now taking place.

Culture

Although Leningrad had to surrender its leading role in politics to Moscow at the beginning of the century, the two cities continue to vie with one another for cultural supremacy within the USSR.

Academy of Sciences

Higher education

There are currently about 280,000 students studying in Leningrad's 41 institutes of higher education, 22,000 being registered at the Zhdanov State University alone. The university is the country's biggest after Moscow's Lomonosov University, with a correspondingly large faculty of 1700. In addition the Academy of Science maintains a number of institutes in Leningrad, making their contribution to Soviet research.

Museums and libraries

Leningrad has over 50 museums, of which the Hermitage and Russian Museum are by far the most famous.
The people of Leningrad are great readers, with 2500 libraries to choose from. The biggest and best known are the Saltykov-Shchedrin Library, with 22 million volumes, and the Library of the Academy of Sciences.

Theatre and music

Some 25 theatres, 5 large concert halls and various smaller venues in clubs and palaces of culture ensure that a taste for theatre and music is well supplied.
The Leningrad Kirov Ballet is famous the world over, while the Vaganova Ballet School, directed from 1934 to 1941 by Agrippina Vaganova, trains a constant stream of new dancers. Vaganova developed a system for teaching classical ballet that is widely used, not only in the USSR.

Notable Personalities

Joseph Brodsky (born 24.5.1940) Russian-American poet

When Joseph Brodsky – actually Iossif Brodskiy – received the Nobel Prize in 1987 he suddenly found himself world famous.
Brodsky, who now lives in the USA, was born in Leningrad in 1940. As a young man he was already in conflict with the Soviet authorities and was sent to prison camp in 1964 for his "parasitic life style"; he was pardoned in 1965, then exiled in 1972. Since then Brodsky has lived in New York where he lectures at several universities. He continues to be a poet and essayist, and a translator.
Brodsky, who calls himself a bad Russian and a bad Jew but a good poet, sees poetry as an end in itself, man's aesthetic destination. In his writings, such as "Memories of Leningrad" he also analyses the experiences of his Leningrad childhood and youth.

Fyodor Dostoievsky (11.11.1821–9.2.1881) Russian novelist

Fyodor M. Dostoievsky was born in Moscow in 1821, the son of a doctor. From 1838 to 1843 he studied at the Military Engineers' Institute in St. Petersburg, then worked from 1844 as a free-lance writer. His first novel "Poor People" published in 1846 as a series of letters, was extremely successful, and was followed by short stories including "White Nights" (1848). Dostoievsky's arrest for conspiracy in 1849 was a turning-point. Facing death, his sentence was commuted at the last moment to four years' exile, although he was not allowed to return to St. Petersburg until 1859. His great novels, including "Crime and Punishment", "The Possessed" and "The Brothers Karamazov" appeared between 1860 and 1880, but even so, apart from the last years of his life, he was permanently plagued by money worries which also forced him into a long stay abroad. Dostoievsky lived in 17 different flats in Leningrad. The last of these, where he wrote "The Brothers Karamazov" and where he died, has been turned into a museum. St. Petersburg is very much present in his work, especially in "Crime and Punishment".

Catherine the Great (II) (2.5.1729–6.11.1796) Empress of Russia

Catherine the Great is one of the most controversial figures in Russian history, posterity's judgements on her ranging from "a model ruler" to "the whore on the throne of Czars" and "the most evil of evil women".
Sophie Auguste Frederike von Anhalt-Zerbst was born on 2 May 1729 in Stettin. At the age of 15 she went to St. Petersburg for the first time, to be married to the heir to the Russian throne, the future Peter III. After her conversion to Russian Orthodoxy she was called Catherine Alexeyevna. The marriage proved to be anything but happy. Peter III was more interested in dolls and playing at soldiers than he was in his wife. In July 1762 Catherine succeeded in ridding herself of the husband she hated. He was forced to abdicate and his murder was sanctioned shortly afterwards.
Catherine, now absolute monarch, liked to appear to the world as a cultured person influenced by the ideas of the "Enlightenment". In 1767 she convened a legislative commission to consider sweeping reforms. None of its liberal proposals were ever set in train, but it was prevailed upon to offer the Empress the title of "the Great", which she

Fyodor M. Dostolevsky

Catherine the Great

Vladimir Lenin

gladly accepted. Under her rule social disparities in Russia intensified, and while the situation of the peasant serfs deteriorated, the privileges of the nobility increased. The abolition of conscription by Peter III in 1762 was reaffirmed in 1785. The general popular discontent was expressed in the Pugachov Uprising of 1773/74, to which the Empress reacted with characteristic harshness.
On the military front she could boast impressive successes. Two wars against the Turks gave Russia possession of the Crimea and other tracts of land reaching to the Black Sea coast, Poland was occupied and there was also a victory against Sweden.
A good proportion of her own memoirs and of the many biographies published about her, is taken up with her love affairs. She did indeed have many amorous adventures throughout her life and several lovers of long standing, including Count Orlov, her gifts to whom included the estate at Gatchina, and Prince Potemkin, on whom she bestowed the Tauride Palace. The latter also remained her close political adviser until his death in 1791
On 6 November 1796 Catherine the Great died suddenly of a stroke. Paul I, the son she never loved, succeeded her.

Vladimir I. Lenin (1870–1924) Soviet politician

Lenin, founder of the world's first Soviet state, a giant figure who changed the face of international politics in the 20th century, was born on 10 April 1870 in Simbirsk (now Ulyanovsk), the son of a school inspector named Ulyanov. He was given the name Lenin later during his period of exile in Siberia.
A happy childhood in a strictly religious household and a successful school career came to an end in 1886 with the death of his father. Fifteen months later his elder brother Alexander was hanged in the St. Petersburg fortress of Schlüsselburg as a member of a revolutionary group which had planned to assassinate Tzar Alexander III. Vladimir Ilyich's sheltered life in a Lutheran family home was now at an end: as he wrote subsequently "My way in life was marked out for me by my brother."
The rest of the family moved to Kazan where Vladimir Ilyich became a student at the University, but after taking part in student demonstrations he was exiled to Kokushkino. In

1891 he was allowed to sit the State examinations at St. Petersburg University as an external student, taking his degree in the following year. He was then employed as an assistant to a St. Petersburg solicitor, but most of his energies went into political activity.
In 1894 Lenin published his first work, "What are the 'Friends of the People'?", a critical analysis of the populist movement. In 1895, during visits to Germany, France and Switzerland, he established his first contacts with Russian exiles, and in the autumn of that year he founded the St. Petersburg League of the Struggle for the Emancipation of the Working Class. He was soon arrested and spent the years 1897–1900 in exile in Siberia, where he married Nadezhda Krupskaya in July 1898.
From 1900 to 1905 Lenin lived outside Russia. In 1902 he published (in Stuttgart) his "What is to be done?", in which he called for an organisation of professional revolutionaries. The Marxist party he had in mind must act as the vanguard of the working class; a socialist consciousness must be introduced into the masses from outside. At a congress held in London in 1903 the Social Democratic Workers' Party of Russia was split into the Bolsheviks (those in the majority) who supported Lenin and the Mensheviks (the minority) who supported Martov. With the support of the Bolsheviks Lenin became *de facto* leader of the party. After returning to Russia during the revolutionary uprising of 1905 Lenin spent a further period in exile from 1907 to 1917, during which time the Bolsheviks consolidated their position as the leaders of a future revolution. On 16 April 1917, after the outbreak of the February Revolution, Lenin returned to Petrograd (as St. Petersburg was now called) where he was given a triumphal reception by the workers. In the same month he published his "April Theses", in which he saw the Russian Revolution as a prologue to world revolution.
Under Lenin's leadership the Bolsheviks seized power on 25 October (7 November). He was elected head of the revolutionary government and, in spite of being crippled by two strokes (in 1922 and 1923), continued as leader of the party until his death. He died on 21 January 1924 of cerebral sclerosis, brought on, according to the official medical report, by "excessive intellectual activity". His embalmed body can be seen in the Lenin Mausoleum in Moscow's Red Square.

Mikhail W. Lomonosov
(19.11.1711–15.4.1765)
Russian scientist and poet

Mikhail W. Lomonosov, the much-quoted intellectual and co-founder of the University of Moscow, lived and worked in St. Petersburg.
Lomonosov came from a Russian peasant family. He left his home village on the White Sea as a teenager and was admitted to the Slav, Greek and Latin Academy in Moscow, transferring later to the Academic Gymnasium or High School in St. Petersburg, and then continuing his education in Marburg and Freiburg (in Saxony). After five years he returned to St. Petersburg where he worked from then on at the Academy of Science housed at that time in the Kunstkamera. In 1745 Lomonosov was appointed Russia's first professor of chemistry, but he was just as intensely concerned with physics, astronomy, and Russian grammar and literature. He also found time to take an interest in a project for a glass and mosaic factory, which was eventually set up

near Oranienbaum. Not inappropriately the whole place, small town as well as summer palace, is now called Lomonosov.

In honour of the "father of Russian science and of Russian grammar and literature" as he is known in the Soviet Union, Lomonosov's workrooms in the Kunstkamera have been turned into a museum.

Peter the Great (I)
(30.5.1672–28.1.1725) Tsar of Russia

In Leningrad the memory of Peter the Great, the founder of the city, is still very much alive. Couples getting married have their photographs taken at his monument in the Square of the Decembrists, and there are always flowers on his sarcophagus in the Cathedral of SS Peter and Paul.

Peter the Great's childhood and youth were dominated by wrangling about the throne. Little attention was given to his education, and so he devoted himself all the more to playing at soldiers and to navigation. Following the death of his half-brother Fyodor in 1682, he and his feeble-minded half-brother Ivan V were adjudged joint successors to the throne, their sister Sophia acting as regent until 1689 since the two young Tsars were not yet of age. When Ivan died in 1696 Peter became sole ruler. In 1697/98 he travelled incognito to Riga, Amsterdam, Vienna and other cities in Europe, an experience which had a great influence on his personal development.

On his return he set out to combat Russia's backwardness by encouraging a thorough rapprochement with the West, and by securing equality of political status with other European countries. The founding of St. Petersburg in 1703 can be seen as part of this process. During the rest of his reign he issued over 3000 ukases (imperial edicts). These did not lead to a unified programme of reform, however, but rather to a series of adjustments to suit changing needs (the creation of a "service nobility", replacement of the Patriarch by a Synod and the Ecclesiastical Council by a Senate, the establishment of a powerful navy, and the introduction of western European clothing, etc.). Through his military successes (in particular victory over Sweden in the Northern War) he made Russia the dominant power in the Baltic region.

Despite Peter the Great's ability as a statesman and commander-in-chief, there are many question-marks raised by his personality. He was capable of extreme cruelty, especially to those close to him: he condemned his own son Alexey to death (though the young man died before the sentence was carried out), and he once presented Catherine I, his wife and successor, with the preserved head of one of her lovers.

It is certainly not on account of his personal attributes therefore that Peter I can be termed "Great", but rather because of the radical changes he instigated. He took Russia a crucial step along the road from a primitive agrarian society to an internationally recognised and, in economic terms, comparatively strong 18th c. monarchy run by the nobility and a bureaucracy.

Alexander Pushkin
(26.5.1799–29.1.1837)
Russian poet

A visitor to Leningrad cannot avoid being introduced to Pushkin: monuments, museums, squares, culture centres and even a small town are reminders of the poet, deemed the creator of Russian literature. Poetry dominates his work, but he also wrote a few plays and particularly after 1830 turned to prose.

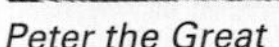

Peter the Great

Alexander N. Pushkin

Dmitry D. Shostakovich

Alexander S. Pushkin, born in Moscow on 26 May 1799, had close ties with St. Petersburg throughout his life, ties which find repeated expression in his work. From 1811 to 1817 he attended the Lyceum, Tsarist Russia's most famous school for the nobility, only a few kilometres from St. Petersburg in Tsarkoye Selo (now Pushkin). Among the friends he made here were some of those who later took part in the Decembrists' Uprising. In 1820 he was forced to leave St. Petersburg on account of his many satirical and political poems, remaining in exile until1826. After that he lived mostly in Moscow and St. Petersburg, his work being subject to the personal censorship of the Tsar. He was only allowed to publish his writings after a certain period of time had elapsed and was constantly short of money, a problem made worse by his high living. Periods of deep depression alternated with phases of excessive *joie de vivre*. There is no knowing how many loves there were in his life.
Even after his marriage in 1831 things went far from smoothly. The couple who had four children, lived first in Tsarkoye Selo, then mostly in St. Petersburg. Married to a woman whose beauty was much admired, not least by Tsar Nicholas I, attacks on his wife's virtue forced Pushkin to take part in a duel on 27 January 1837 in which he was fatally wounded. He died two days later in his apartment on the Moyka at No. 12 (now a museum). His body was taken secretly from the house and interred in the Svyatogorsk Monastery.

Bartolomeo Francesco Rastrelli (about 1700–29.11.1771) Russian-Italian architect

Bartolomeo Francesco Rastrelli, one of the most prestigious of St. Petersburg's architects, was born about 1700 probably in Paris. He first arrived in the Russian capital in 1716 with his father, the sculptor and architect Carlo Rastrelli. He began his studies under his father, and then spent a considerable time in France and Italy continuing them.
After his return to Russia in about 1730 he received his first commission from the Empress Anna Ivanovna. Under the Empress Elizabeth I he was the court's most active and influential architect, also accepting commissions from private clients. He was responsible for many exceptionally splendid buildings in and around St. Petersburg (the

Winter Palace, the Catherine Palace in Tsarkoye Selo, Smolny Convent and Stroganov Palace, among others), and played a decisive role in establishing the Russian Baroque style (see Architecture).
Rastrelli's designs were not to the taste of Catherine the Great, who assumed power in 1762. Angered, he left St. Petersburg and went to Warsaw. He died in 1771 in Courland, in the palace he had built in 1735/40 for the Duke Biron, Anna Ivanovna's lover.

Ilya E. Repin (5.8.1844–29.9.1930) Russian painter

Ilya E. Repin, who was born in Chuguyev, is the foremost representative of the Russian Realist School. His scenes from everyday life, historical paintings and portraits not only gained him recognition but also struck a chord in Russia and abroad. In 1873, after studying at the Academy of Arts in St. Petersburg, Repin painted his best-known work, the "Volga Boatmen" (now in the Russian Museum). His realism caused a sensation in the art world of the day and was soon taken up by the 'Peredvizhniki' (or "Itinerants"). Although the official press criticised his "profanation of painting" his stature was nevertheless recognised and he was awarded a grant to study abroad, mainly in Paris (1873/76). On his return to Russia Repin joined the artists' colony in Abramtsevo near Moscow, which was calling for social and artistic reform. From 1884 to 1907 he taught at the St. Petersburg Academy (becoming a professor in 1893).
After 1899 Repin spent part of his time on his country estate "Penaty", at Kuokkala (now Repino) 45 km/28 miles from Leningrad, later making it his permanent home. He is buried there and his former house has been turned into a museum, with some of his paintings on show. Most of his works, however, are either in the Tretyakov Gallery in Moscow or, of course, the Russian Museum in Leningrad. These include "The Zaporozhets Cossacks writing a letter to the Turkish Sultan", "The Meeting of the State Council", and numerous portraits.

Carlo I. Rossi (29.12.1775–18.4.1849) Russian-Italian architect

Carlo I. Rossi was the outstanding exponent of Alexandrian neo-Classical architecture, as Rastrelli was of Russian Baroque. Rossi was born in Naples, the son of an Italian ballet dancer. In Russia the wildest rumours circulated about his parentage; it was even suggested that his father might be Tsar Paul I.
Rossi completed his studies under the architect Brenna, and assisted him at Gatchina and Pavlovsk, broadening his experience with a stay in Italy from 1801 to 1803. Subsequently he was employed mainly in Moscow, only entering the service of the St. Petersburg court in 1816. In the years that followed he was responsible for many superb buildings and also proved an exceptionally gifted town-planner. Among his designs are the Square of the Arts and its surrounding buildings, the General Staff Building on Palace Square, the former Alexandra Theatre (now the Pushkin Theatre) and the street behind it, which was later named after him.
Rossi's final projects were completed in the early 1830s. He then withdrew from public life, though he continued to live in St. Petersburg where he died in 1849.

Dmitry D. Shostakovich (25.9.1906–9.8.1975) Russian composer
Born in St. Petersburg the composer Dmitry Shostakovich studied at the Petrograd Conservatoire from 1919 to 1930. From 1939 to 1958 he taught music in what had become Leningrad, then from 1943 to 1948 he worked in Moscow. The Symphony No. 1 in F minor (1926) was his first success. Works such as the Leningrad or Seventh Symphony, first performed in the Large Philharmonia Concert Hall which now bears his name, won him recognition as the outstanding Soviet composer of his day.

History of Leningrad

Dating

On 1 January 1700 as part of his programme of Westernization Peter the Great introduced the Julian calendar in place of the Byzantine one. The Gregorian calendar was not introduced into Russia until 14 February 1918. By 1 March 1900 the difference between the Julian calender still in use in Russia and the Gregorian calender long since adopted throughout western Europe had increased to 13 days. Thus the October Revolution took place on 25 October according to the Julian calendar, but on 7 November according to the Gregorian one.
The dates given below follow the Julian calendar until the reform of the calendar in Russia in 1918.

1703

The history of Leningrad, or St. Petersburg, begins on 16 May 1703, the day when the foundation-stone of the Peter and Paul Fortress is laid.
At the beginning of the same month the Russians under Sheremetyev have advanced to the mouth of the Neva and captured the Nyenshants Fortress. It is on this land, inhabited only by a few Finnish peasants, that Peter the Great decides to build the city which he names after his patron saint, St. Peter. (Old documents and maps also show the Dutch "St. Petersburgh" or "St. Petersburch" beside the German "St. Petersburg".) The construction of the city encounters enormous physical and political problems. Costly large-scale drainage is necessary before anything at all can be built on the boggy terrain of the Neva delta. In addition up until 1721, Russia is fighting the Northern War with Sweden, in the course of which there are several skirmishes in the immediate vicinity of the newly founded imperial capital. Nevertheless Peter the Great chooses this site primarily because of its potential as a harbour, and also because it connects with the Russian river system inland. Another important factor is its nearness to western Europe since Peter the Great is concerned, as Pushkin put it, to open up "a window on Europe".

1704

The fact that work on building the Admiralty has already started in 1704 shows how much importance Peter the Great attaches to building a navy. In the same year work begins on the Summer Garden.
The city is given additional protection by the Kronstadt Fortress on the island of Kotlin at the mouth of the Neva.

1706

A special commission assumes control of all building in St. Petersburg.

1707

In Peterhof (now Petrodvorets) the first modest buildings are going up for the Tsar's summer palace.

1709

The city can be regarded as largely secure following the defeat of the Swedes at Poltava.

1710

Everything possible is done to press on with the construction of the city. It is decreed that every inhabitant must supply 100 building stones a year, or pay a large fine.

Tsars of Russia since the founding of St. Petersburg

Name	Year of Birth (birthplace)	Reigned
Peter I, The Great	1672 (Moscow)	1682/1689–1725; (Sophia acts as Regent until 1689; he rules jointly with his feeble-minded brother Ivan V).
Catherine I	1684 (in Lithuania)	1725–1727
Peter II	1715 (St. Petersburg)	1727–1730
Anna Ivanovna	1693 (Moscow)	1730–1740
Ivan VI	1740 (Moscow)	1740/1741 (His mother acts as Regent; he is assassinated in 1764)
Elizabeth I	1709 (Moscow)	1741–1761
Peter III	1728 (Kiel)	1761/1762 (assassinated)
Catherine II, The Great	1729 (Stettin)	1762–1796
Paul I	1754 (St. Petersburg)	1796–1801 (assassinated)
Alexander I	1777 (St. Petersburg)	1801–1825
Nicholas I	1796 (Tsarkoye Selo)	1825–1855
Alexander II	1818 (Moscow)	1855–1881 (assassinated)
Alexander III	1845 (St. Petersburg)	1881–1894
Nicholas II	1868 (Tsarkoye Selo)	1894–1917 (assassinated 1918)

1711

Work begins on laying a road (the Nevsky Prospect as it becomes known in 1788) from the Admiralty to the Alexander Nevsky Monastery (founded 1710).

1712

Peter the Great declares St. Petersburg capital of the Russian Empire.

1712–1716

Throughout this period 50,000 people are permanently engaged in the building of St. Petersburg. Few come to the swampy, mosquito-ridden area of their own free will. Serfs are ordered there and forced labour camps are set up. The members of the nobility are also reluctant to come to the new capital.

History of Leningrad

1714	An imperial ukase forbids building in stone anywhere in Russia except in St. Petersburg (not repealed until 1741).
1717	The plan of St. Petersburg drafted by the architect Leblond envisages the city centred on Vasil'yevskiy Island, with the imperial palace in the middle. However it proves quite impracticable to raise the ground level sufficiently and the plan has to be abandoned.
1725	When Peter the Great dies in 1725 St. Petersburg already has 70,000 inhabitants.
1727	After Peter II, a grandson of Peter the Great, is proclaimed Tsar, the seat of the imperial court is transferred to Moscow.
1732	The reigning Empress Anna Ivanovna, a daughter of Ivan V, designates St. Petersburg capital of the Russian Empire once again. It retains this status until 1918.
1754–1762	In 1754 the Empress Elizabeth commissions her favourite architect Rastrelli to build the fourth (and present) Winter Palace.
1764	The foundations of the Hermitage collection are laid in the Winter Palace by the purchase of a large collection of paintings in Germany. The Smolny Institute in St. Petersburg, founded in the same year, is the first Russian higher educational establishment for the daughters of the nobility.

Festivities on the Neva in May 1863

1801 — A State iron foundry is set up to manufacture firearms. By the end of the century it has become an important metallurgical and mechanical engineering concern (now the Kirov Works).

1811 — In Tsarkoye Selo (now Pushkin) the Lyceum opens, a school specially founded to prepare children of the nobility for important positions in the civil service. The school, which Pushkin attends as one of its first pupils, is later moved to St. Petersburg in 1843.

1819 — The main Institute of Education is reorganised and becomes St. Petersburg University, with three faculties initially.

1824 — On 7 November the Neva reaches its highest recorded level, over 4 m/13 ft above normal. Thousands of people are drowned and countless houses are washed away in the devastating floods.

1825 — Following the sudden death of Alexander I in November, there is doubt about which of his brothers, Konstantin or Nicholas, will succeed him. This uncertainty provides an opportunity for an attempted putsch by a group of officer conspirators, who have been preparing for some time under cover of various secret societies. On 14 December some 3000 soldiers who have refused to swear the oath of allegiance to the new Tsar, Nicholas, gather in Senate Square (now Square of the Decembrists). Within a few

hours the Decembrists' Uprising is put down by loyal Tsarist troops.
The leaders of the revolt are imprisoned in the Peter and Paul Fortress and executed in July 1826.

1835 The population of St. Petersburg reaches 515,000; Moscow's population on the other hand is still only about 300,000.

1837 Russia's first railway line is opened between St. Petersburg and Tsarkoye Selo.

1852 The Hermitage art collection is opened to a wider public as a museum.

1876 The first social revolutionary demonstration on Russian soil takes place in front of the Kazan Cathedral. Those taking part are put on trial.

1895 Lenin and Starkov together found the "Union for the Struggle for the Liberation of the Working Class" in St. Petersburg.

1898 The Russian Museum, founded in 1895, is opened in the Mikhail Palace.

1905 At the very beginning of the year a strike at the Putilov Works (now the Kirov Works) ends in an uprising in which the whole of St. Petersburg takes part. On 9 January, the day that is to go down in history as "Bloody Sunday", there is a mass demonstration in front of the Winter Palace. Nicholas II orders his troops to open fire on the workers who only want to present him with a petition. Hundreds are killed.
During the year, first in St. Petersburg and then in other parts of the Empire, strike committees come together to form soviets, the councils that gradually develop into organs of proletarian self-government.

1914 At the start of the First World War St. Petersburg is renamed Petrograd.

1917 During the war food in Petrograd is in increasingly short supply. In February unrest turns into a general strike. When the Petrograd garrison mutinies as well and joins the demonstrators, the abdication of Nicholas II is inevitable. The so-called First Provisional Government assumes power. Tsar Nicholas and his family are imprisoned in Tsarkoye Selo until July.
With the official help of the German government Lenin returns to Petrograd from Zürich, arriving on 3 April. In his "April Theses", published the following day, he calls for an end to the war, a republic of the worker soviets, and control by the soviets of the means of production and distribution.
The provisional government also proves unable to resolve the shortage of supplies, but embarks nevertheless on a new offensive at the front, which is doomed to failure from the outset.
Mainly owing to war-weariness the Bolsheviks under Lenin's leadership finally manage to gain the upper hand (in 1903 Russia's Social Democratic Workers' Party had split

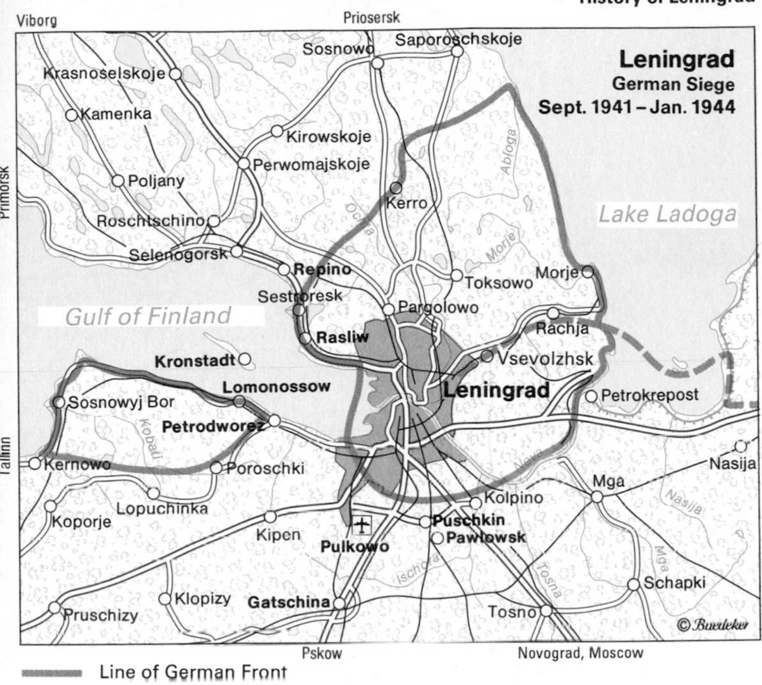

into Bolsheviks, i.e. those in the majority, and Mensheviks, those in the minority). On the night of 24/25 October (6/7 November) the Bolsheviks occupy strategic points in the city; the provisional government retreats to the Winter Palace. The following night the battlecruiser "Aurora" gives the signal to start storming the Winter Palace and the ministers of the provisional government are arrested.

1918 The peace treaty of Brest-Litovsk is signed following a renewed offensive that brings German troops very close to Petrograd. Fearing that the capital is in imminent danger of attack the Soviet government transfers to Moscow.

1920 The population of Petrograd, which in 1916 was still 2.4 million, has fallen to only 722,000.

1924 Following Lenin's death on 21 January, Petrograd is renamed Leningrad on 27 January.

1927 Leningrad becomes the regional capital of the Russian Soviet Federative Socialist Republic.

1936 A new development plan proposes extending the streets leading southwards from the city centre and connecting them by new ring roads.

History of Leningrad

1941–1944

Warning of artillery fire on the Nevsky Prospekt

On 22 June German troops start the assault on Leningrad. Schlüsselburg is taken on 8 September, followed by Peterhof (now Petrodvorets) on 12 September. The city is finally encircled by German troops who embark on a war of attrition against the Soviet troops lasting until January 1944. During this time the people of Leningrad suffer extreme deprivation. Not only do they have to endure daily artillery fire, they also experience terrible starvation and, in winter, terrible cold as well. The city's "lifeline", the only route by which supplies of food and fuel can be brought in, is via Lake Ladoga. Even so provisions for the population are totally inadequate. The daily bread ration for children and those not actively employed is 125 g/less than 4.5 oz. Corpses are an everyday sight on the streets of Leningrad. The greatest losses occur between December 1941 and April 1942 during which period about a 3500 people die of hunger every day.
The successful Soviet counter offensive begins on 15 January 1944. Following the recapture of Gatchina and Oranienbaum (now Lomonosov) the German troops withdraw. On 27 January 1944, after 900 days, the blockade of Leningrad ends.

1955

The first section of the Leningrad Metro is opened.

1959

The world's first nuclear-powered ice-breaker is built in Leningrad.

1965

For its fortitude during the blockade the honorary title of Heroic City is conferred on Leningrad by the Soviet government.

1975

The Monument to the Heroic Defenders of Leningrad is unveiled in Victory Square. It is financed partly by the State and partly through the voluntary labour of the people of Leningrad.

1987

In Leningrad, the "cradle of three revolutions", the seventieth anniversary of the October Revolution is celebrated in grand style; the cruiser "Aurora" and the Museum of the October Revolution are renovated in honour of the occasion.

1988

A fire in the Academy of Sciences destroys or damages over three million books and periodicals, some of which are irreplaceable. The Soviet press descibes the event as "our cultural Chernobyl".

Architecture

No other major European city grew up in quite so deliberate and preconceived a fashion as Leningrad. Peter the Great created the city out of nothing at the beginning of the 18th c., and the programme of building he inaugurated was carried on at such a pace that, within 50 years of its foundation, the Russian capital as it then was had become a metropolis comparable to Paris, Vienna or Rome.
The Tsars brought Europe's foremost architects and artists to St. Petersburg, Italians, Frenchmen, Dutchmen and Germans whose Baroque and neo-Classical buildings give the city its imposing west European character. The development of the capital continued at the same speed and on the same grand scale until the middle of the 19th century. Since then, however, there has been no building of comparable magnificence.
Urban development in Leningrad can be divided into eight phases:

Early Baroque (Beginning of the 18th c.)

In utilising architectural forms from western Europe in their designs for the new imperial palaces, the architects responsible for the creation of St. Petersburg were forced to adapt to both the landscape and their patrons' tastes. They erected functional buildings with simple ground-plans and relatively plain façades. Any exterior ornamentation scarcely projected at all, vertical articulation being limited to flat pilasters (columns connected to the wall, consisting of a base, shaft and capital) or strips (like pilasters but without base or capital). Much use, however, was made of colour, façades being generally painted in two tones. Warm red walls contrasting with white window frames, pilasters, etc. was a frequently used combination.
One of the first architects to be brought to St. Petersburg was Domenico Trezzini (*c.* 1670–1734) who was involved in the construction of the Peter and Paul Fortress, the Summer Palace, the Twelve Colleges and the Alexander Nevsky Monastery. The German architects Andreas Schülter (*c.* 1660–1714), Johann Braunstein and Gottfried Schdel (1680–1752), the Frenchman Jean Baptiste Leblond (1679–1719) and the Italians Giovanni Maria Fontana and Gaetano Chiaveri (1689–1770) also designed buildings in St. Petersburg, as well as at Peterhof, Tsarskoye Selo and Oranienbaum. With the exception of the Menshikov Palace and the Kikin Palace little of their work survives.

Russian Baroque (Mid-18th c.)

As the 18th c. progressed the Tsars and Russian nobility attached increasing importance to their palaces as symbols of power and influence. In consequence ground-plans became more complex, many buildings such as the Smolny Convent and the Winter Palace being designed round enclosed quadrangles. Almost all the palaces of the period have façades articulated by full-height projections extending in front of the building-line. The façades are further broken up by columns, half columns, pilasters, pediments and elaborate window-frames, while corners are emphasised by more columns, often in clusters. Colour came to be given even greater architectural prominence than before, three different shades on the same building being quite usual. Turquoise, azure and deep green were the most frequently used colours, window-frames, etc. remaining white. Ornamental features such as statues and vases along the roofs were often brought into relief in gold or olive.

Unlike its Italian counterpart, Russian Baroque is mainly represented in secular architecture. Some churches were also built, however, the traditional Early Russian arrangement of five domes being incorporated into the Baroque design. The positioning and appearance of the domes varies from church to church. Sometimes they are grouped closely together, as on the Smolny Convent, sometimes spread far apart, as on St. Nicholas's Cathedral. Elsewhere, as on the palace church of the Catherine Palace at Tsarkoye Selo, the domes serve no more than a decorative purpose. The dominant influence on Russian Baroque architecture was Bartolemeo Francesco Rastrelli (see Notable Personalities). Throughout Russia the nobility copied his work in their buildings, "azure walls in a array of white columns". In and around St. Petersburg Rastrelli was responsible for the Winter Palace, the Great Palace at Peterhof, the Catherine Palace at Tsarkoye Selo, the Smolny Convent, and the Stroganov Palace and others. Savva I. Chevakinsky (1713–*c.* 1783), whose greatest achievement was St. Nicholas's Cathedral, was also an influential exponent of the Russian Baroque style.

Late Baroque with neo-Classical elements (1760s and 1770s)

Neo-Classical architecture made its appearance in St. Petersburg in the 1760s when, at first, Baroque and neo-Classical features were combined. The leading architects of the period, Vasily I. Bazhenov (1737–1794), Jean Baptiste Vallin de la Mothe (1729–1800), Antonio Rinaldi (1709–1794) and Yuriy Velten (1730–1801) designed buildings with heavily articulated façades, both vertically and horizontally,

Winter Palace – the zenith of Russian Baroque

but with relatively little in the way of sculptured ornamentation. Examples of the style are the Academy of Arts, the Large Department Store, the Small Hermitage, and St. Catherine's Church on Nevsky Prospekt.

Late neo-Classicism (Late 18th c.)

Neo-Classicism reached the peak of its influence in the 1780s and 1790s. As in ancient Greek and Roman building the arrangement of columns came to dominate the architecture, no longer serving a purely decorative purpose but fulfilling a structural role as well. The central sections of buildings are almost always accentuated by a columned portico (usually projecting) crowned by a triangular pediment. Side wings, too, are decorated with porticos, but with half columns or pilasters reflecting their secondary importance. Ground-plans are based on simple geometric figures and sculptured ornamentation is almost totally lacking, window- and door-frames being very plain. Colouring is also very restrained, commonly a pale yellow or grey against which the white columns and window frames hardly stand out.

The style of the period, sometimes known as "Sentimentalist neo-Classicism", embodied an attempt to harmonise buildings with the landscape. Particularly successful examples can be seen in the great parks of the imperial summer palaces outside St. Petersburg.

Giacomo Quarenghi (1744–1817) and Charles Cameron (1743–1812) were the leading architects of the period. Quarenghi built the Academy of Sciences, the Smolny Institute and the Assignatsionnyy Bank, while Cameron was entrusted by Catherine the Great with numerous projects at Pavlovsk and Tsarkoye Selo. The work of Ivan Starov (*c.* 1743–1808) is also of significance in the period, his buildings, especially the Tauride Palace, being distinguished by their unconventional design.

Architecture

Alexandrian neo-Classicism (Beginning of the 19th c.)

The power and status attained by Russia under Alexander I is reflected in its buildings. As elsewhere in Europe, architects in St. Petersburg no longer almost exclusively invoked Roman traditions, increasingly drawing their inspiration from the Greek originals, especially the Doric style. The new emphasis was on simplicity, size and starkness. As in the Greek Peripteros Temples, columns become heavier and squatter, sometimes completely surrounding the building as they do for example in the Exchange. Windows have no frames, being no more than rectangular slits. Large reliefs gain in decorative importance, especially reliefs with military themes like the victory over Napoleon in 1812, well illustrated by the Admiralty which Andrey Zakharov (1761–1811) completely rebuilt. The Imperial Stables and the barracks for the Paul I regiment, both designed by Vasily Stasov (1769–1849), successfully combine elegance and functionality, typifying his very economical use of architectural detail.
In contrast to previous decades, the preoccupation was no longer with individual buildings but rather with coordination of the whole. Thomas de Thoman's (1754–1813) Exchange, for example, is the focal point of a magnificent ensemble of city buildings. The truly outstanding urban architect of the period, however, was unquestionably Carlo Rossi (see Notable Personalities). As well as Palace Square, Senate Square and the Square of the Arts, Rossi was responsible for the design of an almost complete district around the former Alexandra Theatre.
In the 1830s Neo-Classicism began gradually to decline, its use becoming stereotyped and a mere matter of form. An example can be seen in St Isaçac's Cathedral, built by August Ricard de Montferrand (1798–1877).

Historicism (Last thirty years of the 19th/beginning of the 20th c.)

In Russia, as in Europe generally, neo-Classicism gave way to eclecticism. The leading St. Petersburg architects of the period, Andrey Y. Stakenschneider (1802–1865), Alexander P. Bryullov (1798–1877) and Konstantin A. Thon (1794–1881), designed buildings in a variety of styles (neo-Romantic, neo-Gothic, neo-Renaissance and neo-Baroque), examples of which include the Belosel'skiy-Belozerskiy Palace, the Kirov Theatre, the Moscow Station and the pavilions in the Alexandria Park at Peterhof. Many of the buildings appear extravagant in form, and occasionally in size. Sometimes, too, a single structure has features drawn from different architectural periods.
In other parts of the country there was also something of a revival of early Russian architecture. St. Petersburg, however, remained largely unaffected by it, the only major exception being the Church of the Resurrection.The beginning of the 20th century saw a return to the trusted principles of neo-Classicism. The buildings which resulted are often stylistically very successful, making use of modern construction methods and materials including reinforced concrete and glass.

Art nouveau (*c.* 1900)

There are few buildings in St. Petersburg strictly representative of *art nouveau*, or "the style moderne" as it is known in Russia. The Comedy Theatre on Nevsky Prospekt is one example. Typical are unconventionality of design, windows of various shapes and sizes, and façades which have received different treatments. As well as rendering, some of the buildings are faced with fragments of stone or brick.

Constructivism (1920s)

Following the October Revolution Constructivism became the dominant movement in Russian architecture, seeking a unity of form and function. Well-designed buildings such as the Gorky Palace of Culture were erected on the outskirts of what had become Petrograd (and was soon to become Leningrad), built in functional materials and intended to serve the needs of the people.

Neo-Classicism in the Stalin era (1930s and 1950s)

During the Stalin era architecture stagnated. Following basically neo-Classical principles, huge blocks of flats were constructed like those which can now be seen on Leningrad's Moscow Prospekt .

Today and in the future

Throughout the 1960s and 1970s Leningrad experienced an unusually large expansion of building. In the once outlying communities around the city enormous housing estates mushroomed. Even so the target of 9 sq m^2/95 sq ft^2 of living space per person is still to be achieved. Inevitably, therefore, the city will continue to expand in the decades to come, especially to the north where ever-more drab dormitory towns will be established.

Plan of the Inner City

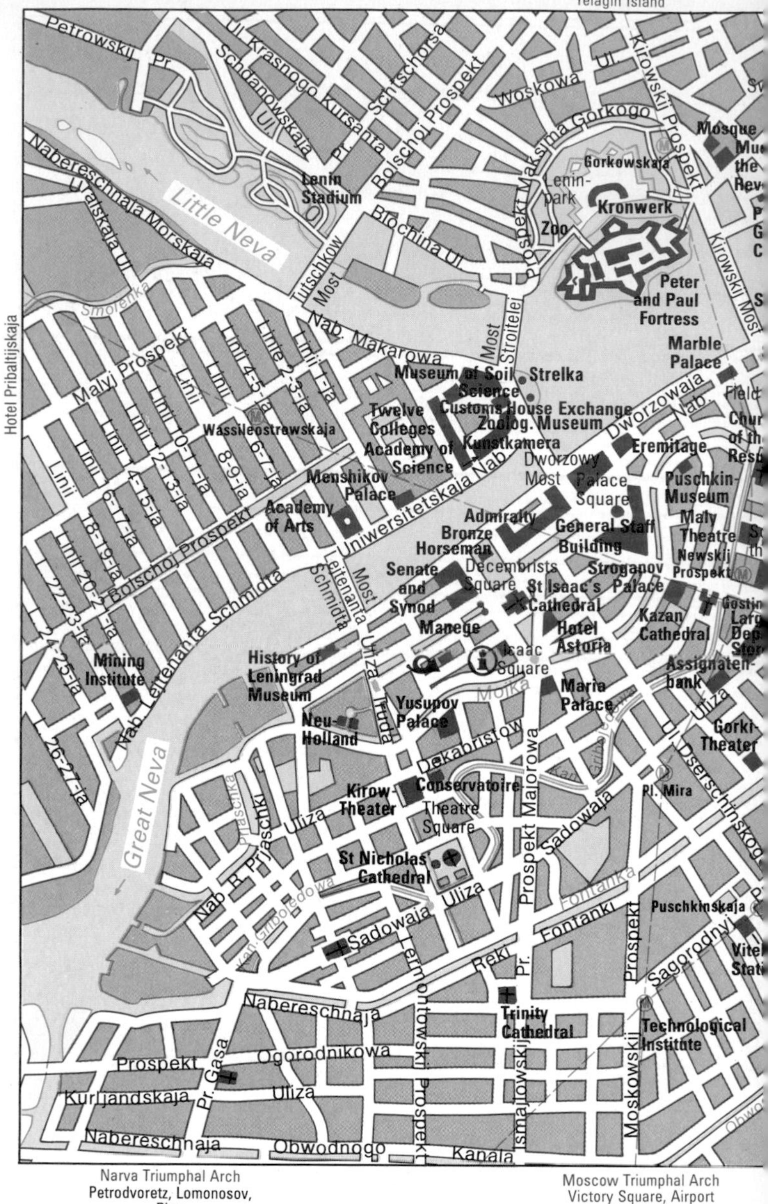

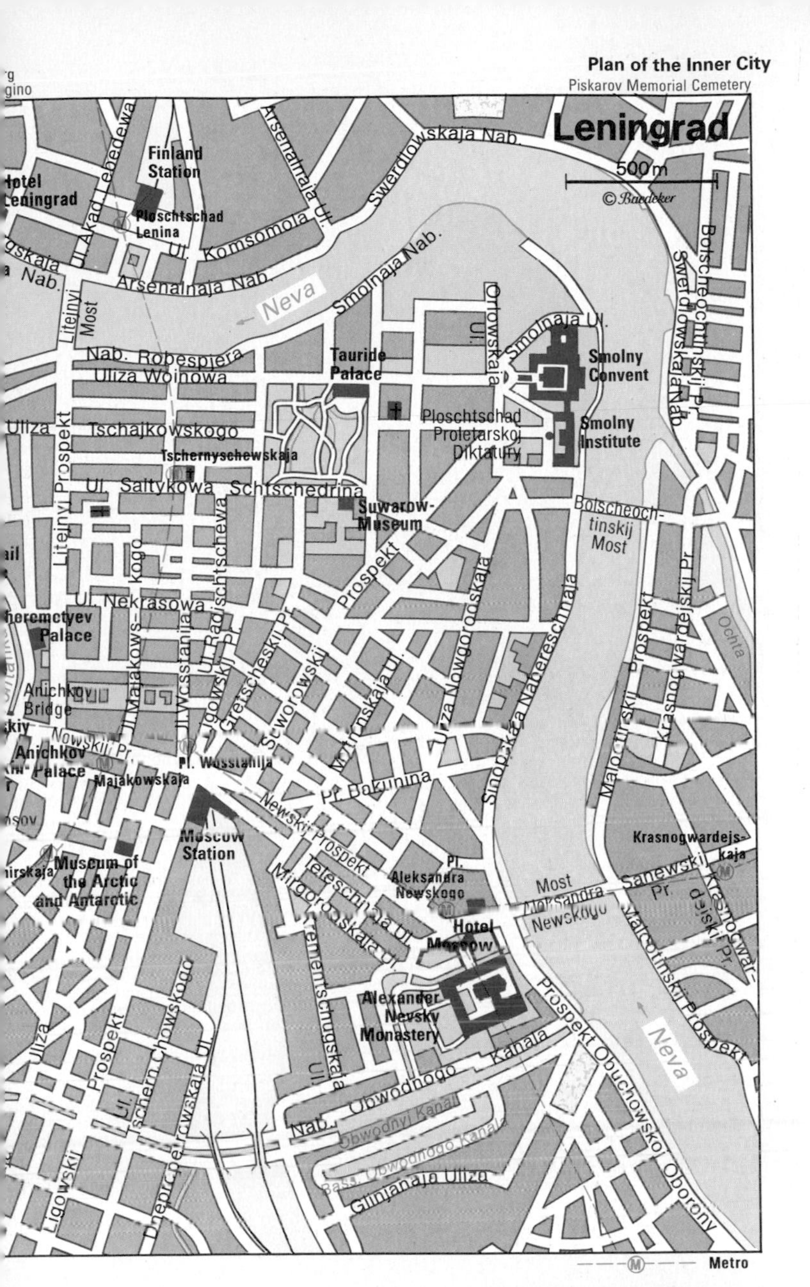
Piskarov Memorial Cemetery
Leningrad
500 m
© Baedeker
Finland Station
Hotel Leningrad
Ploschtschad Lenina
Ul. Akad. Lebedewa
Arsenalnaja Ul.
Swerdlowskaja Nab.
Ul. Komsomola
Arsenalnaja Nab.
Neva
Smolnaja Nab.
Litejnyi Most
Nab. Robespjera
Uliza Woinowa
Tauride Palace
Orlowskaja Ul.
Smolnaja Ul.
Smolny Convent
Smolny Institute
Ploschtschad Proletarskoj Diktatury
Bolscheochtinskij Pr.
Swerdlowskaja Nab.
Uliza Tschajkowskogo
Tschernyschewskaja
Litejnyi Prospekt
Ul. Saltykowa Schtschedrina
Suwarow-Museum
Bolscheochtinskij Most
Prospekt
Ul. Nekrasowa
Ul. Radischtschewa
Scheremetyev Palace
Ul. Majakowskogo
Ul. Wosstanija
Ligowskij Pr.
Gretscheskij Pr.
Sworowskij
Motrinskaja Ul.
Uliza Nowgorodskaja
Sinopskaja Nabereschnaja
Malootinskij Prospekt
Krasnogwardejskij Pr.
Ochta
Anichkov Bridge
Newskij Pr.
Anichkov Palace
Pl. Wosstanija
Majakowskaja
Pr. Bakunina
Newskij Prospekt
Moscow Station
Museum of the Arctic and Antarctic
Teleschnaja Ul.
Mirgorodskaja Ul.
Pl. Aleksandra Newskogo
Most Aleksandra Newskogo
Krasnogwardejskaja
Sanewskij Pr.
Krasnogwardejskij Pr.
Malootinskij Prospekt
Hotel Moscow
Alexander Nevsky Monastery
Ul. Tschernjachowskogo
Dneprpetrowskaja Ul.
Prospekt
Ul. Kremenschugskaja
Nab. Obwodnogo Kanala
Obwodnyj Kanal
Bass. Obwodnogo Kanala
Glinjanaja Uliza
Prospekt Obuchowskoi Oborony
Metro

Sights from A to Z

N.B.

See Practical Information, Sightseeing for suggestions about what to see during a short stay in Leningrad.
See pages 36–37 for a street map of Leningrad.

*Academy of Arts

F8

Akademiya Khudozhestv

Location
Universitetskaya Naberezhnaya 17

Metro
Vasileostrovskaya

Bus
6, 49, 50, 60,

Tram
1, 5, 11, 15, 33, 37, 42, 63

With its main façade fronting the Neva the Academy of Arts is one of Leningrad's finest early neo-Classical buildings. While the Academy itself was founded by the Empress Elizabeth I in 1757, it was Catherine II who a few years later provided money for the building. Sited on University Quay it was constructed between 1764 and 1788 to plans by Kokorinov and Vallin de la Mothe, both of whom taught at the Academy. The design is most unusual: a circular inner courtyard 40 m/130 ft in diameter is enclosed within a large rectangle, with smaller rectangular courtyards in each of the four corners. The façade on to the Neva is heavily articulated both vertically and horizontally, with three projecting porticos. Within the columns of the central portico are two statues of Hercules and Flora.
The Academy produced many famous artists, sculptors and architects, including Repin (see Notable Personalities) who

▲ *Academy of Arts*

◄ *General Staff Headquarters in Palace Square*

also went on to teach there, Surikov, Bryullov, Ivanov, Starov and Martos.
In 1947 the Academy moved to Moscow and the building is now occupied by the Repin Institute of Painting, Sculpture, and Architecture. It continues to house one of the country's oldest art collections belonging to the Academy. The collection includes work presented for examination by former students and copies of famous paintings and Classical sculpture, as well as plans and models of major Leningrad buildings
In front of the Academy, stone steps designed by Konstantin A. Thon and built in 1832/34 lead down to the river. On either side of the steps is a granite plinth bearing a reclining Sphinx 3.6 m/12 ft high, some 5 m/16 ft long and weighing more than 23 tonnes. Hieroglyphs on the plinths honour the Pharaoh Amenophis III (1413–1377 B.C.) The Sphinxes were discovered at Thebes in 1820, acquired by the Russian State, and brought to St. Petersburg in 1832. It took more than a year to bring them by ship from Egypt to the Neva.

Sphinx

*Academy of Sciences — G8

Akademiya Nauk

Location
Universitetskaya
Naberezhnaya 5

Bus
7, 30, 44, 47, 60

The Academy of Sciences building by the architect Giacomo Quarenghi stands on the Neva embankment next to the Kunstkamera (see entry) and was erected between 1783 and 1789. It has an impressive eight-columned Ionic portico in the centre of its 100 m/330 ft wide façade.
The Academy was founded in 1724 by Peter the Great, who however died in 1725 before the first meeting took place. In addition to discharging its primary role of publishing scientific work, the Academy had a major responsibility for Russian history, collecting and analysing source material. A grammar school and a university were affiliated to it. At first the Academy occupied part of the Kunstkamera before moving to Quarenghi's building in 1790. In 1934 the bulk of its activities were transferred to Moscow, leaving only a few departments, including the archives and the institute of linguistics, in Leningrad.

**Admiralty — G8

Admiralteystvo

Location
Admiralteyskaya
Naberezhnaya 2

Bus
6, 7, 10, 30, 44, 45, 60

Tram
31, 63

The Admiralty, on the south bank of the Neva between the Square of the Decembrists (see entry) and Palace Square (see entry), has been the home of the Dzerzhinskiy Naval Academy since 1925 and is not open to visitors. Its superb gilded spire on which Leningrad's three main thoroughfares, Nevsky Prospekt (see entry), Ulitsa Dzerzhinskogo and Prospekt Mayorova converge, is the emblem of the city.

History

In 1704/05, shortly after construction began on the site for the Peter and Paul Fortress (see entry), work was also started on a shipyard. Protected against possible attack by high ramparts and a moat, the original complex of buildings was U-shaped like the present Admiralty, the actual shipyard being in the area enclosed by the three sides. Here the ships of Russia's first fleet were built. By the beginning of the 19th c. the Admiralty had ceased to be of any military significance and magnificent palaces and wide streets had grown up around it. Between 1806 and 1823, under the direction of the architect Zacharov, the moat was filled in, the ramparts were removed, and the shipyard was transformed into the present imposing building.

Exterior

The Admiralty today is in three parts, a main façade 407 m/445 yds long, and two wings each of 163 m/178 yds, neo-Classical in style. The full length of the building can only be seen from the south, across the Gorky Gardens. From the Neva to the north, only the ends of the two wings are visible, the area between having been sold into private ownership at the end of the 19th century and built upon over the years.
The centrepiece of the Admiralty is the tower, rising above a great arch on the two sides of which are nymphs holding globes of the earth and the heavens. A frieze in relief by Terebenyev, "The Establishment of the Russian Fleet", decorates the attic above the archway. It depicts Peter the Great receiving a trident, symbol of power over the sea, from Neptune. Statues of Achilles, Pyrrhus, Ajax and Alexander the Great adorn the corners of the attic. From the base of the tower above the attic rises an Ionic peristyle with 28 columns, above which are a further 28 statues of the four elements, air, earth, fire and water, the four seasons, the four winds, the Egyptian goddess Isis, protectress of shipbuilders, and the Muse Urania, each in duplicate. These in turn are crowned by a gilded dome and finally by the tall gilded spire which reaches to a height of 72.5 m/238 ft above the ground. On top of the spire is a weather vane in the form of a caravel. Apart from the vane the spire is identical to the "Golden Needle" on the Cathedral of SS. Peter and Paul.

Gorky Gardens

About 1870 a small park, known first as the Alexander Park and later as Gorky Gardens, was laid out opposite the south façade of the Admiralty. As well as an attractive fountain there are busts of the writers Gogol (1809–1852) and Lermontov (1814–1841) and the composer Glinka (1804–1857) among others.

Alexander Column

see Palace Square

*Alexander Nevsky Monastery M/N6

Aleksandro Nevskaya Lavra

Location
Ploshchad Aleksandra Nevskovo

The Alexander Nevsky Monastery is one of the most famous in the USSR. It lies at the south-east end of Nevsky Prospekt (see entry) surrounded by walls and moats, and at

Alexander Nevsky Monastery

Metro
Ploshchad Aleksandra Nevskovo

Bus
21, 30, 118, 118a, 160

Tram
7, 13, 17, 24, 27, 38, 44, 48, 59, 65

Opening times
Museum and cemeteries: Mon.–Wed., Fri., Sun. 11 a.m.–7 p.m. (in winter to 6 p.m.)

one time counted twelve churches and a number of chapels among its buildings. The monastery is dominated by the Cathedral of the Trinity in which services are still held. The Church of the Annunciation, in contrast, now houses the Museum of Urban Sculpture.

Of several cemeteries within the Monastery grounds, the Lazarus and the Tikhvin Cemeteries are especially worth visiting.

The monastery was founded in 1710 by Peter the Great on what was believed to be the site of an important victory over the Swedes, on 15 July 1240, by the Novgorod Prince, Alexander Yaroslavich (later called Nevsky). Alexander Nevsky died in 1263 and was later canonised. In 1724 his remains were moved from Vladimir to St. Petersburg where they have been kept ever since in the monastery which bears his name.

At first there was only a simple timber-built church on the monastery site, but in 1717 Peter the Great commissioned the stone Church of the Annunciation. This was followed by the monastery buildings on the east side, but the remainder, including the Cathedral of the Trinity, were only completed at the end of the 18th century.

In 1797 the Monastery was granted the title 'lavra' (monastery of the highest rank) by Tsar Paul I, a status it shared with only three others – in Zagorsk, Kiev and Volhynien.

Monastery Complex

Entrance to the monastery grounds is through the Gate Church (1783/85) designed by Starov, and then along a walled path flanked by the Lazarus and Tikhvin Cemeteries. A second gate on the further side of the moat leads into the

monastery itself. The two-storey gallery-like buildings which make up the monastery complex form a closed quadrangle. To the east, corridors of cells run from the Church of the Annunciation to the Cathedral of the Trinity, which is linked in turn by more cells to the mid-18th c. Fedor Church, modelled on the Church of the Annunciation. The Seminary Building (1756/61) on the south side, the Communion Building (Prosfornyy Korpus 1761/71) on the north side, and the Metropolitan's House (1755/58) on the west side, are similarly integrated into the galleries of cells. All three were designed by the architect Rastorguyev.
The quadrangle is also a cemetery. The graves, under tall trees, are mostly of Second World War soldiers and airmen.

Cathedral of the Trinity

Architecturally the Cathedral of the Trinity, constructed between 1776 and 1790 by Ivan Starov, is the focal point of the whole monastery complex, a neo-Classical building with columned portico, graced by two bell towers and a large central dome.
The magnificent interior has three aisles flanked by massive pillars. The frescoes on the vaultings and in the dome were executed from designs by Giacomo Quarenghi. Copies of works by van Dyck, Rubens and Reni among others adorn the white marble and red agate iconostasis

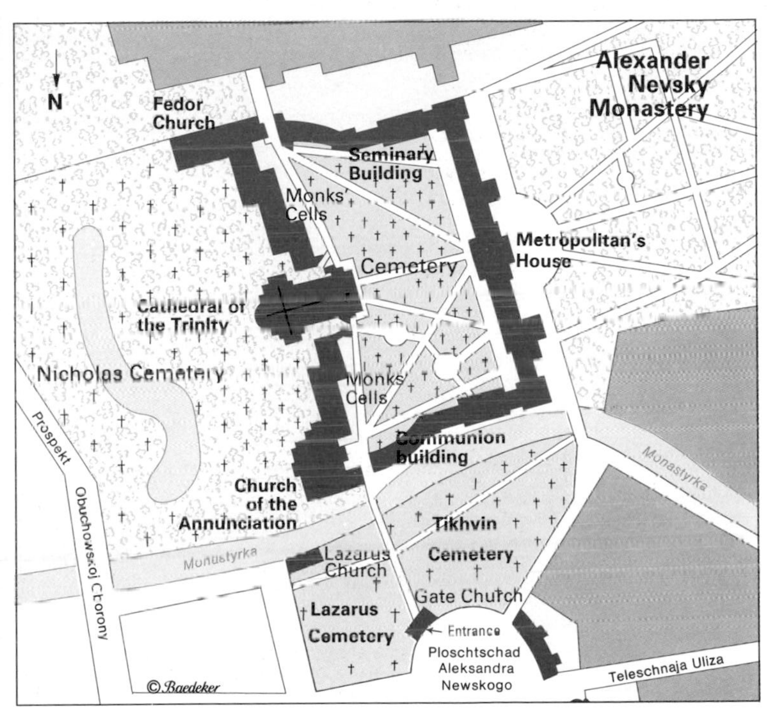

Lazarus Cemetery – Tomb of Lomonosov

Tikhvin Cemetery – Tomb of Dostoievsky

while the "Annunciation" beyond the iconostasis is the work of Anton Raphael Mengs.

Church of the Annunciation (Museum of Urban Sculpture)

The Church of the Annunciation was the first of the monastery buildings, erected between 1717 and 1722 to plans by Domenico Trezzini. With its high stepped roof and large elongated windows, the rectangular, red and white painted church has a rather secular air about it. It was the traditional burial place for members of the imperial family and others of high rank.
Today the church houses the Museum of Urban Sculpture. On the ground floor are the simple grave slabs of royalty, including the son and a sister of Peter the Great, as well as the grave of Generalissimo Suvorov (died 1800). Fine examples of old gravestones and memorial sculpture are on display in the adjacent room. Exhibits on the upper floor include models of famous monuments and sculptures such as the Alexander Column and the Bronze Horseman.

Lazarus and Tikhvin Cemeteries

The Lazarus and Tikhvin Cemeteries lie at the north end of the monastery grounds, the former having been in use since the monastery was founded, the latter opening only in 1823. Famous people are buried in both cemeteries and the remains of a number of artists and composers originally buried elsewhere have been reinterred there (the pianist Anton Rubenstein's grave, for example, was formerly in the Nicholas Cemetery).

Nicholas Cemetery

The Nicholas Cemetery occupies the ground to the east of the Cathedral of the Trinity and contains the graves of many of the monastery's scholars and priests.

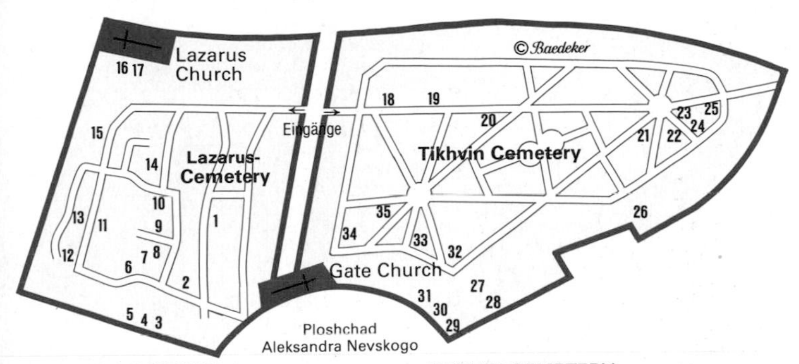

LAZARUS CEMETERY

1 Ivan Martos (sculptor, 1752–1835)
2 Thomas de Thomon (architect, 1754–1813)
3 Countess Lanskaya (first wife of Pushkin)
4 Carlo Rossi (architect, 1775–1849)
5 Giacomo Quarenghi (architect, 1744–1817)
6 Vasily Stasov (architect, 1769–1849)
7 Ivan Starov (architect, 1743–1808)
8 Andrey Voronikhin (architect, 1759–1814)
9 Feodosy Shchedrin (sculptor, 1752–1825)
10 Andrey Zakharov (architect, 1761–1811)
11 Leonard Euler (mathematician, 1707–1783)
12 Vladimir Borovikovsky (painter, 1757–1825)
13 Silvestr Shchedrin (painter, 1791–1830)
14 Mikhail Koslovsky (sculptor, 1753–1802)
15 Mikhail Lomonosov (polymath and writer, 1711–1765)
16 Prince Belosel'skiy-Belozerskiy
17 Princess Belosel'skiy-Belozerskiy
18 Ivan Krylov (poet, 1765–1844)
19 Mikhail Speransky (politician, 1772–1839)

TIKHVIN CEMETERY

20 Marius Petipa (choreographer, 1818–1910)
21 Pavel Fedotov (painter, 1815–1852)
22 Boris Kustodiev (painter, 1878–1927)
23 Ivan Vitali (sculptor, 1794–1855)
24 Vasily Demut-Malinovsky (sculptor, 1779–1846)
25 Peter Klodt von Jürgensburg (sculptor, 1805–1867)
26 Ivan Kramskoy (painter, 1837–1877)
27 Anton Rubenstein (composer, 1829–1894)
28 Peter Tchaikovsky (composer, 1840–1893)
29 Alexander Borodin (composer, 1834–1887)
30 Modest Mussorgsky (composer, 1839–1881)
31 Nikolay Rimsky-Korsakov (composer, 1844–1908)
32 Valentin Serov (painter, 1865–1911)
33 Mikhail Glinka (composer, 1804–1857)
34 Fyodor Dostoievsky (writer, 1821–1881)
35 Nikolay Karamsin (historian, 1766–1826)

Alexandra Theatre

see Ostrovskiy Square: Pushkin Theatre

Andreyevskiy Market

see Bolshoy Prospekt

*Anichkov Bridge J/K7

Anichkov Most

Location
Nevsky Prospekt (between Nos. 39 and 41)

Metro
Gostinyy Dvor

The Anichkov Bridge, some 55 m/60 yds long and 37 m/40 yds wide, carries traffic on Nevsky Prospekt (see entry) over the Fontanka River. In Peter the Great's time the bridge was wooden, although it was four times the length of the present one because of the marshy terrain. It was constructed by Colonel Mikhail Anichkov's regiment, and not only the

Bus
3, 6, 7, 22, 27, 43, 44, 45, 70

bridge but also the nearby palace (see Anichkov Palace) bear his name. At the end of the 18th century the wooden bridge was replaced by a stone one which in turn was widened between 1839 and 1841. The "Horse Trainers", four bronze groups by Peter Klodt von Jürgensburg to which the Anichkov Bridge owes its present fame, were put in place in 1849/50. Each depicts a different stage in the training of horses. Casts of two of the groups were presented by Tsar Nicholas I to his brother-in-law the Prussian King Friedrich Wilhelm IV, and set near the palace in Berlin, while two more casts were also sent as presents to Naples.

Anichkov Palace J7

Anichkovskiy Dvorets

Location
Nevsky Prospekt 39

Metro
Gostinyy Dvor

Bus
3, 6, 7, 22, 27, 43, 44, 45, 70

The Anichkov Palace on Nevsky Prospekt (see entry) is now a centre for the Soviet Youth Organisation, the "Pioneers", having been renamed the Zhdanov Palace of Pioneers in 1937. It took its original name from Mikhail Anichkov whose regiment constructed the first bridge over the Fontanka (see Anichkov Bridge).
The Empress Elizabeth built the palace for her lover Razumovsky, to plans by the architect Zemtsov. The land was acquired in 1741, work started in the same year and was completed in 1750. After Razumovsky's death ownership reverted to the Crown until 1776 when Catherine the Great made a present of the palace to her favourite, Potemkin. He, however, was chronically in debt and sold it. With extraordinary forbearance she bought it back and gave it to him a second time, only to have him sell it again in 1785. From then on, until the Revolution, the palace was the home of several heirs to the throne and other members of the imperial family, the last being Maria Fyodorovna (Dagmar of Denmark), mother of Nicholas II.
Over the years the palace was altered many times and little remains of the original Baroque building. The neo-Classical façade by Starov dates from 1778, and following extensive renovation by Rusca in 1809/10, Carlo Rossi added the two garden Pavilions in 1816 (see Ostrovskiy Square). In 1875 the architect Rahau designed a vestibule extending into the courtyard.

Cabinet

Standing on the embankment of the Fontanka in the grounds of the Palace, the "Cabinet" was erected in 1803/05 by Giacomo Quarenghi. The U-shaped building is of two storeys behind an Ionic colonnade.

Assignatsionnyy Bank H7

Assignatsionnyy Bank

Location
Sadovaya Ulitsa 21

The former Assignatsionnyy Bank faces on to Sadovaya Ulitsa, and at the rear overlooks the Griboyedov Canal, crossed just at this point by Bank Bridge (see entry).

The Bank, which printed the first Russian banknotes, was founded in 1769 by Catherine the Great, who commissioned Giacomo Quarenghi's imposing building (1783/90). The central block is enclosed by horseshoe-shaped depositories. The ends of the "horseshoe" on Sadovaya Ulitsa, which are in the form of loggias (open-sided arcades), were used as guardhouses.
Now the head office of a public authority, the Bank is not open to visitors. A bust of Quearenghi stands in front of it.

Metro
Ploshchad Mira/Gostinyy Dvor

Bus
43

Tram
2, 3, 5, 13, 14

"Aurora" (Cruiser) — J10

Kreyser Avrora

Since 1948 the legendary cruiser "Aurora" has been moored at the point where the Great Nevka (Bolshaya Nevka) branches off from the Neva.
Built in 1900 the ship first saw service in the 1904/05 Russo-Japanese War. In February 1917 during events leading up to the Revolution, the crew sided with the Bolsheviks, and in the following October were instructed by the insurgents to anchor near the Lieutenant Shmidta Bridge to prevent its being raised, so keeping open their route into the city. At 9.45 on the evening of 25 October she fired the shot which signalled the storming of the Winter Palace.
From 1923 the "Aurora" was used as a training ship, but also played a part in the defence of Leningrad in the Second World War.

Location
Petrogradskaya Naberezhnaya 4

Bus
49

Tram
6, 30, 51

Opening times
Tues.–Thur., Sat., Sun.
10.30 a.m.–4.30 p.m.

Cruiser "Aurora"

After a thorough overhaul she was fitted out in 1956 as an annex of the Central Naval Museum (see Exchange). The crew's quarters and officers' cabins are open to view and there is also a display of items which have been presented by the many different Socialist countries.

*Bank Bridge — H7

Bankovskiy Most

Location
Naberezhnaya Kanala Griboyedova

Metro
Nevsky Prospekt

Bank Bridge is one of Leningrad's most attractive foot-bridges, spanning the Griboyedov Canal behind the Assignatsionnyy Bank (see entry). Built by George Traitteur in 1825/26, the iron suspension cables disappear into the jaws of four seated griffins with gilded wings, by the sculptor Pavel Sokolov.

Bolshoy Prospekt — C–F7/8

Bolshoy Prospekt

Location
Vasil'yevskiy Island

Metro
Vasileostrovskaya

Bus
6, 49, 50

A walk along the Bolshoy Prospekt on Vasil'yevskiy Island introduces the visitor to a rather different, typically Russian, Leningrad. Some of the city's oldest houses can be seen here and, while there are also a number of shops along the wide avenue it is much quieter than the busy Nevsky Prospekt.

St. Andrew's Cathedral

St. Andrew's Cathedral, designed by A. F. Vist, stands in a side street off the Bolshoy Prospekt (6-ya Liniya 11). Constructed between 1764 and 1780 on the site of an earlier building, it has a large central dome on a raised drum, with four side domes. Above the nave is a bell-tower with a tall spire.

Andreyevskiy Market

The Andreyevskiy Market at 6-ya Liniya 9 is a two-storey shopping arcade. During the summer half-year fruit and vegetables are sold in the inner courtyard.

Bronze Horseman

see Square of the Decembrists

Central Exhibition Hall

see Manège

Central Lenin Museum

see Marble Palace

Central Naval Museum

see Exchange

*Chesma Church

Chesmenskaya Tserkov

Location
Ulitsa Lensoveta between Nos. 14 and 16

Metro
Park Pobedy/Moskowskaya

Bus
13, 16, 61

Opening times
Wed.–Sun. 10 a.m.–5 p.m.

As the Imperial court moved from residence to residence, staging-posts were needed where horses were changed and people could rest. These staging-posts were themselves palaces, among them Chesma Palace to the south of Leningrad, commissioned by Catherine the Great in 1773 and sited near what is now the Moscow Victory Park. Here the court would break the journey from St. Petersburg to Pushkin or Pavlovsk (see respective entries). The name commemorates the victory of the Russian fleet over the Turks at Chesma in the Aegean in 1770. Chesma Church belonged to the palace.The church was built between 1777 and 1780 under the direction of Yuriy Velten, to a most unusual design. A Western style spire rises above each of the church's four apses pointing to the four main compass points. The "four-apse" pattern is normal for orthodox churches. The spires are not. A central dome, again with spire, completes the five-dome arrangement also normal for Orthodox churches. The exterior decoration of narrow white vertical mouldings, terminating in small pointed arches, make Chesma a rare example of 18th century Russian Gothic.

The church now serves as an annex of the Central Naval Museum (see Exchange) housing exhibits from the naval battle at Chesma.

Chesma Church

Soldiers who fell during the Second World War and also veterans of the war are buried in the graveyard at the rear of the church.

Chesma Palace

Chesma Palace opposite the church was converted in the 1830s into a hospital for war veterans. Triangular in shape with a tower at each corner, three new wings were added and some of the Gothic features removed. It is still a home for the elderly and not open to the public.

Church of the Redeemer

see Church of the Resurrection

*Church of the Resurrection (Church of the Redeemer) J8

Khram Voskreseniya Kristova

Location
Naberezhnaya Kanala Griboyedova

Metro
Nevsky Prospekt

Bus
1, 2, 14, 26, 46, 100

Tram
51, 53

Clearly visible from Nevsky Prospekt (see entry), the splendidly colourful Church of the Resurrection, also known as the Church of the Redeemer or the Church of Blood, was built by Alexander III beside the Griboyedov Canal, marking the spot where his father, Alexander II, was assassinated on 1 March 1881. The Tsar died in a bomb attack by members of a group calling themselves "the People's Will".
The architect, Alfred Parland, created a church in the Old Russian style, modelled on St. Basil's Cathedral in Moscow which, like the Church of the Resurrection (1883/1907), has a primarily commemorative function. Mosaics are a dominant feature of the church both inside and out, so it is appropriate that a museum of mosaic art is to be installed there.

Cruiser "Aurora"

see "Aurora"

Decembrists' Square

see Square of the Decembrists

Engineers' Castle

see Mikhail Castle

Ethnographic Museum

Ethnographic Museum of the Peoples of the USSR J8

Muzey Etnografii Narodov SSSR

With its 250,000 exhibits, the Ethnographic Museum of the Peoples of the USSR is the most important museum of its kind in the Soviet Union. Orginally established as a branch of the Russian Museum (see entry) it became an independent collection in 1934. The present building, adjacent to the east wing of the Russian Museum, was designed by the architect Svinyin and dates from 1900/11.

The history, life and culture of the different peoples and ethnic groups of the USSR is brought to life by the collection of art and craftwork, clothes, jewellery, tools, toys, and other everyday things.

Location
Inzhenernaya Ulitsa 4a

Metro
Nevsky Prospekt/Gostinyy Dvor

Bus
2, 14, 25, 26, 100

Tram
2, 3, 5, 12, 14, 34

Opening times
Tues.–Sun. 10 a.m.–6 p.m.

*Exchange (Central Naval Museum) G9

Birzha (Zentralnyy Voyenno-Morskoy Muzey)

The former Exchange, now the Central Naval Museum, dominates the Strelka (see entry), the most easterly point of Vasil'yevskiy Island.
The neo-Classical building, reminiscent of a Greek temple, was constructed in 1805/10 by the French architect Thomon. Forty-four Doric columns rising above a granite base

Location
Pushkinskaya Ploshchad 4

Bus
10, 45

The Exchange

Tram
31, 63

Opening Times
Wed.–Sun. 10.30 a.m.–4.45 p.m.

surround the main rectangle, while wide steps lead up on the two shorter sides. Above the entablature at each end of the building are fine groups of statues by Prokofyev and Shchedrin. The group facing the Neva depicts Neptune emerging from the waves amidst figures representing the rivers Neva and Volkhov. Mercury the god of commerce, and personifications of the rivers Volga and Dnieper, can be seen at the opposite end.

Almost the whole interior of the building is taken up by a 900 sq. m/1076 sq. yds hall adorned with marble and sculptures, where until 1885 stocks and shares were traded. It became the Central Naval Museum in 1940.

Founded in 1805 the origins of the Museum go back even further. From 1709 models were made of every ship launched in any of Peter the Great's dockyards. These were formed into a collection together with drawings and models of other ships and kept at the Admiralty (see entry). Today the Museum has grown to include over 500,000 exhibits, of which the 1500 ship models remain an important part. They show the development of the Russian fleet from its earliest beginnings to the most modern ships of war. Still to be seen is the "grandame" of the Russian navy, the little vessel in which Peter the Great practised navigation on the river Yausa. The collection also includes uniforms, weaponry, and documents relating to Russian and Soviet shipping.

Field of Mars J9

Marsova Pole

Bus
1, 2, 25, 46, 65, 100, 134

Tram
2, 3, 12, 34, 51, 53

The Field of Mars is a large green park extending over some 12 hectares/30 acres. It was known in the 18th century as "the Field of Pleasure" because firework displays were held there, and also as "the Tsarina's Field" because of its proximity to the palace. It acquired its present name in about 1800 when it first began to be used as a parade and exercise ground.
Bordering the Field to the north are the Marble Palace (see entry), Suvorov Square, and Betskoy's and Saltykov's houses (built in 1784/87 and 1784/88 respectively). To the west are the barracks of the Pavlovskiy Regiment. The river Moyka forms the boundary to the south and the Field is separated from the Summer Garden (see entry) to the east by Sadovaya Ulitsa.

Memorial to the Dead of the Revolution

In April 1917 a hundred and eighty victims of the February Revolution were buried on the Field of Mars, and by 1919 a wall of massive granite blocks had been built round the graves. Today the dead are also commemorated by an Eternal Flame first lit in 1957. Newly-married couples often have their wedding photographs taken at the memorial.

Suvorov Square

A monument to General Alexander Suvorov (1729–1800), architect of many Russian victories in the Russo-Turkish War of 1768/74, stands in the centre of this busy square. Unveiled in 1801, the monument depicts the General in the guise of Mars, god of war.

Barracks of Pavlovskiy Regiment

The barracks were constructed in 1817/21 by Stasov for Paul I's regiment which had acquitted itself gloriously in the campaign against Napoleon (1812/14). The long façade is given distinction by its porticos with Doric columns. Now used as offices the barracks are the headquarters of the Leningrad energy authority.

Field of Mars

Gatchina

Gatchina

Location
45 km/28 miles south-west of Leningrad

Gatchina, one of the former imperial summer residences, is situated in very attractive countryside 45km/28 miles south-west of Leningrad. Because there are military installations near by the palace cannot be visited by foreign tourists, in contrast to the summer residences at Pavlovsk, Petrodvorets, Pushkin and Lomonosov (see respective entries).
While the name Gatchina appears earlier in imperial documents, the palace itself was built between 1766 and 1781 by one of Catherine the Great's lovers, Grigoriy G. Orlov, who also had an extensive landscaped park with many small pavilions and bridges laid out on the estate she had presented to him.
The palace, with its rather plain exterior, was unique in its magnificent and unusual interior décor. Erotic wall-paintings and furniture carved with erotic motifs made it an appropriate setting for meetings between Catherine and Orlov.
After Orlov's death Catherine gave the estate to her son, later Paul I. Although he hated almost everything connected with his mother, Gatchina became his favourite summer home.
The palace was badly damaged in the Second World War, though it has since been largely restored. The unusual furnishings are supposed to have been destroyed by fire or otherwise lost without trace.

General Staff Building

see Palace Square

**Hermitage G/H8/9

Ermitazh

Location
Dvortsovaya Naberezhnaya 34–36

Bus
7, 10, 30, 44, 45, 47, 60

Tram
31, 63

Opening times
Tues.–Sun. 11 a.m–6 p.m.

The Hermitage, on the south embankment of the Neva opposite the Peter and Paul Fortress (see entry), is one of the world's largest and most famous museums. Over three and a half million people visit it each year.
The museum occupies four buildings dating from the 18th and 19th c. The oldest and most important is the Winter Palace, to which the other three, the Small Hermitage, the Old, or Large Hermitage, and the New Hermitage are all connected. A further building, the Hermitage Theatre, joined to the Old Hermitage by a covered bridge across the Winter Canal, is sometimes used for lectures or for special exhibitions held in the foyer.

The name Hermitage

The name "hermitage", from the French *hermitage*, was used in 18th c. Europe to refer to small pavilions which were built in palace grounds. The upper floor was a dining-room for a small number of guests. The table, already laid with food by the servants below, could be raised to the upper

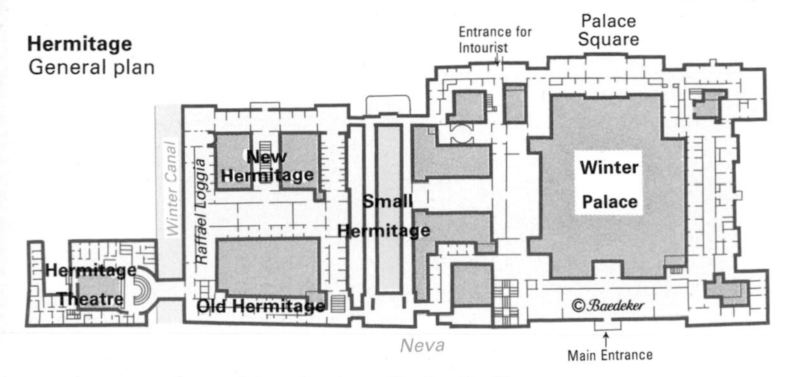

room by means of a special mechanism, allowing the illustrious gathering above to dine completely undisturbed. Catherine the Great commissioned Vallin de la Mothe to build such a hermitage in St. Petersburg (the Small Hermitage), later arranging for the walls of the little palace to be hung with paintings. As the collection of paintings grew it became necessary to create a larger gallery and so the building known today as the Old Hermitage took shape under Velten's direction. In time, all the buildings housing the ever-growing collection came to be known as the Hermitage.

Winter Palace

History

The first Winter Palace, a small two-storeyed building, was completed on Peter the Great's instructions in 1711. The second, built ten years later, was also of modest dimensions. It was in this palace that Peter the Great died in 1725. The third Winter Palace was considerably more imposing, erected to plans by Dominico Trezzini on the site of the present Hermitage Theatre. Alterations and extensions were then set in train under the direction of Bartolomeo Francesco Rastrelli, but in 1754 the Empress Elizabeth gave her approval to plans for a whole new building, finished in 1762. Rastrelli's magnificent palace, which on the outside has remained largely unchanged since its completion, is one of the masterpieces of Russian Baroque architecture.
Following the palace conspiracy which brought Catherine the Great to power Rastrelli left Russia, though he never theless drew the plans for the main staircase and the Throne Room. Work on the rest of the palace interior was entrusted to Vallin de la Motthe, Rinaldi, Velten and Quarenghi, and was continued in the first quarter of the 19th c. by Rossi, Montferrand and, above all, Stasov. In 1838/39 Stasov and Bryullov together carried out extensive renovation work after fire had completely destroyed the inside of the building.
Considerable damage was also caused in the Second World War, but repairs began immediately after the German retreat, and by 1950 the Winter Palace was almost fully restored.

Winter Palace

Exterior

With its undoubted aura of romance, due not least to the pale green and white walls, the Winter Palace is built round a large square quadrangle, each of the façades having received different treatment. The north façade overlooking the Neva is essentially a long, almost straight colonnade, without any major projections. At the centre of the south façade, opening on to Palace Square, there is in contrast a prominent triple-arched entrance giving access to the quadrangle, while to the east and west both façades are deeply indented.

All the outer walls have protruding columns and pilasters. The window surrounds differ from floor to floor and from façade to façade, with one of Rastrelli's characteristic motifs – often a mask, sometimes a shell – above every window. Round the roof the balustrade and pediments are adorned with statues and urns. A small gilded dome marks the position of the chapel.

Interior

Originally the ground floor was taken up with all the palace services, including offices and domestic quarters for staff and soldiers. The state rooms occupied the first floor while on the upper floor were bedrooms and other accommodation for the large retinue of ladies-in-waiting and courtiers. The state rooms were at first decorated in the Russian Baroque style, but after the fire in 1837 only a few were restored to their original form and today most are neo-Classical in appearance.

Jordan or Ambassadors' Staircase

Visitors normally reach the state rooms on the first floor of the Winter Palace by ascending the Jordan or Ambassadors' Staircase (see plan pp. 60–63), formerly used by

ambassadors coming to present their credentials. The staircase owed its other name to the "Jordan Feast", celebrated by the Orthodox Church at Epiphany (6 January) each year, at which the waters of the Neva were blessed. The imperial family walked down the "Jordan Staircase" to take part in the ceremony.
After the fire in 1837 Stasov rebuilt the divided staircase to Rastrelli's original design, but using different materials.

Peter I's Hall

Peter I's Hall, also called the Small Throne Room, was likewise restored to the original, using Montferrand's plans drawn in 1833 in honour of Peter the Great. The painting (1730) behind the throne shows the Tsar in the company of Minerva.

Armorial Hall

The Armorial Hall, intended for receptions and balls, was laid out as a gallery by Rastrelli, and extended by Velten. Few of the original furnishings, emblazoned with the coats of arms of the Russian provincial governors, now remain.

Gallery of the 1812 War

Hung in the gallery are some 329 portraits, mostly of generals who took part in the 1812 war against Napoleon, but also of the three allied monarchs, Alexander I of Russia, Francis I of Austria and Frederick William III of Prussia.

Large Throne Room

The Large Throne Room or St. George's Hall was altered many times, on the last occasion by Stasov. The gilt ornamentation of the ceiling is repeated in the parquet flooring, elaborately laid with 16 different kinds of rare wood. A mosaic map of the USSR made from semi-precious stones

Jordan or Ambassadors' Staircase

Peter I's Hall

Armorial Hall

(1937) now occupies the place where the imperial throne once stood. Above it is a marble relief of St. George slaying the dragon.

Ballroom

From the head of the Jordan Staircase, on the Neva side, a large ante-room leads into an *enfilade* of interconnecting state rooms, the first of which, the Ballroom (1103 sq. m/1320 sq. yds), is the largest hall in the entire palace. It was created in 1793 by Quarenghi who combined three existing rooms.

Malachite Hall

Designed by Bryulov this room is decorated with eight malachite columns and eight malachite pilasters. It also contains some spectacular malachite ornaments including a large bowl, candelabra and vases. The Malachite room was used as a salon by the wife of Nicholas I.

White Dining-Room

In October 1917 the Malachite Hall and the nearby White Dining-Room were the venue for what was to be the last meeting of the Kerensky Government. It was in the White Dining-Room on the night of 25/26 October that government ministers were taken prisoner by the Bolsheviks, after the storming of the Winter Palace. The time at which this happened is still shown by the clock on the mantelpiece.

Small Hermitage

The Small Hermitage, early neo-Classical in style, was erected immediately to the east of the Winter Palace, be-

Small Hermitage

New Hermitage

tween 1764 and 1775, by Vallin de la Mothe and Velten. Paintings belonging to the imperial court were hung in the long narrow building, in the centre of which a hanging garden was created. The short façades at either end are graced by six Corinthian columns and decorated attics.

Pavilion Hall

Stakenschneider's Pavilion Hall (1856) is the most beautiful room in the palace. The slender white marble pillars harmonise superbly with the Moorish wall fountains also in marble, the magnificent chandeliers and the mosaic floor panel copied from a Roman original.

Old Hermitage

The Old or Large Hermitage (1771/87) with its relatively plain façade is the work of Yuriy Velten. It was built to accommodate the fast-growing collection of paintings hitherto housed in the Small Hermitage, but it also included State Council chambers on the ground floor. In 1783 Quarenghi was commissioned to enlarge the building. He added the wing along the west embankment of the Winter Canal, a copy of Raphael's Loggia in the Vatican.

New Hermitage

The New Hermitage was built between 1839 and 1852 to plans by the German architect Leo von Klenze, a two-storeyed, rectangular building with a series of inner quadrangles. A distinctive feature of the main façade on

Ulitsa Chalturina is the portico with its ten Atlas figures. Standing 5 m/16 ft tall they are carved from blocks of grey granite and are the work of Terebenyev.

Hermitage Theatre

At the furthermost end of the complex of buildings extending along the Neva embankment from the Winter Palace, the Hermitage Theatre was erected in 1783/87 by Giacomo Quarenghi. The strictly neo-Classical structure is connected to the rest of the Hermitage by an arched gallery, formerly the theatre foyer, which bridges the Winter Canal. The auditorium is in the form of an amphitheatre.

The Hermitage Collection

History of the collection

Visitors to the Hermitage now have access to 350 rooms, and in all there are some 2.7 million items on exhibition.

Hermitage
GROUND FLOOR

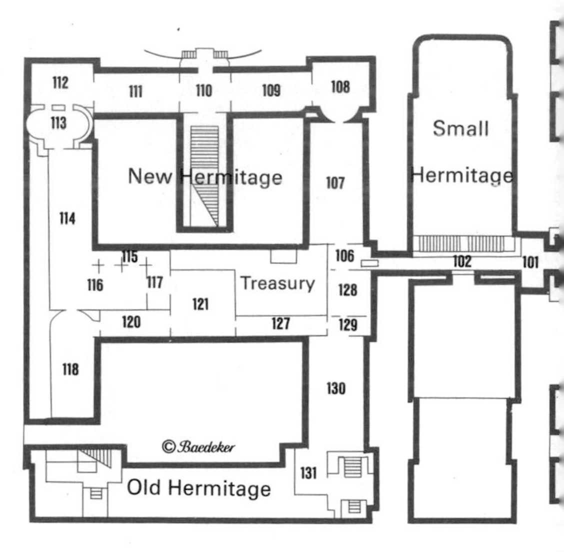

PREHISTORY

11–14 Early Stone Age to Iron Age finds from excavations within the Soviet Union
15–21 Scythian Art and Culture 7th–2nd c. B.C.
22–33 Altai Mountain Culture (finds from the Pasyryk tumuli: 5th–3rd c. B.C.

NEAR EASTERN AND ORIENTA ART AND CULTURE

34–54 Central Asia: 4th c. B.C. –beginning of 20th c. A.D.
55–66 Caucasus: 11th c. B.C. –19th c. A.D.
67–69 Golden Horde: 13th/14th c. A.D.
85–89 Egypt: 4th c. B.C.–4th c. A.D.

This huge art collection grew out of a small palace gallery. Although individual works of art were acquired under Peter the Great, collecting only began systematically in the second half of the 18th century and the Hermitage was officially founded in 1764, when 225 paintings were purchased from the Berlin merchant Gotzkowski. In the decades which followed the collection grew apace, so that from numbering 2089 items in 1774, at the death of Catherine the Great in 1796 the figure had almost doubled to 3986.
At first only the imperial family and their guests were able to enjoy the incomparable treasures, but early in the 19th century the Hermitage was opened to other patrons of the arts though visitors still required permission from the court administration.
Finally, in 1852 Nicholas turned the Hermitage into a museum and the Small Hermitage, the Old Hermitage and the New Hermitage became accessible to the public. Following the October Revolution the collection was enlarged

89,90 Babylonian, Assyrian and neighbouring countries: 4th c. B.C.–3rd c. A.D.

ART AND CULTURE OF ANTIQUITY

100 Black Sea Region 7th c. B.C.–3rd c. A.D. (Finds from Olbia)

101, 102 Italy and Rome: 7th c. B.C.–4th c. A.D.
106, 107 Italy and Rome: 7th c. B.C.–4th c. A.D.
108–114 Greece: 8th–2nd c. B.C.
115–117 Black Sea Region: 7th c. B.C.–3rd c. A.D.
118–121 Greece: 8th–2nd c. B.C.
127–131 Italy and Rome: 7th c. B.C.–4th c. A.D.

by confiscated works of art formerly in private hands, and the Winter Palace was also made into a museum.
The art treasures in the Hermitage survived the Second World War undamaged, the most valuable being moved into store, the others kept in the cellars. A turning-point in the history of the museum occurred in 1948 when it took over a large part of the collection from the Moscow Museum of Modern Western Art. For the first time turn-of-the-century French paintings made their appearance in the Hermitage collection.
Today the collection embraces works of art from all over the world and dating from the Stone Age to the present. It is divided into six departments of which west European art

HERMITAGE
FIRST FLOOR

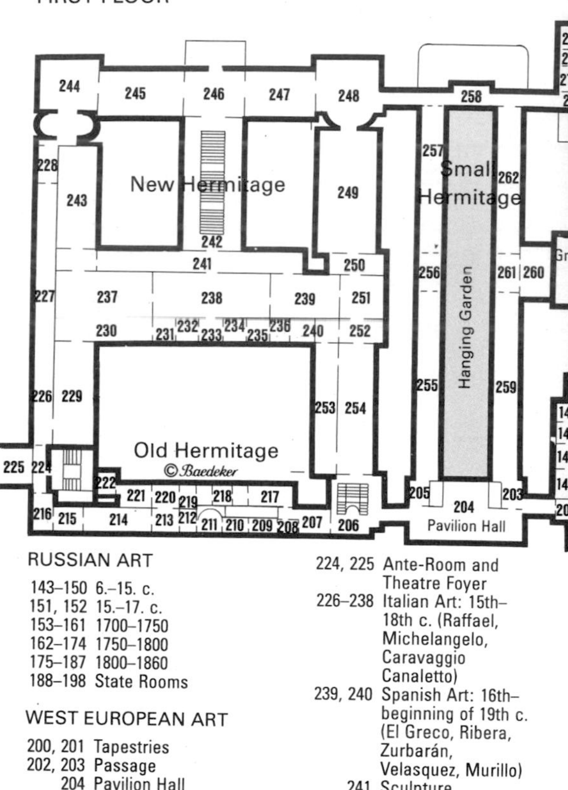

RUSSIAN ART

143–150	6.–15. c.
151, 152	15.–17. c.
153–161	1700–1750
162–174	1750–1800
175–187	1800–1860
188–198	State Rooms

WEST EUROPEAN ART

200, 201	Tapestries
202, 203	Passage
204	Pavilion Hall
205	Passage
206–222	Italian Art: 13. 16th c. (Fra Angelico, Lippi Leonardo da Vinci Titian, Veronese)
224, 225	Ante-Room and Theatre Foyer
226–238	Italian Art: 15th–18th c. (Raffael, Michelangelo, Caravaggio Canaletto)
239, 240	Spanish Art: 16th–beginning of 19th c. (El Greco, Ribera, Zurbarán, Velasquez, Murillo)
241	Sculpture 18th/19th c.
242	Staircase
243	Weapons and armour 15th–17th c.
244	Closed temporarily
245–247	Flemish Art: 17th c.

remains the most important, in particular west European painting.

N.B.

It is quite impossible for the visitor to view all the museum's most important pieces in a single day. The best plan is to concentrate on individual departments and perhaps to visit the State Rooms. A special permit is required to view the Crown Jewels.

Prehistory

The department of prehistory contains archaeological finds from excavations within the Soviet Union. The oldest exhibits date from the Early and Middle Stone Age, the most recent from the Bronze and Iron Ages.

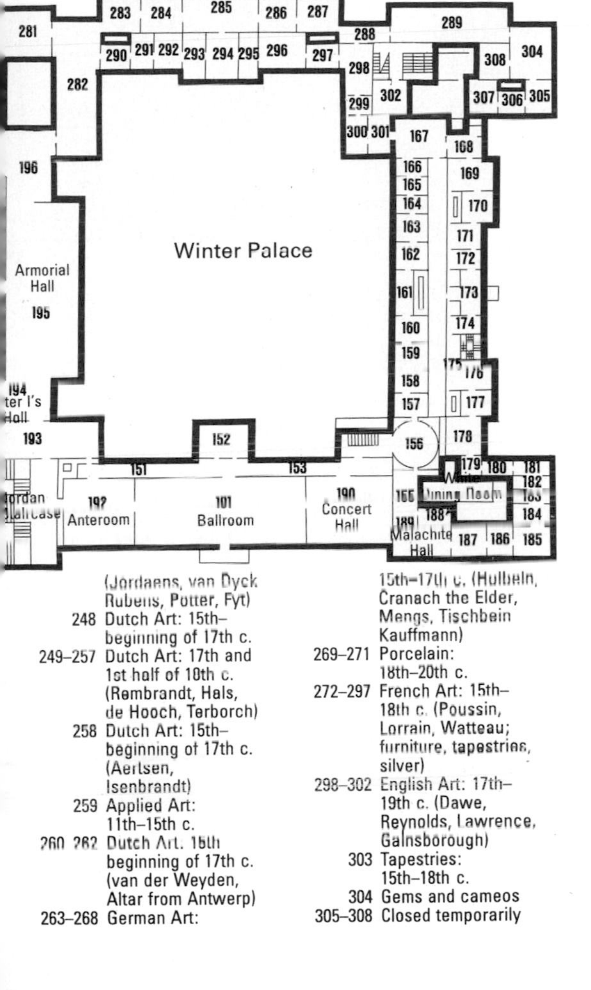

(Jordaens, van Dyck Rubens, Potter, Fyt)

248 Dutch Art: 15th–beginning of 17th c.

249–257 Dutch Art: 17th and 1st half of 18th c. (Rembrandt, Hals, de Hooch, Terborch)

258 Dutch Art: 15th–beginning of 17th c. (Aertsen, Isenbrandt)

259 Applied Art: 11th–15th c.

260–262 Dutch Art: 15th–beginning of 17th c. (van der Weyden, Altar from Antwerp)

263–268 German Art: 15th–17th c. (Holbein, Cranach the Elder, Mengs, Tischbein Kauffmann)

269–271 Porcelain: 18th–20th c.

272–297 French Art: 15th–18th c. (Poussin, Lorrain, Watteau; furniture, tapestries, silver)

298–302 English Art: 17th–19th c. (Dawe, Reynolds, Lawrence, Gainsborough)

303 Tapestries: 15th–18th c.

304 Gems and cameos

305–308 Closed temporarily

Winter Canal

They are arranged geographically and chronologically. The section concerned with Scythian art and culture is of special interest. The first evidence to be discovered of this cultured people from the steppes and forests north of the Black Sea dates from the 7th century B.C., but most of the objects on display date from the 6th to 3rd centuries B.C.. Animals locked in combat, panthers and reclining stags are typical motifs in their art.
The finds from the Pasyryk tumuli in the Altai Mountains are equally exciting. Thanks to the region's permafrost, objects of wood, cloth, skin and fur found in the chief's grave have remained in a good state of preservation; they include a large woven carpet, dated about 2500 B.C., said to be the oldest in the world.

Ancient Greece and Rome

The exhibits in this department belong to the period 800 B.C. to A.D. 400 and include objects from the northern Black Sea coast where there were Greek colonies from the 6th century B.C. onwards, as well as treasures from classical antiquity purchased in Italy and other European countries. The sculptures are primarily Roman, though many are copies of Greek originals. One such copy is the world-famous "Tauride Venus" (3rd century A.D.), which in 1720 became the first Classical statue to be taken to Russia. Peter the Great received it from Pope Clement XI in exchange for St. Brigit's remains. The statue stood first in the Summer Garden (see entry), then later in the Tauride Palace (see entry) from which it took its name.
The development of Roman portraiture from the 1st century B.C. to the 4th century A.D. is illustrated in the numerous

exhibits which also include sarcophagi, marble and other stone reliefs, stelae, ceramics, jewellery, gemstones and a collection of terracotta.

Near Eastern and Oriental Art

This department was established in 1920, prior to which the museum possessed only individual items. These have since been greatly augmented, largely as a result of archaeological expeditions undertaken on behalf of the Hermitage. The Egyptian collection deserves special attention, particularly the Coptic finds dating from the 4th to 6th centuries A.D. which are unique, as is the papyrus telling the story of a shipwreck. On display in the Byzantine section are icons from the 12th to 15th centuries, including mosaic icons. Chinese art is represented for the most part by porcelain, lacquer-work, enamels and wood-carvings.

West European art

The collection of west European paintings is the oldest and most famous of all the museum's departments. French painting from the 15th to the 20th century is well represented by Lorrain, Watteau, Delacroix, Courbet, Corot, Sisley, Rousseau, Monet and Renoir. The Italian section contains works from the 13th to the 18th century by Beato Angelico, Leonardo da Vinci, Raphael, Titian and Veronese, while El Greco, Velázquez, Ribera and Murillo feature among the many Spanish painters. The Hermitage owns works by all the most important Flemish and Dutch Masters, including 25 paintings by Rembrandt. England and Germany are also represented with masterpieces by Gainsborough, Lukas Cranach the Elder, Holbein, C. D. Friedrich and others.

Italian painting in the Hermitage

Although the paintings are certainly the most spectacular section of the department of west European Art there are other sections which contain items of equal merit. There is a valuable collection of drawings by old masters, Rubens and van Dyck for example, and architectural drawings by Quarenghi and Cameron. Among the many sculptures dating from the 15th to the 20th century, Michelangelo's "Squatting Youth" is one of the most important. Also on display are porcelain and ceramics, Venetian, Spanish and German glass, carpets, and rare pieces of furniture.

Hermitage

SECOND FLOOR

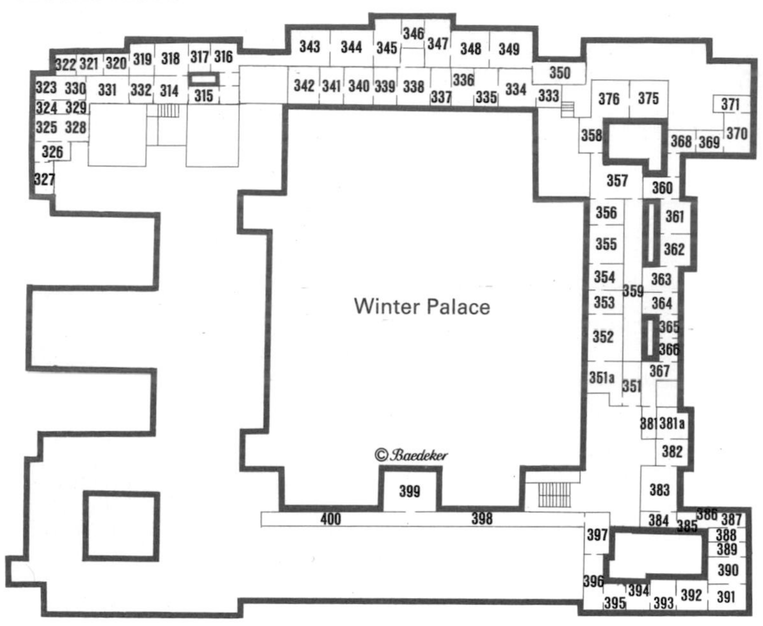

WEST EUROPEAN ART

- 314–332 French Art 19th–20th c. (Gaugin, Rousseau, van Gogh, Cézanne, Monet, Sisley, Renoir, Degas, Daubigny, Delacroix, Ingrès, Gros.)
- 333 Passage
- 334, 335 Art in the Eastern Block
- 336 Art in the USA
- 337 Art in Belgium
- 338 Italian Art
- 339 German, Spanish and Finnish Art
- 340 Dutch Art
- 341, 342 German and Swiss Art in the 19th c.
- 343–350 French Art 19th–20th c. (Picasso, Matisse, Léger, Bonnard)

ART AND CULTURE OF THE PEOPLES OF THE EAST

- 351–363 China; 2 c. B.C.–19th c. A.D.
- 364 Closed temporarily
- 365–367 Mongolia; late B.C.–19th c. A.D.
- 368–371 India; 3rd c. B.C.–20th c. A.D.
- 375–376 Japan; 14th–20th c.
- 381–382 Byzantium; 4th–15th c.
- 383–397 Near and Middle East; 3rd–19th c.

NUMISMATICS

- 398–400 Coins, Orders, Insignia

Russian art

The complete Hermitage collection of Russian paintings was transferred to the Russian Museum (see entry) at the time of its foundation. Russian art and culture continues to be represented in the Hermitage only by a small collection of 14th- to 17th-century icons, a few pictures of historical interest, such as portraits and views of palace interiors, some archaeological material, art and craft work and porcelain.
However, a substantial quantity of furnishings do remain and lamps, pictures, crockery and costumes are displayed to particular advantage. In addition the different styles of furniture from Baroque to modern are illustrated by pieces brought together from the Winter Palace, the New Hermitage and various other palaces.

Numismatic collection

The Numismatic department of the Hermitage collects and researches into coins and other forms of currency, medals, decorations, badges and seals. The coins on display (which with the medals number over 900,000) are classified geographically and chronologically into Ancient, Oriental, Russian and European sections.

History of Leningrad Museum (Rumyantsev House) F7

Musey Istorii Leningrada (Dom Rumyantseva)

Location
Naberezhnaya Krasnogo Flota 44

Bus
6, 49, 50

Tram
1, 5, 11, 15, 33, 42, 63

Opening times
Mon., Thur.–Sun.
11 a.m.–6 p.m.; Tues.
11 a.m.–4 p.m.

The former Rumyantsev House on the south bank of the Neva near the Lieutenant Shmidta Bridge became the History of Leningrad Museum in 1950.
The house is built in the neo Classical Alexandrian style with a portico of 12 Corinthian columns extending across the whole width of the main façade. On the pediment is a relief "Apollo on Parnassus" by Martos.
The history of the city since 1917 is traced through pictures, documents and many other exhibits, with a special section devoted to the blockade during the Second World War.
There are further branches of the museum covering the period from 1703 to 1917 housed in various buildings in the Peter and Paul Fortress (see entry).

Aurora Plaque

The Aurora Plaque was erected in 1939 on the Neva embankment opposite Rumyantsev House. On 25 October 1917 while moored at this spot, the cruiser "Aurora" (see entry) fired the shot which signalled the storming of the Winter Palace.

Imperial Stables H8/9

Konyushennoye Vedomstvo

Location
Konyushennaya Ploshchad 1

Metro
Nevsky Prospekt

Bus
1, 2, 14, 26, 46, 47, 100

The imperial mews, on the bank of the Moyka near the Church of the Resurrection (see entry), provided both stabling and administrative accommodation. Stasov's design of 1817/23 incorporated earlier stables into a long, polygonal building with a large inner courtyard. The main façade on Konyushennaya Ploshchad is distinguished by the domed Equerries' Church in the centre, flanked by slightly angled wings ending in pavilions. One side of the

Tram
51, 53

building is embellished with a row of 22 plain Doric columns.
A funeral service for Pushkin was held in the Equerries' Church on 1 February 1837.

Isaac Square

G7

Isaakievskaya Ploshchad

Location
between the Neva and the Moyka

Bus
2, 3, 10, 22, 27, 60, 100

The north side of Isaac Square borders the Square of the Decembrists (see entry). Dominated by St. Isaac's Cathedral (see entry) from which it takes its name, the Square took shape only gradually following construction of the massive church. Used in the 1830s and 1840s as a market-place it owes its present atmosphere to the late 19th and early 20th century buildings which surround it.

Nicholas I Monument

Montferrand, the architect responsible for St. Isaac's Cathedral, also designed the equestrian statue of Nicholas I (1796–1855) which stands in the centre of the Square. It was actually cast by the sculptor Peter Klodt von Jürgensburg. Unveiled in 1859 the statue shows the Czar in the uniform of the Horse Guards astride a rearing mount. The faces of the four female figures at the base, allegories of Justice, Strength, Wisdom and Faith, are those of Nicholas I's wife and three daughters who commissioned the monument. The bronze bas-reliefs round the base depict events from Nicholas I's reign (the Decembrists' Uprising, civil unrest during the cholera epidemic in 1831, a presentation to the

Mariya Palace and Blue Bridge at Isaac Square

statesman Speransky, and the inauguration of the Moscow to Leningrad Railway.

Lobanov-Rostovskiy House

Montferrand was also the architect of Lobanov-Rostovskiy House, built between 1817 and 1820. The house with its eight-column portico faces Admiralty Prospekt while one side overlooks the east façade of St. Isaac's Cathedral.

Hotel Astoria

The Hotel Astoria was constructed in 1910/12 and opened in 1913. Recently completely renovated, it has over 343 rooms including some in an adjacent building.
Somewhat prematurely as it turned out, Hitler planned to celebrate the fall of Leningrad in the banqueting hall of the Hotel. Invitations were already prepared giving the time of the function, only the date remained to be written in!

Ministry of Agriculture houses

Two almost identical buildings standing opposite one another (Nos. 4 and 13) were formerly the Ministry of Agriculture. Built between 1844 and 1853, they now house the Institute of Botany and Plant Conservation.

Mariya Palace

At the south end of Isaac Square, the Mariya Palace serves as the Town Hall and offices of the Leningrad City Soviet. It was commissioned in 1839 by Nicholas I for his eldest daughter, Maria, designed by Stakenschneider and completed in 1844. Sold to the State in 1894 by Maria's heirs, the palace was put at the disposal of the Imperial Council.
The long façade is heavily articulated with three projecting bays, the central one of which is crowned by a great attic decorated with medals awarded to the city. The flag of the Russian Soviet Republic flies from the roof.

The Blue Bridge

The Blue Bridge over the Moyka opposite the Mariya Palace is almost 100 m/110 yds wide but spans only about 35 m/38 yds and does not really have the appearance of a bridge. It takes its name from the blue paintwork on the underside.

Obelisk

High-water marks on the Obelisk at the Blue Bridge indicate flood levels reached by the Moyka. In the worst flood recorded the water level rose more than 4 m/13 ft.

German Embassy

No. 11 Isaac Square, now the Head Office of Intourist, was for a short time the German Embassy. Embassy staff only occupied the building (by the architect Peter Behrens) from its completion in 1912 until the outbreak of the First World War.

Myatlev House

Myatlev House (No. 9), which dates from the 1760s, is the oldest building in Isaac Square. The architect is assumed to have been Rinaldi. Pushkin, who was a friend of the writer Myatlev, often stayed there.

**Kazan Cathedral (Museum of Religion and Atheism) H7/8

Kazanskiy Sobor (Muzey Istorii Religii i Ateisma)

Location
Kazanskaya Ploshchad 2

The Kazan Cathedral (Cathedral of Our Lady of Kazan) on Nevsky Prospekt (see entry), is one of Leningrad's most

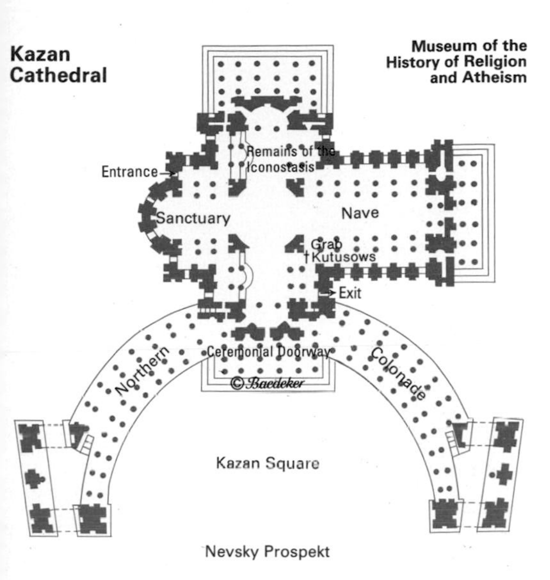

remarkable buildings. It has been the Museum of Religion and Atheism since 1932.
Shortly before his death Paul I, filled with admiration for the Church of St. Peter in Rome, commissioned a similar church for the Russian capital. The neo-Classical Alexandrian-style building, created between 1801 and 1811 by master builder Andrey Voronikhin, turned out in the event to be wholly original, only the dome and colonnade being at all reminiscent of its Roman model.

Metro
Nevsky Prospekt

Bus
3, 6, 7, 14, 22, 27, 44, 45

Opening times
Mon., Tues., Thur.–Sun.
11 a.m.–6 p.m.

Exterior

On the north side of the cruciform building, facing Nevsky Prospekt, there is a semicircular colonnade of Corinthian columns, 13 m/43 ft high and arranged in rows four deep. At either end of the colonnade are huge portals capped by attics. (Voronikhin's original design showed an identical colonnade on the south front.) Above the intersection of the cross a dome rises to a height of 71 m/233 ft. The three entrances to the cathedral are embellished with massive porticos. The bronze doors of the north entrance are copies of "The Gates of Paradise" from the Baptistery in Florence. Set in niches on either side of the doors are statues of John the Baptist, Prince Vladimir, Alexander Nevsky and St. Andrew the Apostle, the work of the sculptors Martos and Pimenov.

Interior

In the interior of the Cathedral, more like the hall of a palace than a church, double rows of columns, each cut from a single block of pink Finnish granite, support the vaulting over the nave and transept. The "miraculous image of Our Lady of Kazan", an icon reputed to have materialised in the

◀ *Kazan Cathedral, facing the Nevsky Prospekt*

Volga town of Kazan in 1579, used to be displayed on the iconostasis, part of which remains. The icon itself was stolen in 1904.
In the north transept, near where he is supposed to have prayed before setting out in 1812 for the war against Napoleon, Field Marshal Kutuzov is buried. Captured regimental colours, keys to surrendered towns and fortresses and other trophies around his tomb are reminders of Russian successes in war.
The Museum of Religion and Atheism housed in the Cathedral is divided into several sections. Pictures, sculptures, photos, documents, models and other exhibits trace, the origin of the different religions, for example, and the history of religion and atheism in classical times as well as in Russia.

Kazan Square

On 6 December 1876 the first revolutionary demonstration on Russian soil took place in the square in front of the Kazan Cathedral. Those who took part in it were subsequently put on trial. In what was later to prove a singularly unsuccessful attempt to prevent any recurrence, the square was laid out as a garden at the turn of the century. The statues of Mikhail Kutuzov (1745–1813) and Mikhail Barclay de Tolly (1761–1818), both distinguished Russian generals in the war against Napoleon, were placed at either end of the Cathedral colonnade in 1837.

Kikin Palace

see Tauride Palace

Kirov Bridge H/J9/10

Kirovskiy Most

Bus
1, 2, 25, 46, 65, 100, 134

Tram
2, 3, 12, 34, 51, 53

The Kirov Bridge, with its six arches one of the city's longest (600 m/656 yds), and almost 45 m/50 yds wide, crosses the Neva near the Peter and Paul Fortress (see entry). Originally called Trinity Bridge, it was opened to traffic in 1903 and is noteworthy for its pretty *art nouveau* design. In 1934 it was renamed after a leading Leningrad Communist, Sergey Kirov.

Kronverk

see Peter and Paul Fortress

*Kunstkamera G8/9

Kunstkamera

Location
Universitetskaya
Naberezhnaya 3

The first in the row of magnificent buildings on University Quay, the former Kunstkamera now houses the Museum of Anthropology and Ethnography and the Lomonosov Museum. It was commissioned by Peter the Great in 1718

The Kunstkamera on the University Embankment

for his collection of curiosities, displayed at that time in the Kikin Palace (see Tauride Palace). Work was finished in 1734 but a fire in 1747 meant that the Kunstkamera had to be almost completely rebuilt to the original plans and in fact it was not until the middle of this century that the upper floors of the tower were restored.

Bus
7, 30, 44, 47, 60

Exterior

Today the green and white three-storeyed building, its two wings linked by a projecting central tower, looks almost as it did in Peter the Great's time. The economy of decoration on the façade is typical of the early 18th century, any vertical articulation being limited to window-frames and shallow recesses. In the complicated design of the tower, on the other hand, Baroque elements are already visible.

Museum of Anthropology and Ethnography

Opening times
Mon.–Thur., Sun.
11 a.m.–5 p.m.

A visit to the Museum of Anthropology and Ethnography starts on the second floor where tools from the Stone, Bronze and Iron Ages are on display, together with reconstructions of prehistoric man. The first floor is given over to the cultures of the Near and Middle East, Australia and China while on the ground floor there is one of the most comprehensive collections anywhere of North American Indian and Eskimo culture. Among the most important exhibits are an Eskimo fish-skin coat for ceremonial wear, and an Indian cape of black ravens' feathers from California.
Also on the ground floor Peter the Great's collection of curiosities includes a remarkable variety of extraordinary oddities gathered on his foreign travels. A number of freaks

and monstrosities acquired in Amsterdam formed the basis of the collection, together with such items as deformed foetuses preserved in spirit, stuffed animals, and a large selection of strange instruments and gadgets. The collection was constantly being enlarged since Peter the Great issued instructions for anything odd or unusual to be brought to the Kunstkamera.

Lomonosov Museum

Opening times
Mon.–Thur., Sun.
11 a.m.–5 p.m.

This museum commemorating Lomonosov has been established in the tower of the Kunstkamera. Mikhail Lomonosov (see Notable Personalities), scholar-scientist, founder of the University of Moscow, worked in the building from 1741 to 1765. His books and personal effects are on display as well as rare 18th-century scientific instruments. One of the tower rooms contains a copy of the so-called Gottorp Globe. Showing the earth's surface on the outside, the hollow globe, 3 m/10 ft in diameter, can also be entered to reveal the heavens on the inside. Made for the Duke of Holstein-Gottorp, it was a gift to Peter the Great from the King of Denmark. The original was destroyed in a fire, and Lomonosov was involved in making the mid-18th-century copy.

*Large Department Store — J7

Gostinyy Dvor

Location
Nevsky Prospekt 35

Metro
Gostinyy Dvor

The Large Department Store, or Gostinyy Dvor, is Leningrad's equivalent of the GUM in Moscow. Biggest of its kind in the city it is quite unlike a Western department store. Traditionally, itinerant merchants in Russia sold their goods in a bazaar, or "gostinyy dvor", and in the Large Depart-

Large Department Store

Lion Bridge

ment Store clothes, household goods, food and many other products are sold from stalls.
Facing Nevsky Prospekt (see entry), the trapezoidal early neo-Classical building was erected between 1761 and 1785 to plans by Rastrelli and Vallin de la Mothe, although Rastrelli had sketched the ground-plan as early as 1748. It occupies a whole block, the combined length of the façade being over one kilometre. Restoration work at the end of the 19th century and in the 1950s and 1960s has left the exterior of the building, with its open arches on two storeys, almost unchanged, but the interior has been completely transformed.

Bus
3, 6, 7, 14, 22, 25, 27, 43, 44, 45, 70

Tram
2, 3, 5, 13, 14

Lenin Museum

see Marble Palace

Lion Bridge G7

Lvinyy Most

The Lion Bridge over the Griboyedov Canal near Theatre Square (see entry) was constructed by Traitteur in 1825/26. It is a suspension bridge similar to his Bank Bridge (see entry) but this time the steel cables disappear into the jaws of four lions, again by the Russian sculptor Sokolov.

Location
Naberezhnaya Kanala Griboyedova

Bus
3, 27, 43, 49, 50

*Lomonosov (Oranienbaum)

Lomonosov (Oranienbaum)

Location
40 km/25 miles west of Leningrad

Train
from Baltic Station (Baltiskaya Metro Station) to Lomonosov

The former imperial summer palace near the small town of Lomonosov (formerly Oranienbaum) 40 km/25 miles west of Leningrad has now been opened to foreign tourists. As at Pavlovsk, Petrodvorets, Pushkin and Gatchina (see respective entries) there are several palaces, pavilions, and other buildings set in an extensive park. Lomonosov may appear less grand than the other summer palaces, but it nevertheless has some buildings well worth seeing, and its park is relatively unspoiled, with fine old trees.

The town is now named after the Russian intellectual and writer Mikhail Lomonosov (see Notable Personalities) who established a factory there for making mosaics. The name Oranienbaum (as the railway station is still called), meaning "orange tree", comes from the large orangery once attached to the palace.

At the time when Peter the Great was building his first small palace at Petrodvorets, one of the Tsar's closest friends Prince Menshikov was intent on also owning a palace on the Gulf of Finland. Preliminary work began in 1710 but by 1728 when the interior was still not quite finished Menshikov was financially ruined and the estate passed to the Crown. The Empress Elizabeth gave it to her nephew the

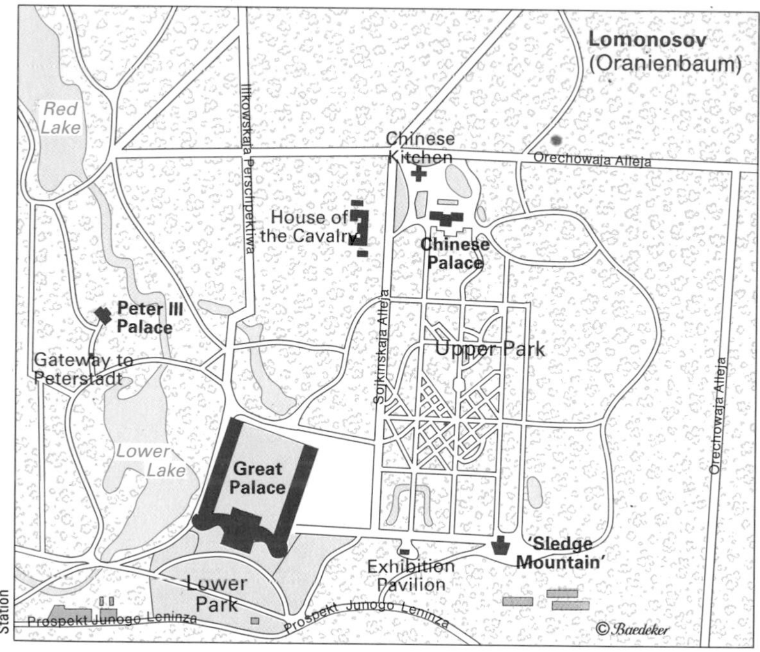

Great Palace; The Pavilion

Peterstadt Gateway

future Tsar Peter III, and during his reign and the reign of his wife and successor, Catherine the Great, other buildings were erected in the spacious grounds.

The Great Palace

The Great Palace, sited on a terrace overlooking the sea, was constructed between 1710 and 1725 under the direction of the architects Giovanni Maria Fontana and Gottfried Schädel. Curved galleries terminating in octagonal pavilions lead off from either side of the main building. About 1750 Rastrelli added new estate buildings, extending from the pavilions to form a large entrance court. The Great Palace is not open to the public.

The Sledge Mountain (Katalnaya Gorka)

The most interesting of the Lomonosov buildings is the so-called Katalnaya Gorka, the "Sledge Mountain". Built between 1762 and 1777, it is a tall, tapering three-storeyed pleasure pavilion, crowned by a bell-shaped tower. Each floor is encircled by a balustraded balcony which seems to demand that the visitor take advantage of the view, as indeed was the intention. The name recalls a favourite pastime enjoyed by St. Petersburg society, sledging. In Catherine the Great's time a great wooden switchback stood in front of the pavilion, down which in winter members of the court and their friends slid at great speed on small sledges. In summer specially built carriages were used. Between slides members of the court could take refreshment and rest in Katalnaya Gorka. The switchback itself was dismantled in the 19th century but a model is now on show in the pavilion. (Open in summer: Mon. 11 a.m.–5 p.m., Wed.–Sun. 11 a.m.–6 p.m.)

Katalnaya Gorka

Lomonosov Bridge

Peterstadt Gateway

Peter III, who liked to indulge his taste for military pursuits, had a cantonment, Peterstadt, built at Oranienbaum. Nothing remains of it but Rinaldi's delightful gate with its iron grilles and octogonal spire, dating from the 1750s.

Peter III's Palace

Peter III's Palace which Rinaldi built between 1758 and 1762 is a very modest two-storey building. The Czar's private apartments were on the upper floor, the ground floor being occupied by the domestic quarters. (Open in summer: Tues.–Fri. 11 a.m.–6 p.m., Sat., Sun. 10 a.m.–6 p.m.)

The Chinese Palace

Despite its name the exterior of the Chinese Palace (built between 1762 and 1768 on Catherine the Great's instructions) shows not a trace of Chinese influence. A few of the rooms are furnished in the Chinese Rococo style however and others are clearly inspired by the Orient. In the Russia of the time anything at all exotic was referred to as "Chinese" and this accounts for the name. Although the interior was exceptionally beautiful Catherine the Great is reputed to have spent only forty-eight days there in the whole of her thirty-four-year reign. (Open in summer: Mon., Wed.–Fri. 11 a.m.–6 p.m., Sat., Sun. 10 a.m.–6 p.m.)

Lomonosov Bridge J7

Most Lomonosova

Lomonosov Bridge, named after the Russian scholar and writer Mikhail Lomonosov, (see Notable Personalities) crosses the Fontanka near Rossi Street (see entry). Built in 1785/87 the middle span between the four squat towers was once a wooden drawbridge.

Location
Fontanka/Ploshchad Lomonosova

Bus
14, 25

Lomonosov Museum

see Kunstkamera

Lutheran Church

see St. Peter's Lutheran Church

Manège (Central Exhibition Hall) G7/8

Manezh (Tsentralnyy Vystavochnyy Zal)

The long neo-Classical structure of the former Manège (Horse Guards' Riding School) between Isaac Square (see entry) and the Square of the Decembrists (see entry) now serves as the city's largest exhibition hall. Built between 1804 and 1807 by Giacomo Quarenghi, an eight-column portico embellishes the Isaac Square façade. In 1817 statues of the Dioscuri were placed on either side of the entrance, copies of the Classical statues of Castor and Pollux with their horses which stand in front of the Quirinal Palace in Rome.

Location
Isaakievskaya Ploshchad 1

Bus
2, 3, 10, 22, 27, 60, 100

*Marble Palace (Central Lenin Museum) H/J9

Mramornyy Dvorets
(Leningradskiy Filial Zentralnovo Muzeya V. I. Lenina

Location
Ulitsa Chalturina 5/1

Bus
1, 2, 25, 46, 65, 100, 134

Tram
2, 3, 12, 34, 51, 53

Opening times
Mon., Tues., Thurs.–Sun.
10.30 a.m.–7 p.m.

One side of the Marble Palace extends along the Neva embankment opposite the Peter and Paul Fortress (see entry) but the main façade with its enclosed entrance court overlooks Suvorov Square. Since 1937 this magnificent building, access to which is from Ulitsa Chalturina, has been a branch of Moscow's Central Lenin Museum.

Field of Mars

The palace was built by Catherine the Great between 1768 and 1785 for her lover of many years, Grigoriy Orlov, who died before it was finished. In constructing it – Antonio Rinaldi carried out the work – nothing seems to have been too costly, the early neo-Classical front being faced entirely with marble and granite, exceptional even by St. Petersburg standards. A total of 32 different types of marble were used for the interior and exterior decoration. In contrast there is little in the way of sculptured ornamentation, the side façades being embellished only by the flattest of pilasters with Corinthian capitals, and only the main façade having columns. Above the main entrance is a clock tower, the hands of the clock permanently indicating 6.50 p.m. the time at which Lenin died on 21 January 1924 (see Notable Personalities).

Plan of the Marble Palace

Of the original interior only the staircase and part of the Marble Hall remain. Almost 7000 exhibits documenting the life of Vladimir Ilyich Lenin are on display in 25 of the palace rooms. Among the items, in addition to personal effects, are first editions of his books, photocopies of his manuscripts, and paintings, drawings and photographs connected with his life.

Marble Palace

The armoured car from which Lenin made his speech at Finland Station on 3 April 1917 now stands in the entrance court to the Marble Palace. He had just returned from exile and spoke urging that the bourgeois revolution be transformed into a socialist one.

Mariya Palace

see Isaac Square

Marsova Pole

see Field of Mars

Memorial to the Dead of the Revolution

see Field of Mars

*Menshikov Palace F8

Menshikovskiy Dvorets

Location
Universitetskaya Naberezhnaya 15

Bus
7, 30, 44, 47, 60

Tram
5, 37

The former home of Alexander Menshikov (1673–1729) was the first palace in St. Petersburg to be built of stone. Today the building on University Quay is a branch of the Hermitage (see entry), housing the collection of Russian culture in the first third of the 18th century.
Menshikov, Peter the Great's favourite and trusted friend, built the palace, large and splendid by the standards of the day, on Vasil'yevskiy Island, on land presented to him by the Tsar. Constructed between 1710 and 1720 the initial architect was the Italian Fontana, but later the Hamburg architect Schädel also worked on the project. On the Neva embankment opposite the main façade there was a landing stage, and the house was surrounded by an extensive park. Peter the Great, who owned nothing so luxurious, held official receptions there on numerous occasions. After Menshikov's downfall – he was banished to Siberia in 1727 – the palace became the property of the State, and in 1732 was handed over to the 1st Cadet Corps, an élite school for the nobility. In the course of the 18th century renovation work completely changed the exterior of the building. Eventually, it was left to deteriorate, measures being taken to restore it again only in 1967. The work proved to be extraordinarily difficult, particularly because the level of the embankment had since been raised and major excavation was required to expose the ground floor once again. Since then the exterior has been partly restored to its Petrine original.

Menshikov Palace

Exterior

The ground-plan of the Menshikov Palace, a large central section with projecting bays either side, is typical of early St. Petersburg buildings. The three-storeyed façade is decorated by tiers of white pilasters. Originally deep red, the colour has been changed to a dark yellow.

Interior

Over the years the interior of the palace, like the façade, has undergone many changes. As part of the restoration process of recent decades furniture and works of art were transferred from the Hermitage collection in 1981 with the aim of re-creating as far as possible the Petrine era. Menshikov's former living-room, panelled in oak, deserves special note: the fresco on the ceiling "Warrior in Armour" depicts the 20-year-old Peter the Great, while the small mirror in the amber frame is a relic of the Amber Room in Pushkin (see entry) which has disappeared without trace. A great many of the other rooms are lined with Dutch and Russian tiles. When first built it soon proved too costly to decorate whole rooms with Delft tiles, so Peter the Great arranged for two skilled Dutch tile-makers to set up workshops in St. Petersburg. The folk motifs on these tiles do not really compare with the fine examples from Delft.

Rumyantsevskiy Obelisk

The Rumyantsevskiy Obelisk, crowned with an eagle on a bronze sphere, stands in the park to the west of the Menshikov Palace. It was erected in 1799 to commemorate General Rumyantsev's (1725–1796) victories in the Russo-Turkish War of 1768 to 1774.

Mikhail Castle

*Mikhail Castle (Engineers' Castle) J8

Mikhaylovskiy Zamok (Inzhenernyy Zamok)

Location
Sadovaya Ulitsa 2

Bus
1, 2, 14, 25, 26, 46, 47, 65, 100, 134

Tram
2, 3, 12, 34

The Mikhail Castle, also known as Engineers' Castle, is set in pleasant gardens, its north façade overlooking the Summer Garden (see entry). Access to the central courtyard, leading to several institutes and a library, is through the south entrance.
It is by no mere chance that the Mikhail Castle has more the air of a medieval fortress than a palace. The intention of Paul I, Catherine the Great's son, was precisely to create a refuge safe from his enemies. He claimed the Archangel Michael appeared to him in a dream telling him to build a palace and a church dedicated to St. Michael at his birthplace. So the Summer Palace which stood on the site was pulled down and the Mikhail Castle commissioned.
The general design was by Bazhenov, but between 1797 and 1800 Brenna supervised work on the building which was much more fortress-like then than today. To the north and east the Fontanka and the Moyka provided protection from possible intruders, while moats, since filled in, guarded the palace on the west and south. Nevertheless, Paul's fortress failed to give him the security he sought and he was unable to enjoy it for long, for in March 1801 he was murdered in his bed. Afterwards no member of the imperial family wanted to live there, and it remained empty for many years. Following extensive restoration the Military Engineering Academy was set up in the huge building in 1823,

and it acquired the name by which it was later known, Engineers' Castle.

Exterior

The Mikhail Castle is square in plan, with a central octagonal courtyard. Each façade of the dark salmon-pink building is different. While the north front is dominated by a colonnade of pink marble columns, the west and east façades have arc-shaped bays. The golden dome of the palace church rises above the bay on the west façade. The main façade to the south is decorated with a bas-relief depicting the glory of Russia and also with the imperial Arms.

Peter the Great Monument

At the south entrance to the Mikhail Castle stands an equestrian statue of Peter the Great which is rather more conventional than the Bronze Horseman (see Square of the Decembrists). Cast between 1745 and 1747 during the reign of the Empress Elizabeth, it was only much later that Paul I decide to erect it. The inscription on it "To a great-grandfather from a great-grandson 1800" recalls a similar inscription on the Bronze Horseman.

Pavilions

Twin pavilions built between 1798 and 1800 flank the avenue leading to the south entrance of the palace. They are of a most unusual oval-shaped design with "flattened" ends.

Mining Institute — E7

Gornyy Institut

Location
Naberezhnaya Leytenanta Shmidta 45

Tram
15, 37, 63

The Mining Institute (see photo p. 178), one of the first mining academies in Europe, was founded in 1773. Its present building on the Neva embankment on Vasil'yevskiy Island was constructed by Voronkhin between 1806 and 1811, and follows the line of the river as it bends. An impressive portico with 12 Doric columns enhances the central block, while sculptured groups "Heracles and Antaeus" and the "The Rape of Persephone" flank the entrance steps. The Institute possesses an interesting museum. Large pieces of malachite, beryl, topaz and quartz are on display, as well as petrified wood, shells and cut stones.

Moscow Triumphal Arch — H2

Moskovskiye Triumfalnyye Vorota

Location
Moskovskiy Prospekt/ Ligovskiy Prospekt

Metro
Moskovskiye Vorota

Most visitors to Leningrad see the impressive Moscow Triumphal Arch as they drive from the airport to the city centre. It was erected between 1834 and 1838 by Stasov to commemorate victories in the Russo-Turkish War of 1828/29, taken down in 1936 and re-erected in 1959 to 1961. The cast-iron double colonnade is crowned by a cast-iron entablature and attic.

Mosque H10

Mechet

The mosque, built between 1910 and 1912 and at present undergoing renovation, is situated to the north-east of the Peter and Paul Fortress (see entry) near the Square of the Revolution. It is still a place of worship for Muslims who have also provided funds for the extensive renovation work.
With its faience-covered dome the mosque is reminiscent of the famous Tamerlane Mausoleum in Samarkand. The entrance is graced by two tall, slender minarets. Both the interior and the exterior are wholly Islamic in style.

Location
Pr. Maksima Gorkoga 7

Metro
Gorkovskaya

Bus
1, 25, 46, 65, 134

Tram
2, 3, 6, 12, 26, 34, 51, 53

Museum of Anthropology and Ethnography

see Kunstkamera

Museum of Religion and Atheism

see Kazan Cathedral

Narva Triumphal Arch E3

Narvskiye Triumfalnyye Vorota

The Narva Triumphal Arch stands in the middle of the Square of Strikes.
In 1814 Quarenghi erected a wooden arch for the triumphal return of the Russian army from the war against Napoleon. This monument soon fell into disrepair and was replaced between 1828 and 1834 by the present brick gateway covered with metal plates, the work of the architect Stasov. The raised attic is crowned by an imposing statue of the goddess Victory driving a chariot drawn by six horses. The names of battlefields and regiments are engraved on the arch.

Location
Ploshchad Stachek

Metro
Narvskaya

**Nevsky Prospekt H–M6–8

Nevsky Prospekt

Nevsky Prospekt, Leningrad's main thoroughfare and principal shopping area, extends for some 4.5 km/2.7 miles from the Admiralty (see entry) to the Alexander Nevsky Monastery (see entry).
Work started as early as 1712 on the wide virtually straight road between the Admiralty and the newly established monastery. On completion in 1718 it was known as the Great Perspective Road and at that time was a tree-lined avenue. The trees disappeared over the centuries and were replaced by an array of magnificent buildings along the

Location
runs from the Admiralty to the Alexander Nevsky Monastery

Metro
Nevsky Prospekt/Gostinyy Dvor/Mayakovskaya/
Ploshchad Vosstaniya/
Ploshchad Alexandra Nevskovo

ДОМ
М

Bus
3, 6, 7, 22, 27, 44, 45

grand thoroughfare. It was called Nevsky Perspektive from about 1738, and from 1783 Nevsky Prospekt.
The most impressive buildings, including shops, houses, palaces and banks, lie between the Admiralty and the small river Fontanka which for many years formed the city boundary.
Many poets and writers have sought to convey Nevsky's fascination, and time devoted to a walk along it is certainly well rewarded. Starting from the Admiralty the following buildings deserve special notice (N.B. even numbers are on the north side of the street):

No. 7/9. Wollenberg Banking House

This 1912 building was originally the St. Petersburg Commercial Bank. Today it houses an office of Aeroflot and a Beriozka shop. The ornamentation on the grey granite façade, suggestive perhaps of the Doge's Palace in Venice, is quite untypical of Leningrad.

No. 14. School building

Constructed in 1939 this is the only building on Nevsky Prospekt west of Ploshchad Vosstaniya to date from after the October Revolution. A sign on one of its outside walls (see photo p. 00) continues to warn of the danger of artillery bombardment, a sobering reminder of the blockade of Leningrad.

No. 15. House with the pillars

This house, built in the 1760s, clearly shows the architectural influence of the Winter Palace (see Hermitage).

No. 18. Kotomin House

Built by the architect Stasov between 1812 and 1816, Kotomin House is named after its first owner. During the 19th century it was a coffee-house frequented by artists and writers, including Pushkin. On the morning of 27 January 1837 he spent some time there, before taking part in the duel which led to his death. The coffee-house has been reopened and furnished with items from the Pushkin Museum.

No. 20. Dutch Church

The church was erected between 1834 and 1839. Only the central part under the dome was used for worship, the side wings serving the social needs of the Dutch community. In the church today are a library and some shops, including a bookshop.

No. 17.

The Stroganov Palace (see entry).

Nos. 22–24. St. Peter's Lutheran Church

Bryullov constructed St. Peter's in the years from 1832 to 1838 on the site of an older Lutheran church. He incorporated Romanesque elements which reflect the prevailing Romantic movement in European architecture, enhancing the façade with simple twin towers.
Next on the opposite (south) side is the great Kazan Cathedral (see entry).

No. 28. House of Books

Built in 1912/14 what is now the House of Books, the largest bookshop in Leningrad, formerly belonged to the Singer Sewing Machine Company of America.
From just across the bridge over the Griboyedov Canal the delightful Church of the Resurrection (Church of the Redeemer) can be seen some distance away on the left (see entry).

◀ *View of Nevsky Prospekt*

St. Peter's Lutheran Church

St. Catherine's Church

No. 30. Small Shostakovich Philharmonia Concert Hall

Rastrelli's turquoise mid-18th-century building was altered in 1829 by Jacquot. In the 19th century it played an important part in the musical life of the capital, with Liszt and Wagner among the famous musicians invited to give concerts there. It was badly damaged during the blockade. Following restoration in 1949 it became the Glinka Hall, the smaller of the two Philharmonia concert halls (named after the composer Glinka). The Large Concert Hall is in the Square of the Arts (see entry).

Nos. 32–34. St. Catherine's Church

The Catholic Church of St. Catherine was designed and built by Vallin de la Mothe. Construction of the domed cruciform church began in 1762 and was completed in 1783. The main façade is in the form of a triumphal arch. Statues of the Evangelists and of angels holding the Cross line the attic.

Nos. 31–33. Silver Row and the Town Duma tower

Silver Row, built by Quarenghi in 1784/87 as a trading house, is joined to the Town Duma tower. The tower, completed in 1804, served at first as an alarm tower from which warning of fire and sea floods was given. At the end of the 19th century it housed the heliograph, part of the signalling system which connected the capital with the summer palaces, and by means of which the arrival or departure of the Tsar was communicated.

No. 35.

The Large Department Store, Leningrad's best shopping centre (see entry).

Between Nos. 40 and 42. The Armenian Church

Built by Velten in the years from 1771 to 1780, the Armenian Church facing Nevsky Prospekt has a pedimented portico with four Corinthian columns. A small dome on a raised drum rises above it.

No. 48. Arcade

The "Passage" is by far the most interesting department store in Leningrad (see photo p. 188). A glass roof covers the 19th-century arcade which connects Nevsky Prospekt and Ulitsa Rakova.

No. 56. Comedy Theatre

The *art nouveau* building dates from 1903/07. A famous delicatessen (now Gastronom No. 1) used to occupy the ground floor, while above was a theatre (now the Comedy Theatre).
Next on the south side across the street is Ploshchad Ostrovskovo (see Ostrovskiy Square) with the monument to Catherine the Great. Then come No. 39 the Anichkov Palace (see entry) and Anichkov Bridge (see entry).

No. 41 Belosel'skiy-Belozerskiy Palace

The bright red Belosel'skiy-Belozerskiy Palace on the other side of Anichkov Bridge faces Nevsky Prospekt, with a side façade overlooking the Fontanka. The Belosel'skiy-Belozerskiy family, one of the richest in Russia, acquired the site in 1797. Stakenschneider erected the palace in the mid 19th century replacing an earlier building. He was an admirer of Russian Baroque, and enriched the façade with typical 18th-century detail. The palace is now a local authority headquarters.

Belosel'skiy-Belozerskiy Palace

*New Holland F7

Novaya Gollandiya

Location
Naberezhnaya Reki Moyki 103

Bus
2, 3, 22, 27, 49, 50, 100

Tram
1, 5, 11, 15, 31, 33, 42

New Holland is on an island formed by the Moyka and the Kryukov and Krushteyn canals. It consists of an assortment of red-brick buildings originally used to store timber for the Admiralty. Chevakinsky designed the functional buildings in 1765, work continuing on them until the late 1780s though they were never completed. The stone arch over the Moyka designed by Vallin de la Mothe is especially attractive, flanked on each side by a pair of Tuscan granite columns.
In the first half of the 19th century a prison was also erected on the island.

Oranienbaum

see Lomonosov

Ostrovskiy Square J7

Ploshchad Ostrovskogo

Location
south of Nevsky Prospekt

Metro
Gostinyy Dvor

Bus
3, 6, 7, 14, 22, 25, 27, 43, 44, 45

Tram
2, 3, 5, 13, 14

Ostrovskiy Square, just off Nevsky Prospekt (see entry), is dominated by the Pushkin Theatre on its south side. On the west side stands the Saltykov-Shchedrin Library and on the east side are two pavilions belonging to the Anichkov Palace (see entry). A monument to Catherine the Great was set in the centre of the square in the second half of the 19th century. The square and its surrounding buildings were designed by Carlo Rossi at the beginning of the 19th century. He drew up several plans for the then vacant space between the Anichkov Palace and the existing part of what is now the Saltykov-Shchedrin Library. The square was originally named after Nicholas I's wife, Alexandra. It was given its present name in 1923 to commemorate the dramatist, Alexander Ostrovskiy (1823–1886), considered to be the founder of Russian national theatre.

Catherine the Great Monument

The monument to Catherine the Great, unveiled in 1873, depicts the Empress in ermine robes holding the imperial sceptre in her right hand and a garland in her left. Round the bell-shaped base are nine larger than life-sized bronze figures of famous contemporaries, among them General Suvorov.

Anichkov Palace Pavilions

In 1816/18, on the eastern edge of Ostrovskiy Square in the gardens of the Anichkov Palace, Rossi erected two pavilions, connected by a wrought-iron railing which he also designed. On the façades overlooking the Square the identical small pavilions are decorated with Ionic columns and further embellished with statues of warriors.

Saltykov-Shchedrin Library

The Saltykov-Shchedrin Library which extends along the west side of Ostrovskiy Square consists of three wings. The main building, on the corner of Nevsky Prospekt and Sadovaya Ulitsa, was constructed between 1796 and 1801. The block facing Ostrovskiy Square was erected some thirty years later (1828/34) by Carlo Rossi as part of his scheme for the Square. Between the Ionic columns of the façade stand statues of philosophers and poets, including Homer, Vergil, Tacitus and Cicero. A further neo-Classical extension was added at the turn of the century (1896/1901). The library is named after the Russian writer Mikhail J. Saltykov (1826–1889) who wrote under the pseudonym Shchedrin. Opened in 1914 it is the oldest Russian public library and also second largest in the country after the Lenin Library in Moscow. It has 22 million books and periodicals among which are some valuable *incunabula* (early printed books) and important historical documents, including some in Peter the Great's handwriting. Voltaire's private library of about 7000 volumes, bought by Catherine the Great for an incredibly small sum, and the earliest dated Russian manuscript, the Ostromir Evangeliar, are also kept there.

*Pushkin Theatre

Built between 1828 and 1832 the Alexandra Theatre was the architectural centrepiece of Rossi's design for the Square in which it stands, taking its name like the Square from the wife of Nicholas I. It was renamed the Pushkin Theatre, or

Pushkin Theatre

Akademicheskiy Teatr Dramy im A. S. Pushkina to give the full Russian name, in 1937.
When it was opened the theatre became the home of Russia's permanent drama company, established by the ukase (imperial edict) of 1756 from a theatre-troupe formed by the Empress Elizabeth I from among the students of the Cadet Corps. Prior to moving into the Alexandra Theatre the company performed at different venues.
The building is square in plan. The principal façade on Ostrovskiy Square has six Corinthian columns forming a loggia, on either side of which is a niche containing the statue of a Muse. The attic is crowned by a statue of Apollo driving a chariot and four horses. The rear façade of the theatre forms the end of Rossi Street (see entry).
Parts of the splendid auditorium still appear as they did when new. The boxes and the stage are richly ornamented with velvet and gold-painted carvings.

**Palace Square — H8

Dvortsovaya Ploshchad

Location
east of the Admiralty

Bus
7, 10, 30, 44, 45, 47, 60

Tram
31, 63

Despite variations in architectural style Palace Square is one of the most magnificent of the world's great squares. Its most distinctive buildings are the Winter Palace on the north side (see Hermitage) and the General Staff building to the south. On the west the square is bordered by a wing of the Admiralty (see entry) while to the east side lie the former Guards Headquarters. In the centre stands the Alexandor Column.
The square was created in very much its present form in the first half of the 19th century. Previously plans for the area immediately to the south of the Winter Palace had been drawn up by Rastrelli, architect of the palace, but these had never come to fruition and a medley of timber buildings of various heights and styles stood on the site of the present General Staff building. In 1819 Alexander I commissioned new plans from Carlo Rossi. Rossi's bow-shaped design for the General Staff building resulted in a square of unusual shape and size, an ideal venue for marches and parades. In 1977 the square was resurfaced in stone for the sixtieth anniversary of the October Revolution, restoring it to its appearance in Alexander I's time.

Alexander Column

Like the triumphal arch of the General Staff building, the Alexander Column, designed by the architect Montferrand and built between 1829 and 1834, is a monument to the Russian victory over Napolean. Montferrand, finding inspiration in Roman tradition, created a tall Doric column surmounted by the figure of an angel crushing a snake underfoot, a symbol of the Russian triumph. With his left hand the angel, whose features are said to be those of Alexander I, supports a cross 6 m/20 ft tall. The overall height of the monument is 47.5 m/156 ft, even higher than

Alexander Column in Palace Square ▶

General Staff Headquarters on Palace Square

Trajan's Column in Rome. Supported only by its own weight, the column, cut from a single block of granite, rests on a bronze plinth, and with a dead weight of about 650 tonnes is so stable that it remained upright despite damage to the granite during the Second World War. Round the plinth are allegorical bas-reliefs of events during the Napoleonic campaign. The side facing the Winter Palace bears the inscription: "Alexander I, Russia's Gratitude".

General Staff Headquarters

Between 1819 and 1829, on the opposite side of the square to the Winter Palace, Rossi built the General Staff Headquarters, which also housed the Ministry of Foreign Affairs. The bow-shaped neo-Classical design is in distinct contrast to Rastrelli's Baroque palace.

The General Staff Headquarters consists of two wings divided by a massive double arch beneath which runs a carriageway linking Palace Square with Nevsky Prospekt. Conceived as a triumphal arch to commemorate the Russian victory over Napoleon, it is decorated with martial emblems, warriors, winged figures and allegories of glory. On the attic above the arch, symbolising Victory, is a huge sculpture of a female figure, standing in a chariot drawn by six horses. 10 m/32 ft high and 15 m/49 ft wide this was for a long time held to be the largest of its kind in Europe. All the decorative sculptures are by Pimenov and Demut-Malinovskiy. To Rossi's contemporaries the arch with its crowning group of figures seemed so immense that many believed it liable to collapse under its own weight. Rossi however had complete confidence in his architectural ability declaring to the Tsar, "If it falls, I will fall with it". The building is now used for administrative purposes.

Guards Headquarters

Bryullov's Guards Headquarters (1837/43) was the last building to be erected in Palace Square. Its unpretentious façade forms a successful transition between the Winter Palace and the General Staff Headquarters.

Passage

see Nevsky Prospect

**Pavlovsk

Pavlovsk

Location
30 km/19 miles south of Leningrad

Rail
from Vitebsk Station (Pushkinskaya Metro Station)

Pavlovsk (from "Pavel" meaning Paul), the last of the imperial summer palaces to be built, stands in exceptionally picturesque grounds 30 km/19 miles south of Leningrad, and only 5 km/3 miles from Pushkin. Of all the summer residences Pavlovsk is many people's favourite, preferred even to the great palaces at Pushkin, Petrodvorets and Lomonosov (see respective entries).
After the completion in 1837 of Russia's first railway, which ran between St. Petersburg, Tsarkoye Selo (now Pushkin) and Pavlovsk, excursions to the little town of Pavlovsk became popular with St. Petersburg society. This was largely due to the presence of a concert hall next to the station. Concerts were held there several times a week, a practice which continued into the present century. The station itself was modelled on London's Vauxhall (from which the Russian word for station "voksal" is derived).
In 1777 Catherine the Great presented 600 hectares/1500 acres of land with two tiny villages on it, south-east of Tsarkoye Selo, to her son the future Tsar Paul I and his wife Maria Fyodorovna (until her marriage Princess Sophie of Württemburg). The occasion of the gift was the birth of their first child, later Tsar Alexander I. At first only two modest wooden houses, Marienthal (Maria's Valley) and Paullust (Paul's Joy), were erected on the estate, but in 1782 work on a stone palace commenced under the direction of the Scottish architect Charles Cameron. At the same time the park was landscaped and a number of smaller pavilions were also built.
When later Paul was given the palace at Gatchina (see entry) by his mother he lost interest in Pavlovsk, and on becoming Tsar handed over the estate to his wife. Maria Fyodorovna took a very active interest in furnishing the palace and in laying out the park. She stayed there regularly until her death in 1828 when the estate passed to her youngest son, Grand Duke Mikhail Pavlovich. It remained in imperial ownership right up to the October Revolution.
During the Second World War Pavlovsk, like Petrodvorets

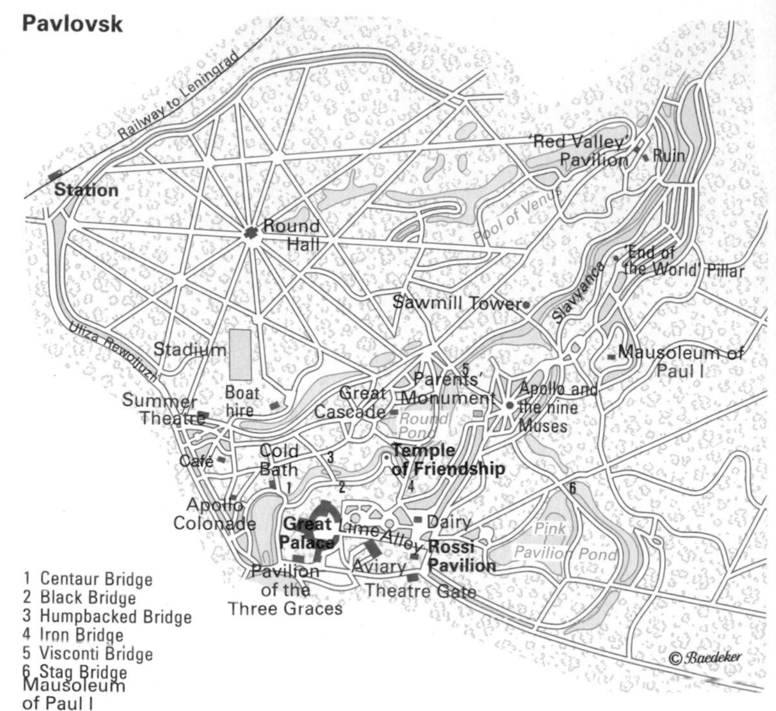

and Pushkin, was occupied by German troops and quite wantonly left in ruins. Work began on restoring the park and palace immediately after the German withdrawal. The park was reopened to the public in 1950 and the first rooms opened in 1957.

Great Palace

Opening times
Mon.–Wed., Sat., Sun.
10 a.m.–6 p.m.;
Thurs. (State Rooms only)
10 a.m.–4 p.m.

The Great Palace was erected between 1782 and 1786 on the site of Paullust, one of the wooden houses. Cameron's original design, based on a Roman villa, soon proved too small so in 1796/99 Vincenzo Brenna added a second storey to the galleries and end pavilions. One of the pavilions was also extended and two curved administrative wings were built.

Exterior

The central block of the neo-Classical palace is a rectangular three-storeyed building, crowned by a cupola in the form of a colonnaded drum supporting a flattened dome. From this central block curved galleries run out on either side terminating in pavilions, from which the service wings extend in turn to form an almost enclosed court. Both the façade overlooking the park and the façade fronting the entrance court are embellished with porticos of Corinthian columns.

Paul I Monument

A monument to Paul I erected in 1872 stands in the centre of the entrance court. It was cast from a statue by Giovanni Vitale made for the Gatchina Palace and depicts the Tsar in Prussian military uniform.

Interior

The strictly neo-Classical interior was the work of some of the most influential architects of the period. As well as Cameron and his successor Brenna who were responsible for a number of rooms, they included Quarenghi, who designed at least two, Voronikhin who redesigned several after fire had badly damaged the palace in 1803, and Carlo Rossi.
The private apartments on the ground floor and the State Rooms on the first floor are open to the public. In what used to be the staff quarters on the second floor there is now a permanent exhibition of 19th-century Russian furniture and interior design.

Private apartments of Paul I and Maria Fyodorovna

Entrance to the private apartments is through the Egyptian Vestibule, so called because of its Egyptian statues, allegories of the twelve months of the year. The largest of the ground-floor rooms, the dining-room, is dominated by four scenes of the park at Pavlovsk, painted by Martynov in 1800. Also on display is a dinner-service, originally of about 1000 pieces, made in 1827 at the imperial porcelain factory in St. Petersburg. Paul I's private study, the Old Study or Raspberry Room, is noted for its paintings of the Tsar's favourite palace Gatchina, dating from between 1797 and 1800.

State Vestibule

Access to the State Rooms on the first floor is via the State Vestibule, decorated with bas-reliefs of banners, weapons and armour. Brenna who designed the staircase could be guaranteed the approval of his patron Paul I, whose favourite recreation was to play at being the General!

Great Palace in Pavlovsk

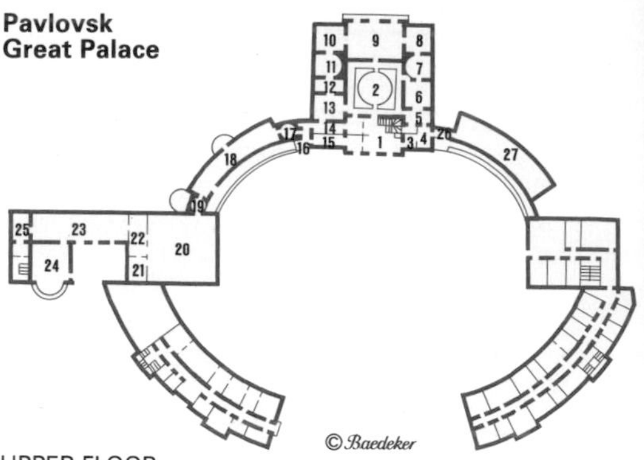

1 State Vestibule
2 Italian hall
3 Valet's Room
4 Dressing Room
5 Small Study
6 Paul I's Library
7 Gobelin Room
8 Hall of War
9 Grecian Hall
10 Hall of Peace
11 Maria Fyodorovna's Library
12 Boudoir
13 State Bedchamber
14 Dressing Room
15 Ladies-in-Waiting Room
16 First Lobby
17 Second Lobby
18 Portrait Gallery
19 Third Lobby
20 State Dining-Room
21 Servery
22 Orchestra Room
23 Hall of the Knights
24 Palace Church
25 Horseguards' Room
26 Lobby
27 Rossi Library

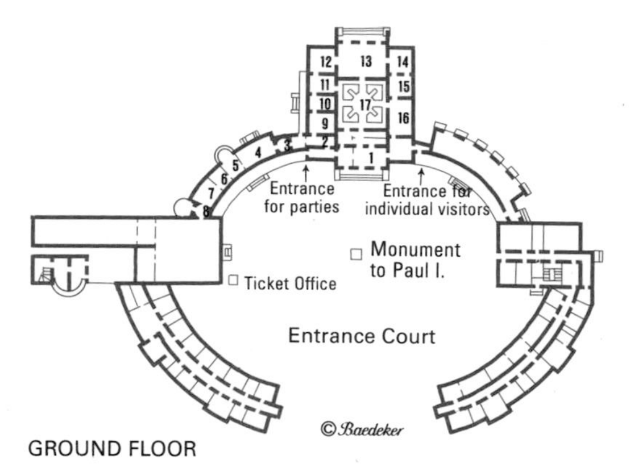

1 Egyptian Vestibule
2 Ante-Room
3 Valet's Room
4 Pilaster Room
5 Lantern Room
6 Dressing Room
7 Bedroom
8 Lobby
9 Old Study (Raspberry Room)
10 General Study
11 New Study
12 Corner Room
13 Dining-Room
14 Billiard Room
15 Old Drawing Room
16 Small Ballroom
17 Cloakroom

Tapestry in the Gobelin Room

Grecian Hall

Italian Hall

The Italian Hall in the centre of the building, designed by Cameron, extends upwards from first-floor level into the cupola, daylight streaming through the lantern windows in the circular drum. The elaborately inlaid mahogany and rosewood doors with gilded bronze ornamentation are exceptionally fine.

Paul I's State Rooms

Paul I's State Rooms are through the Valet's Room and the Dressing Room. In the Library there is a portrait of Maria Fyodorovna by the Austrian court painter Lampi, who for a time worked for the Russian imperial family. The tapestries in the Library were a present from Louis XVI, as were those which hang on the curved wall in the Gobelin Room. The latter, and the two Gobelin tapestries on the side walls, depict scenes from Don Quixote. The Hall of War, used for official receptions, again has decorations designed by Brenna.

Grecian Hall

The Grecian Hall separates Paul I's apartments from those of Maria Fyodorovna. Resembling a Greek temple in its design and ornamentation, the Hall is considered by many to be the most beautiful room in the palace. Fluted green marble columns constrast sharply with the white artificial marble-covered walls, while copies of classical statues adorn the niches round the room. The two white marble fireplaces are embellished with lapis lazuli and decorated with bronze ornaments.

Maria Fyodorovna's State Rooms

The Hall of Peace in Maria Fyodorovna's suite corresponds to Paul I's Hall of War. Symbolic garlands of flowers,

Temple of Friendship

kets of fruit, musical instruments and cornucopias feature among the decorative mouldings. The *pièce de résistance* in the library is a mahogany writing table with twelve ivory legs made by David Roentgen in 1784. The matching chair was designed by Voronikhin, the cornucopias in the back being intended for cut flowers. There is no record of Maria Fyodorovna ever having slept in her State Bedchamber although, by her own account, she thought the room and its furnishings wonderfully fine. The toilet set was a present from Marie Antoinette.

Picture Gallery

Entrance to the Picture Gallery is through a small lobby. Many of the paintings in the gallery were acquired by Paul I and his wife while travelling in Europe. For the most part, however, the furniture, candelabra and vases are of considerably greater interest.

State Dining-Room (Throne Room)

At the end of Paul I's short reign the Tsar's and Tsarina's thrones which stood in the State Dining-Room were removed. The ceiling of this the largest of the palace rooms is painted to give the illusion of open sky above a classical colonnade. The idea for the ceiling originally came from the Russian stage designer Gonzago at the end of the 18th century, but it remained unexecuted until his drawings were found quite by chance during restoration work following the Second World War. So, almost two hundred years later, the painting was finally completed.

The Hall of the Knights

Following Napoleon's capture of Malta, the Order of the Knights of St. John sought refuge in Russia and invited Paul

I to be their Grand Master. The Tsar had the hall built for meetings of the Order.

Pavlovsk Park

Opening times
Daily 9 a.m.–8 p.m.; garden pavilions: June–Oct., daily 10.30 a.m.–6.30 p.m.

Simultaneously with the construction of the palace, the park, through which flows the small river Slavyanka, was landscaped. It underwent a continuous process of alteration and improvement well into the 19th century. Trees and flowers were brought from abroad, oaks from Finland, limes from Lübeck, and bulbs from Holland and England. Maria Fyodorovna also had numerous pavilions built; a number of these are monuments – to her parents, her children and, of course, her husband, for whom she built the Mausoleum. In all, 17 pavilions, 12 bridges and many statues ornament the extensive grounds (see map page 96). Some of the pavilions are now used for temporary exhibitions

Temple of Friendship

The most noteworthy building in the park is the Temple of Friendship, designed by Cameron and erected in 1780/82. The circular structure is surrounded by fluted Doric columns with a freize above, decorated with dolphins and garlands, symbols of friendship. The interior consists of a single room the encircling wall of which is broken up by niches. Daylight enters from above through windows in the cupola.

Monument to My Parents

In 1786 Maria Fyodorovna had Cameron build this pavilion in memory of her parents Friedrich Eugen and Fredericke Sophia Dorothea, Duke and Duchess of Württemberg.

Dairy

The Dairy (1782) was also built by Cameron, on the model of a Swiss farm. It was large enough for six cows and had a cold room, despite which it was never intended to be more than a pleasure pavilion, being fitted out like the others with gilded furniture and valuable porcelain.

Rossi Pavilion

The Rossi Pavilion to the east of the Great Palace was only erected in 1913/14 to plans originally drawn by Carlo Rossi a hundred years earlier. A monument to Maria Fyodorovna stands in the semi-rotunda.

Theatre Gate

The Theatre Gate at the south-east side entrance to the park was built by Brenna in 1802. It once led to a wooden theatre – hence the name – which was pulled down in the mid 19th century.

Aviary

The rectangular Aviary, designed by Cameron in 1782, is a single-storeyed building, the central room with its cupola being connected to smaller side rooms by colonnaded galleries. In the 18th and 19th centuries song birds were kept in one of the galleries. The rooms were used for small receptions and for serving meals.

Pavilion of the Three Graces

The Pavilion of the Three Graces (1801) was Cameron's final contribution to Pavlovsk. "The Three Graces", a group hewn from a single piece of marble by the sculptor Paolo Triscorni in 1803, is surrounded by 16 Ionic columns.

Apollo Colonnade

Another of Cameron's pavilions, the Apollo Colonnade, was built in 1782/83. The statue of Apollo was originally encircled by columns, but in 1817, following flooding caused by a storm, the ground subsided and part of the colonnade collapsed. The appearance of a ruin was then deliberately preserved.

Peterhof

see Petrodvorets

**Peter and Paul Fortress G/H9/10

Petropavlovskaya Krepost

Entrance
Ploshchad Revolyutsii

Metro
Gorkovskaya

Bus
1, 25, 46, 65, 134

Tram
2, 3, 6, 12, 26, 34, 51, 53

Opening times
Mon., Tues., Thur.–Sun.
11 a.m.–6 p.m.

Standing on a small island in the centre of what is in effect the Neva delta, the Peter and Paul Fortress was the nucleus around which Leningrad as we know it today has grown. Work on the foundations is said to have begun on 16 May 1703, and in the autumn of that year some 20,000 men were engaged in building the ramparts, earthen mounds with wooden fortification towers. In 1706 the Swiss architect Domenico Trezzini replaced the earthworks with a stone wall, 2.5 to 4 m/8 to 13 ft thick, in the shape of an irregular hexagon, with bastions at the corners named after the various noblemen who were in charge of the building.
All the fortifications, including the outer defences, were completed in the first half of the 18th century, the Alexander Ravelin at the western end being named after Peter the Great's father, and the Ivan Ravelin at the eastern end after

Peter and Paul Fortress and bathing beach

his brother. The Kronverk provided extra protection to the north.
The building which is the heart of the fortress, the Cathedral of SS Peter and Paul, was constructed between 1712 and 1733, the other buildings being erected in the course of the 18th and 19th centuries. The fortified walls overlooking the Neva were faced in granite between 1770 and 1780.
The fortress was never required to fulfil the purpose for which it was intended, but from 1717 onwards part of the complex was used as a prison. Peter the Great's son was the first of a long line of prominent political prisoners to be held there. Among those who followed were Radishchev, whose "Journey from St. Petersburg to Moscow" brought imperial displeasure upon his head, the Decembrists, Maxim Gorky, Lenin's brother A. I. Ulanov, and many others. The last political prisoners of the Tsarist régime were the soldiers of the Paul I Regiment, freed after the February Revolution.
Every day at 12 noon precisely a cannon is fired from the Naryshkin Bastion signalling the time to the inhabitants of Leningrad, a custom which goes back to the 18th century.
The main access to the Peter and Paul Fortress is by the Peter Gate at the eastern end, reached via the Ivan Bridge and the Ivan Gate in the outer fortifications. Entrance to the fortress itself is free, a charge being made only for the museum and the Cathedral of SS Peter and Paul (ticket office to the right immediately through the Ivan Gate).

Peter Gate

The first wooden Peter Gate (1708) was replaced in 1717/18 by a stone gate in the form of a triumphal arch. Above the gateway is a relief of the double-headed Russian eagle, and above that a bas-relief by Konrad Osner "Simon Magus being cast down by the Apostle Peter". The Apostle was

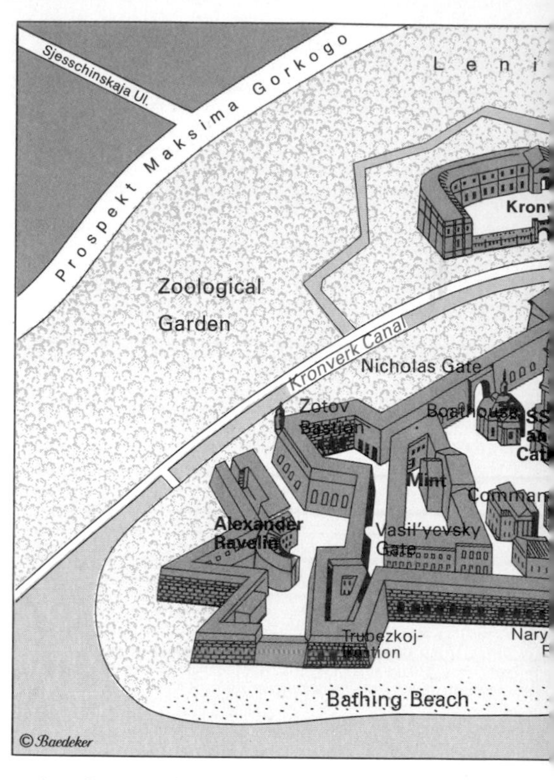

given Peter the Great's features by the sculptor, the relief symbolising the Tsar's superiority over his enemies. Statues of Bellona the goddess of war and Minerva the goddess of wisdom stand in niches on either side of the arch.

Engineer's House

Built in 1748/49 the Engineer's House is now a branch of the History of Leningrad Museum (see entry) featuring the architecture of St. Petersburg and Petrograd from the beginning of the 18th to the beginning of the 20th century. The exhibits include numerous draft plans and models of major buildings.

Guardhouse

The original Guardhouse was built in 1743 but later underwent considerable changes inspired by the neo-Classical revival at the turn of the 20th century. It is now used for the museum offices.

Neva Gate

Visitors arriving at the Peter and Paul Fortress by boat land at the Commandant's Pier and enter by the Neva Gate. It was constructed in 1730 and rebuilt in about 1785. On each side of the gateway are two Doric columns mounted on granite blocks. Levels reached by the Neva in flood are

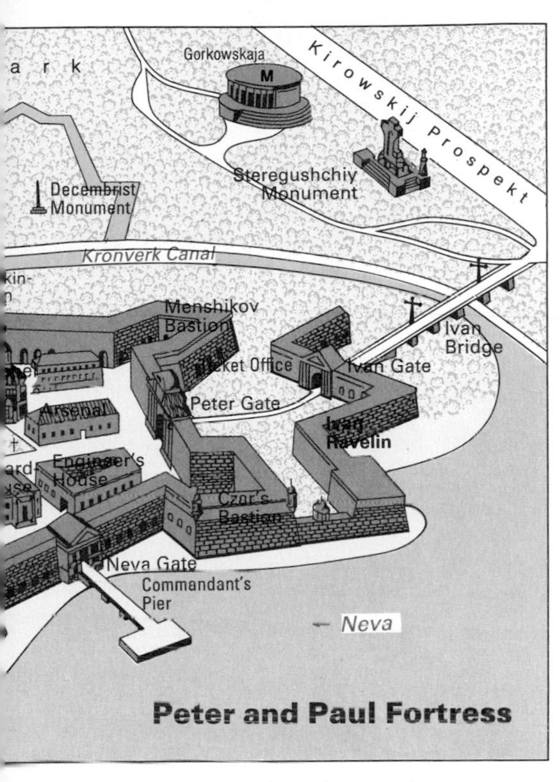

marked on a wall underneath the arch. The Neva Gate was used for taking condemned prisoners from the Fortress at night to be executed in the Schlüsselburg Fortress or some out-of-the-way place.

Commandant's House

Built in 1743/46 the former Commandant's House also contained the offices of the the fortress administration and the courtroom in which prisoners were tried. In 1975 it became another branch of the History of Leningrad Museum, covering the history of St. Petersburg and Petrograd from 1703 to 1917. The courtroom has been restored to its appearance in July 1826 when the verdicts were reached in the trial of the Decembrists. The place where the conspirators stood while sentence was passed is marked by a slab of marble.

Cathedral of SS Peter and Paul

At almost the same time as the original earth ramparts and wooden fortification towers were constructed, a timber church was built in the inner precinct of the fortress. Between 1712 and 1733 this was replaced by the Cathedral, which was to became the burial place of the Tsars.
Designed by the Swiss architect Dominico Trezzini, the Cathedral is quite untypical of Russian ecclesiastical

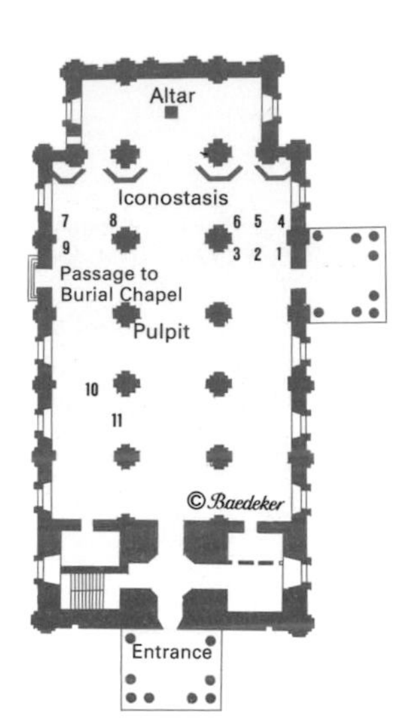

Cathedral of SS Peter and Paul

Starting with Peter the Great all the Tsars except Peter II and Ivan VI are buried in the Cathedral of SS Peter and Paul.
The sarcophagi are white Carrera marble apart from those of Alexander II and his wife which are red and green marble respectively.

TOMBS OF THE TSARS
1 Peter the Great (1672–1725)
2 Catherine I (1684–1727)
3 Elizabeth I (1709–1761)
4 Anna Ivanovna (1693–1740)
5 Peter III (1728–1762)
6 Catherine the Great (1729–1796)
7 Paul I (1754–1801)
8 Alexander I (1777–1825)
9 Nicolaus I (1796–1855)
10 Alexander II (1818–1881)
11 Alexander III (1845–1894)

architecture. The otherwise plain exterior is dominated by a bell tower and spire, 122 m/400 ft high, one of Leningrad's most prominent landmarks. Peter the Great decreed that the church should remain the city's tallest structure, and even today only the television tower exceeds it in height. The gilded spire is crowned by a weather vane in the shape of an angel, the cross the angel carries being 7 m/22 ft high. When in 1830 the original wooden spire was damaged by a storm it was thought too expensive to erect scaffolding, so someone prepared to risk life and limb had to be found to return the angel and cross to the top of the spire. For this brave deed one Tyolushkin, a farmer, received money and clothes from the Tsar and, according to legend, the "Golden Cup", which allowed him to drink as much as he liked free of charge in any inn in the land. He soon died from too much vodka! In 1857/58 the wooden spire was replaced by a slightly taller metal one, identical, except for the weather vane, to the spire on the Admiralty (see entry) the vane of which is in the shape of a caravel. At the far end of the nave from the tower there is a dome rising above a raised drum. The unusual interior of the church, a great hall 64 m/210 ft long and 30 m/98 ft wide, is divided into three aisles, separated by pillars. It is decorated with murals and reproductions of regimental colours captured in the Northern War against the Swedes.
The pulpit is another feature unusual in an Orthodox church. It is believed to have been used only once, in 1902 when Tolstoy was excommunicated following the publication of his novel "Resurrection", a work severely critical of Russian Orthodoxy.
The gilded carved wooden iconostasis resembles a triumphal arch, yet another allusion to victory in the Northern War. Designed by Zarudny and made in 1722/26, the

Baroque iconostasis is decorated with detached statuary, an innovation in Russian art.

Mausoleum

A covered passageway leads north-east from the Cathedral of SS Peter and Paul to the Mausoleum (built 1896/1908) where there is now a permanent exhibition tracing the architectural history of the Cathedral. On display are construction plans, a model of the spire, bells, cannon, pictures showing different phases of restoration, and much more besides.

Boat House

In 1762/66 a small single-storeyed building was erected next to the front of the Cathedral of SS Peter and Paul to house the boat in which Peter the Great first learnt the art of navigation. Today the boat itself can be seen at the Central Naval Museum (see Exchange).

Combining Baroque and neo-Classical features, the little pavilion with Doric pilasters and tall rectangular windows is further embellished by Doric porticos on the east and west façades. On the roof a wooden female figure, carved in 1891, symbolises Navigation.

Mint

Opposite the main façade of the Cathedral is the Mint, founded in 1716, where small coins, medals and decorations are still produced. Prior to completion of the present building in 1806 coins were minted in one of the fortress bastions.

Trubetskoy Bastion

Until the October Revolution the Trubetskoy Bastion, like the Alexander Ravelin, was used as a prison. It has now been turned into a museum and the former prison cells can

Peter Gate

SS Peter and Paul Cathedral

be visited. There were more cells, including a condemned cell, in the outer ramparts between the Trubetskoy and Naryshkin Bastions, where there were also rooms for those visiting the prison.

Kronverk (Military Museum of Artillery, Engineers, and Signals)

Opening times
Wed.–Sat. 11 a.m.–6 p.m., Sun. 10.30–6 p.m.

The Kronverk, immediately to the north, provided additional protection for the Peter and Paul Fortress. The first building was constructed in 1707/08, the present horseshoe-shaped edifice dating from the first half of the 19th century. Originally used as an arsenal it became an artillery museum in 1872. Now known as the Museum of Artillery, Engineers, and Signals there is a display of military equipment ranging from old instruments of war to the most modern rocketry.

Monument to the Decembrists

The obelisk to the east of the Kronverk was erected in 1975 to commemorate the Decembrists. It marks the place where the five young aristocrats, leaders of the 1825 conspiracy, were executed. A poem by Alexander Pushkin (see Notable Personalities), who was a close friend of some of the Decembrists, is carved on the plinth.

Steregushchiy Monument

The Steregushchiy Monument commemorates two sailors from the torpedo-destroyer "Steregushchiy" who, in 1904 during the Russo-Japanese War, scuttled their ship to prevent her falling into Japanese hands.

Peter the Great's Cottage J10

Domik Petra I

Location
Petrovskaya Naberezhnaya 6

Metro
Gorkovskaya

Bus
1, 25, 46, 65, 134

Tram
2, 3, 6, 12, 26, 34, 51, 53

Opening times
Mon., Wed.–Sun. 10 a.m.–6 p.m. (closed from 11 Nov. to 30 April)

Peter the Great's Cottage, the city's oldest building, was begun in May 1703 on a site to the east of the Peter and Paul Fortress (see entry) which was then in process of construction. The timber cottage with high shingle roof was erected in less than three days and except for its large windows resembles a traditional Russian farmhouse. In 1784 a stone structure, renewed again in the mid 19th century, was built over the wooden one to protect it from the elements.
The timber-built cottage is divided into three rooms, a work room, a dining-room and a tiny bedroom, separated from one another by a small hall. The ceilings are unusually low (2.5 m/8 ft) because although Peter the Great was tall he disliked high rooms, sometimes having his bed draped with sail cloth when travelling to create the illusion of a low ceiling. Furniture from the period and some of the Tsar's personal effects are on view.
Other items, including a boat believed to have been built by Peter the Great himself, are displayed in the space between the walls of the stone building and the timber cottage.

Bust of Peter the Great

In 1875 a bust of Peter the Great by P. Sabello was placed in front of the entrance.

**Petrodvorets (Peterhof)

Petrodvorets (Peterhof)

Petrodvorets, until 1944 known as Peterhof, is one of the most delightful of all the places to visit in the Leningrad area. Intourist offer guided tours of the extensive parks and some of the magnificent palaces but the tours are generally much too short. It is far better to visit Petrodvorets in your own time, preferably during the week when it can be enjoyed in peace. At week-ends it is a popular excursion for Leningrad people. The journey by hydrofoil takes about 30 minutes (see Practical Information, Boat Trips).

Location
30 km/19 miles west of Leningrad

Hydrofoil
from the Square of the Decembrists, the Hermitage or Tuchkov Bridge (from end of May to end of August only)

Train
from Baltic Station (Baltiskaya Metro Station)

With its lovely palaces, extensive gardens, and numerous fountains and cascades, Petrodvorets unquestionably invites comparison with Versailles from which came much of its inspiration. As at Versailles the parks are strictly formal, laid out geometrically in long straight lines. The Great Palace stands on a ridge some 20 m/65 ft high, below which the Lower Park with its smaller palace buildings and fountains extends 400 m/1300 ft or so to the sea.

History

The origins of Peterhof date back to 1704 when Peter the Great had a modest timber house built close to the shore. From 1713 onwards intense effort went into transforming the site in keeping with the Tsar's growing ambitions for it. Forests were cleared, avenues planted and the first palace buildings erected. Johann Braunstein and Jean Baptiste Alexander Leblond were the architects largely responsible.

Great Palace

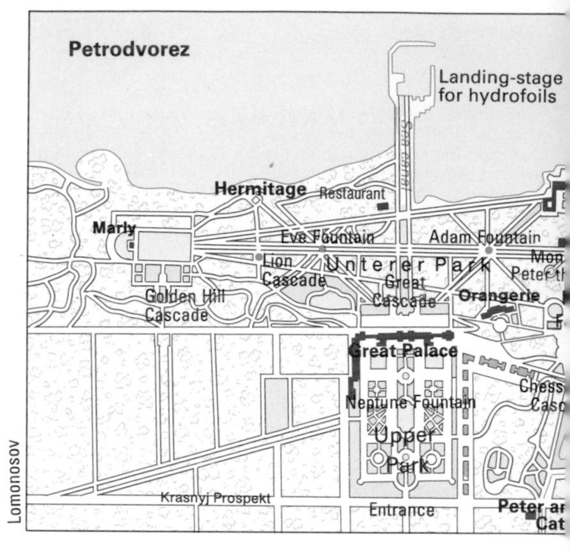

Huge numbers of workers were brought in, so that it was possible for Peterhof to be ceremonially inaugurated as the imperial palace in 1723. The Upper Park, the Lower Park, the Great Palace and the smaller palaces of Monplaisir and Marly were all completed about the same time, while the Hermitage was also in process of construction. Following Peter the Great's death in 1725 however work on Peterhof was halted. It began again only in the mid 18th century during the reign of his daughter the Empress Elizabeth, when additions and alterations were entrusted to Bartolomeo Franscesco Rastrelli.

During the Second World War the Germans occupied Peterhof and almost razed it to the ground. The palaces were set on fire, the parks completely devastated, and numerous art treasures disappeared. Immediately after the German withdrawal the painstaking task of reconstruction began, and with the help of photos and scraps of wallpaper great efforts were made to re-create the previous splendour. By the beginning of the 1960s the parks and palaces had all but been restored to their original appearance.

Some restoration work is still going on. At the present time, for instance, the fountains in the Lower Park are being renovated from the old plans.

Great Palace

Opening times
Tues.–Sun. 11 a.m.–6 p.m.

The two-storeyed house built by Peter the Great between 1714 and 1725 was quite modest compared with the grand palace the visitor sees today. To begin with construction was in the hands of the French architect Leblond, but after his death in 1719 Braunstein and Michetti took charge until work was halted in 1725. Within a relatively short space of

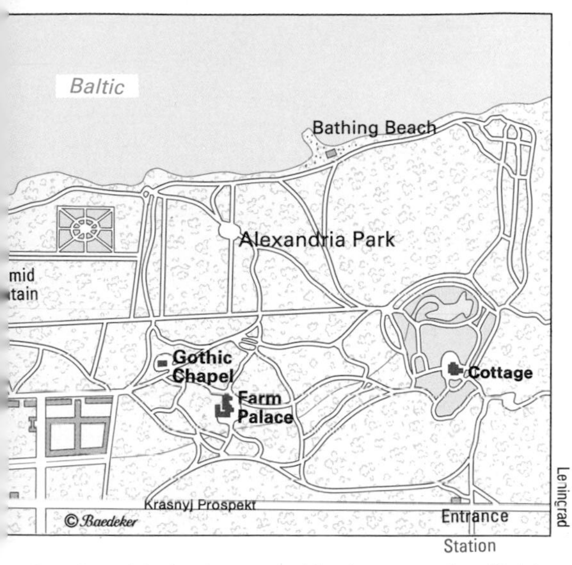

time the original palace proved inadequate to the official needs of the imperial court and so between 1747 and 1752 it was considerably enlarged under the direction of Rastrelli.

Exterior

Today the façade of the Great Palace is 275 m/895 ft long, with galleries extending on either side of the three-storeyed main building, terminating in pavilions. The cupola of the palace church in the east pavilion is crowned with a cross, while the Russian double eagle rises above the cupola on the west pavilion.

For the most part the ornamentation on the façade of the Early Baroque building is relatively restrained, amounting to no more than plain white frames round the windows, simple white pilasters, and pediments over the bays. The central bay has a distinctive triangular pediment capped by a gilded ornamental vase. The pavilions, in contrast, are somewhat more ornate, their roofs draped with gilded garlands.

Interior

In extending the palace Rastrelli largely kept to the style of Leblond's Early Baroque façade, but he departed considerably from the original conception in his reconstruction of the interior. The rooms he designed are full of gilded carvings, large murals and ceiling-paintings, only the Oak Study remaining unchanged from the time of Peter the Great. Throughout the second half of the 18th century the interior underwent further modification, several rooms being redesigned in the neo-Classical style.

Only the most important rooms are mentioned below, starting with the Oak Study where a tour of the Great Palace usually begins.

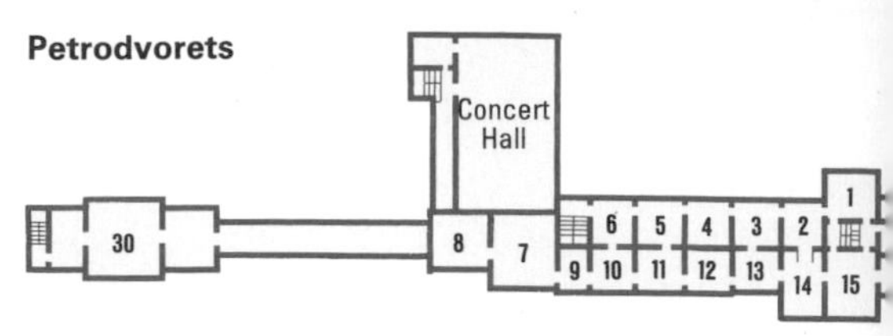

1 Oak Study
2 Crown Room
3–6 Guest Rooms
7 Blue Guest Room
8 Secretary's Office
9 Lobby
10 Cavalier Room
11 Standards Room
12 Study
13 Dressing Room
14 Divan Room
15 Partridge Room
16 Eastern Chinese Study
17 Portrait Gallery

Oak Study

The study takes its name from the oak panelling on the walls. Part of the original panelling carved by Nicholas Pineau in 1718/20 has survived. Also of interest is the travelling clock, thought to have belonged to Peter the Great.

Crown Room

The Crown Room and the Divan Room (see below) were at one time part of a single chamber, divided in the 1770s by creating alcoves back-to-back. The Crown Room is so called because the imperial crown was kept there when the Tsar or Empress were in residence. The gilded bed is from the 18th century.

Great Palace; fountains

Palace Church

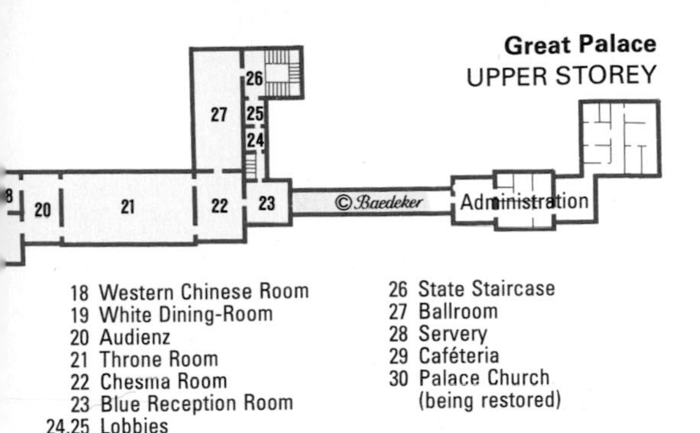

Blue Reception Room

The walls of this salon are covered with pale blue silk and hung with large paintings of Catherine the Great and Maria Fyodorovna, wife of Paul I. The service on display was made about 1850 in the imperial porcelain factory and used for State receptions.

Divan Room

The Divan Room, like the Crown Room, is panelled with Chinese silk. Of particular interest are the inlaid tables, Chinese vases, and a porcelain model of Semira, Catherine the Great's favourite greyhound, made in 1770.

Partridge Room

The silk wall-coverings decorated with garlands of flowers, ears of corn and partridges on a pale blue background are very fine. The room was originally hung with silk from Lyons, but this was replaced in the 19th century with silk woven in Moscow. Following restoration the west wall has been re-covered with the 19th-century fabric while the others are lined with new silk in the original pattern. Most of the furniture is from the 18th century. The harp was made in London in the first half of the 19th century.

Portrait Gallery

The Portrait Gallery, sometimes called the Rotari Room, was designed by Rastrelli as one of the main State Rooms. The walls are covered with 368 portraits of young girls painted by Pietro Rotari who worked in St. Petersburg from 1757 till his death in 1762. Only eight girls modelled for the artist, each being portrayed in a great variety of different costumes and poses.

White Dining-Room

The décor of this room is typically neo-Classical, everything from the walls to the dinner-service being predominantly cream-coloured. The Wedgwood service was made in 1770 and the Russian and Bohemian glassware is also from the 18th century.

Throne Room

The Throne Room occupies the whole width of the building, light streaming in through rows of windows on the two longer sides. Mirrors are hung between the lower windows, portraits of the Tsars and the imperial families between the upper ones. Behind the throne, which was made by Russian master craftsmen at the beginning of the 18th century, there is a great painting of Catherine the Great mounted on a white horse. On the wall opposite the throne are four paintings showing scenes from the Battle of Chesma.

Upper Park

Opening times
Daily 9 a.m.–9 p.m.

The Upper Park is overlooked by the south façade of the Great Palace. It is laid out symmetrically and surrounded by elaborate railings designed by Rastrelli between 1755 and 1759.

Neptune Fountain

The centrepiece of the formal garden is a fountain with an unusual history, the Neptune Fountain. It was designed for the market-place in Nuremberg by two German sculptors, Richter and Schneider. Not until the individual parts had been cast in 1660 was it realised that insufficient water was available to operate it. The useless product of this abortive scheme was ignominiously consigned to storage in Nuremberg, where it remained for over a century until Paul I acquired it on his travels in 1782. In 1799 it was finally assembled and installed at Petrodvorets.

Lower Park

Opening times
Daily from 9 a.m.–9 p.m.
(the fountains operate in summer Mon.–Sat. 11 a.m.–8 p.m., Sun. 11 a.m.–9 p.m.)

The Lower Park, a formal Baroque garden, occupies the ground between the ridge on which the Great Palace stands and the sea. Work on laying it out began in 1714. At one time the Tsars were able to proceed by boat as far as the Great Palace, along the 400 m/1300 ft sea canal which splits the park from north to south.

Sun Fountain

Garden of Monplaisir

Hermitage

Fountains

The Lower Park at Petrodvorets owes its uniqueness to the glorious play of water from its 144 fountains and 3 cascades. Underground conduits from the river Kovasha supply the reservoirs, from where water is piped to the various fountains before finally flowing into the canal and away to the sea. There are no pumps, water pressure depending entirely on the gradient between the reservoirs and fountains. The gradient is steepest closest to the reservoirs, so as the distance increases the jets become less powerful.
The Adam and Eve Fountains (1771/72) are among the oldest in the park, with avenues leading away from each like the spokes of a wheel. Particularly spectacular are the Sun Fountain and the Pyramid Fountain shooting plumes of water to different heights. Near the pavilion Monplaisir there are "trick" fountains, quite common in the 18th century, which spray the unsuspecting visitor who sits on a certain bench or treads on a particular stone. The Oak and Umbrella Fountains near the Peter the Great Monument behave like that, too.

Great Cascade

The Great Cascade, constructed between 1715 and 1724, is one of the most impressive fountain complexes in the world. Water tumbles down a divided aquatic staircase from the terrace in front of the palace to a marble basin below. The staircase and the grotto in the middle are flanked by gilded statues and numerous jets and sprays.
The Samson Fountain, set in the centre of the basin at the foot of the staircase, is one of the principal features of the Cascade. It was commissioned in 1734 to commemorate the Russian victory over Sweden at the Battle of Poltava, on St. Samson's day 1709. The sculptured group is a copy of the original which was stolen during the Second World War. Samson stands victorious over a lion from the mouth of which a jet of water is thrown 22 m/72 ft into the air.

Monplaisir

The first building to be erected at Peterhof, Monplaisir – meaning "my joy" – was sited directly on the shore and is evidence of Peter the Great's liking for plain Dutch-style houses. Extended galleries with round-topped windows lead off from the central block, terminating in small pavilions. In the mid 18th century Rastrelli built the Catherine wing, close to the west pavilion.
The style of the interior has largely survived from Peter the Great's time, when the Tsar was wont to drink his guests quite literally under the table. The bulk of a collection of paintings acquired by Peter, mostly works by 17th-century and early 18th-century Dutch and Flemish masters, still hang in the galleries, while the remainder can be seen in the various rooms. A Dutch garden with flower-beds and fountains is laid out in front of the little palace, some "trick" fountains having been added in the 19th century. (Open: Mon., Tues., Thur.–Sun. 10.30 a.m.–6 p.m.)

Hermitage

Designed by Braunstein in 1722/25 the moated Hermitage is in the western part of the Lower Park. The two-storeyed pavilion consists of a ground-floor kitchen and a dining-room on the upper floor. Originally there was no stairway, the guests and the already laid table being carried up by means of a special lift. In this way the invited guests were able to dine in complete privacy, undisturbed even by the staff who served them. (Open: Mon., Tues., Thur.–Sun. 10.30 a.m.–6 p.m.)

Marly

The most westerly of the buildings in the Lower Park, the small palace known as Marly, was built in 1720/23 and used primarily to accommodate guests. Following restoration the furniture and objets d'art are once again from the Petrine period. (Open: May–Sept., Mon., Wed.–Sun. 11 a.m.–6 p.m.; Oct.–Apr., Tues.--Sun. 11 a.m.–6 p.m.).

Alexandria Park

The Alexandria Park borders the Lower Park on its eastern side. Laid out in the style of an English landscape garden it was a gift from Tsar Nicholas I to his wife Alexandra in 1825. In the subsequent decades estate buildings, pavilions, towers and bridges were added.

Gothic Chapel

The Gothic Chapel dedicated to Alexander Nevsky was designed by the German master builder K. F. Schinkel in 1831/33. Each side of the square building has a rose-window above a Gothic stepped portal.

Farm

When first erected in 1829 the Farm was no more than a little pavilion intended to enhance the idyllic, pastoral character of the park. In 1838, however, it was enlarged to provide a small palace for the heir to the throne, the future Tsar Alexander II.

Cottage

The Cottage (1826/29) was the first of the Alexandria Park pavilions. It was built in the then fashionable pseudo-Gothic style of English country houses, with an intricate array of roofs, terraces, balconies and bays. The same style was also carried into the design of the interior. (Open: May–Oct., Mon.–Thur., Sat., Sun. 10.30 a.m.–6 p.m.; Nov.–Apr. Tues.–Sun. 10.30 a.m.–6 p.m.)

Piskarov Cemetery

Bronze statue of the "Motherland"

Piskarov Memorial Cemetery O/P14

Piskarovskoye Memorialnoye Kladbische

The Piskarov Memorial Cemetery in north-east Leningrad was opened on 9 May 1960, the fifteenth anniversary of the Allied victory in the Second World War. More than 500,000 people from the Leningrad area lie buried there, killed during the blockade of the city.
The mass graves are inscribed only with the year. At one end of the rows of graves an Eternal Flame is kept burning while at the other end a granite wall decorated with reliefs bears the inscription "No one is forgotten, nothing is forgotten." On a tall podium in front of the wall there is a bronze female statue representing the Motherland.

Location
Prospekt Nepokorennych 74

Metro
Ploshchad Muzhestva (first bus 101, then bus 75 or 178; or about 40 minutes on foot)

**Pushkin (Tsarskoye Selo)

Pushkin (Tsarskoye Selo)

Pushkin, formerly Tsarkoye Selo meaning "Tsar's village", is today a town of 80,000 inhabitants. In 1710 when Peter the Great gave the land to his wife Catherine I, it had been a Finnish estate called "Saari Muis" or "farm on high ground", being 65 m/213 ft above sea-level. It then became known as "Saarskoye Selo" which eventually turned into "Tsarskoye Selo". In 1918, because of the large convalescent home for children there, the name was changed to

Location
25 km/16 miles south of Leningrad

Train
from Vitebsk Station (Pushkinskaya Metro Station) to Detskoye Selo

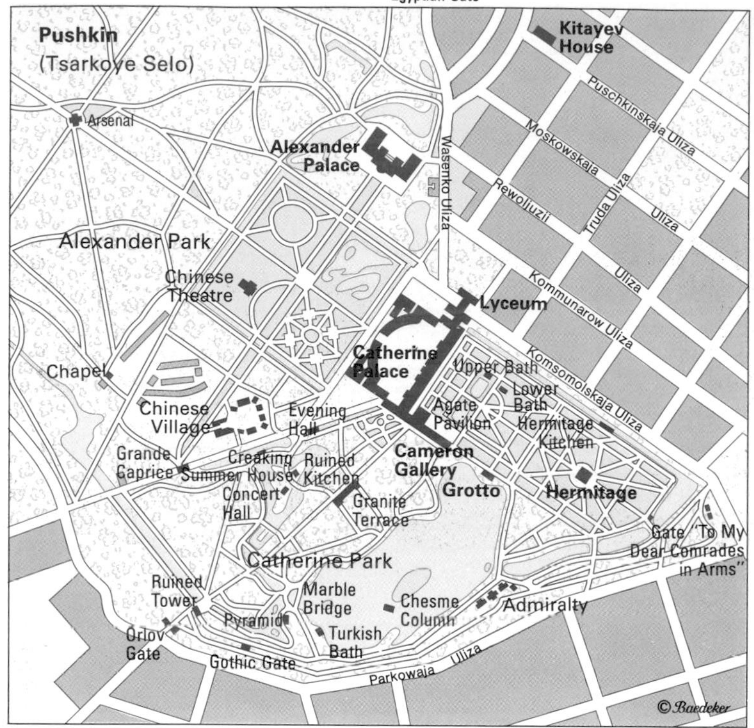

"Detskoye Selo" meaning "children's village" (the railway station is still known by that name). Finally, in 1937, the town became Pushkin on the centenary of Alexander Pushkin's death (see Notable Personalities).

Pushkin is well worth visiting for its two palaces (only the Catherine Palace is open to the public) and beautiful parks, and for the opportunity to walk the paths trodden in his schooldays by one of Russia's greatest poets. There are two museums and two monuments dedicated to him.

Catherine Palace

Opening times
Mon., Wed.–Sun. 10 a.m.–5 p.m. (in summer 11 a.m.–6 p.m.)

The origins of the Catherine Palace date from the year 1717 when Catherine I commissioned the German architect Johann Braunstein to build a stone house on the estate. After Catherine's death her daughter the future Empress Elizabeth inherited the property. Further extensive work was carried out creating a magnificent palace dedicated, as the inscription over the pediment testifies, to "Catherine I, in eternal and happy memory". Elizabeth entrusted the task of enlarging and embellishing the palace to the architects

Zemzov, Kvazov and Chevakinsky, but between 1752 and 1756 Francesco Bartolomeo Rastrelli took charge, raising the height of the building and extending the façade. Like Elizabeth, Catherine the Great was also fond of Pushkin and often stayed there. She employed the Scottish architect Charles Cameron to alter several rooms and to erect more buildings in the park. In the 1820s and 1830s following a fire the Russian architect Stasov was responsible for further alterations to the interior.
During the Second World War the Germans almost completely destroyed the Catherine Palace. The work of rebuilding is still not complete, but the splendour of the façade and most of the State Rooms has been restored.

Exterior

Now once again in its original blue and white colouring the main façade of the Catherine Palace measures more than 300 m/980 ft, from the palace church with its five domes at the north end to the single-domed pavilion to the south. This incredible length is broken up by projecting bays and richly embellished with columns, pilasters and decorative window-frames.
Immediately west of the palace two blocks of administrative buildings form great arcs enclosing the entrance court. The main gateway into the court was designed by Rastrelli, the gilded wrought-iron gates themselves being the work of Cordoni. The gates are ornamented with the double-headed Russian eagle and a crown.
The Agate Pavilion and the Cameron Gallery stand close to the south wing, while at the north end a passageway connects the palace church to the Lyceum.

Catherine's Palace in Pushkin

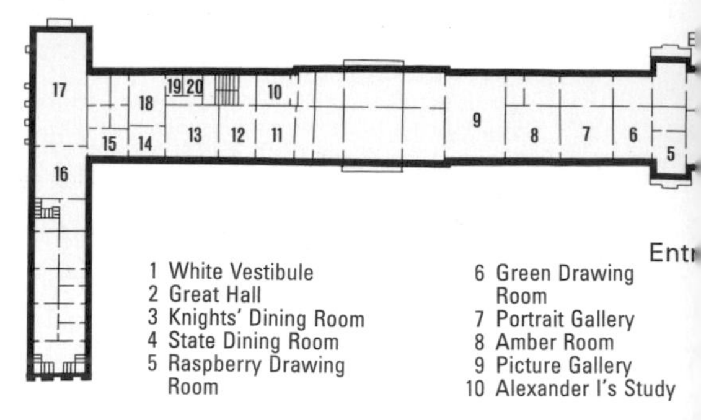

Interior

Although the interior of the palace, like the façade, had already been completely redesigned by Rastrelli, in the latter part of the 18th century and first half of the 19th, first Cameron and then Stasov rebuilt many of his Baroque rooms in the increasingly fashionable neo-Classical style. Today the State Rooms and Tsar's private apartments on the first floor are reached via the White Vestibule, the staircase which was designed by Monighetti in 1860.
Among the most beautiful rooms to have been painstakingly restored since the Second World War are:

Great Hall

Rastrelli's Great Hall is 47 m/154 ft long and some 18 m/59 ft wide. For receptions and balls it was formerly lit by 696 candles in huge candelabra. Mirrors in gilded wood frames with arabesque carvings are hung between the windows along the full extent of the two longer sides. The considerable effect created by the sheer size of the room is dramatically increased by the painted ceiling, "Russia's Triumph", which gives an illusion of unusual height. Painted from a sketch by Guiseppi Valeriani, it is a series of allegories glorifying Russian victories in war and achievements in the arts and sciences.

Knights' Dining-Room

This room takes its name from its use as a meeting-place for the Order of the Knights of St. Andrew, founded by Peter the Great in 1698. The gilded carvings on the walls are complemented by the Baroque chairs, reproductions from old designs.

State Dining-Room

The State Dining-Room was used for ceremonial State dinners. The table is laid with a dinner-service decorated with hunting scenes in green and brown on a white background, made in the imperial porcelain factory in the 1760s.

Amber room

The carved amber panelling by Andreas Schülter, which once almost completely covered the walls of this room, was presented to Peter the Great in 1716 by Friedrich Wilhelm of Prussia. During the Second World War the extremely valuable panels were removed by the occupying Germans and sent first to Königsberg and then to an unknown destination further west. They have never been found. In 1979 the

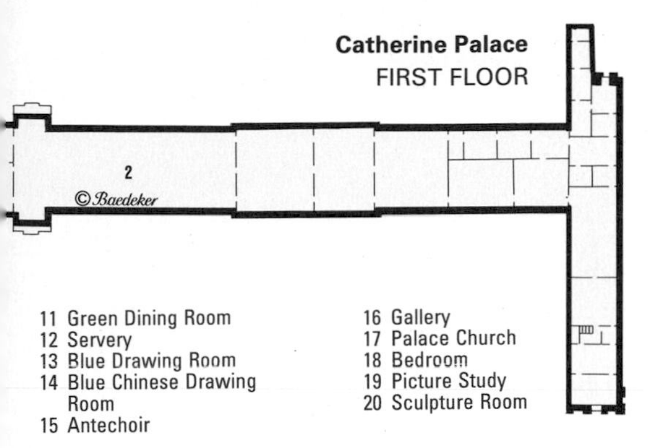

Russian Government decided to restore the unique room and soon visitors will once again be able to marvel at its splendour. An area of 25 m²/265 ft² will be completely lined with amber pieces of different sizes and colours.

Picture Gallery

The walls of the gallery are hung with some 130 pictures, of which 114 are original works by Flemish, German, Italian and French masters from the 17th and early 18th centuries.

Blue Drawing Room

The Blue Drawing Room was designed by Cameron for Tsar Paul I. The blue on white pattern of the silk on the walls is repeated in the curtains and chair coverings, and complemented by the dark blue glass torchères dating from the late 18th century. Portraits of a forceful looking Peter the Great by the Russian painter Ivan Nikitin, and of Catherine I by an unknown artist, are among those hanging in the room.

Blue Chinese Room

Designed once again by Cameron this room has walls covered exotically in blue Chinese silk with an idyllic landscape pattern, despite which the rest of the furnishings are almost all strictly neo-Classical. There is a portrait of the eight year old future Empress Elizabeth, depicted as Flora.

The Antechoir

The Antechoir is decorated with yellow silk, woven with pheasants, peacocks and other birds. Unlike the fabrics in most of the rooms, which are of recent manufacture from old designs, this silk is completely original. The pattern apparently failed to meet with imperial approval when it was first made, and instead of being hung the silk remained stored away in the Winter Palace (see Hermitage) until used in the restoration of the room following the Second World War.

Palace Church

The Palace Church, designed by Chevakinsky, was commissioned by the Empress Elizabeth in the 1740s. The dark blue walls with gilded decorations were retained by Rastrelli when he otherwise transformed the church in 1752/56, creating a Baroque interior.

Bedroom

This was the bedroom of Alexander I's wife Elizabeth. One of the features of the room is the fifty graceful pillars on

The Great Hall in Catherine Palace

which the ceiling appears to be supported, ornamented with leaves and garlands winding round the shafts. Some of the eight doors are purely decorative.

Catherine Park

Opening times
Daily 9 a.m.–8 p.m.

The Catherine Park, extending east and south of the Catherine Palace, took shape gradually during the course of the 18th and 19th centuries. It is in two parts, the French Garden laid out in geometric patterns in front of the east façade and the landscaped English garden with its Great Pond to the south. Neatly pruned trees and precisely arranged parterres, some of which are laid with coloured fragments of anthracite, brick and stone, establish the typically formal ambience of the French Garden. Catherine the Great was responsible for the creation of the English Garden, landscaped in 1768. She disliked straight avenues, fountains and canals, and considered the interior of a building to be the appropriate setting for statuary. In the open air, in contrast, Catherine thought the beauty of nature should be allowed to hold sway.
Scattered across the large expanse of the Catherine Park are several pavilions, monuments and bridges in a variety of styles, Chinese mixing with Baroque, neo-Classical and neo-Gothic.

Agate Pavilion

The Agate Pavilion, situated south-east of the Catherine Palace, was built between 1780 and 1787. It took its name from the opulent interior, ornamented with agate, jasper,

The Great Pond in Catherine Park

porphyry and marble. The living and reception rooms were on the upper floor, the ground floor being reserved in Roman fashion for baths. Although the pavilion is often referred to as "the Cold Bath" there were in fact warm and hot baths, too. (Open in summer: Mon., Wed.–Sun. 11 a.m.–5 p.m.)

Cameron Gallery

Charles Cameron was responsible both for the Agate Pavilion and the nearby gallery which bears his name. The upper floor is enclosed within a colonnade of Ionic columns forming a covered walk on either side. At the east end a divided flight of curved steps leads down to the garden. On the walls which flank the foot of the stairs stand bronze figures of Hercules and Flora, cast in 1786 from Classical statues in the Villa Farnese in Rome. The Gallery now contains a permanent exhibition of costumes and military uniforms from the 18th to the 20th century. (Open in summer: Mon.–Wed., Fri.–Sun. 11 a.m.–5 p.m.)

Upper Bath

The small rectangular Upper Bath was built in 1777/79 by I. Neyelov. In contrast to its plain exterior the interior is especially sumptuous.

Hermitage

The main path through the terraced French Garden leads to the Hermitage. Erected between 1744 and 1755 it was completed by Rastrelli and like the Hermitage at Petrodvorets (see entry) had a device for raising both dinner table and guests to the upper floor. In this way privacy was ensured for those dining at the invitation of the Tsar. After the meal the table was lowered again and the upper room became a ballroom.

The Hermitage Kitchens

The Hermitage Kitchens (1775) on the north side of the French Garden also incorporated a side entrance to the park. The red-brick walls are surmounted by small spires and, on one side, by turrets.

Grotto

The Grotto, on the north side of the Great Pond, was built by Rastrelli in 1753/57. The elaborate Baroque exterior, decorated with fishes, sea monsters and dolphins, is largely original. A collection of carriages dating from the 17th to the 19th centuries is now on display in the pavilion.

Admiralty

With its red-brick walls, little spires and arched windows, the Admiralty on the east side of the Great Pond has an almost Gothic air about it, despite having been designed by V. Neyelov in the 1770s. It was called "the Admiralty" because boats used on the Great Pond and the other waterways in the park were kept there. The building is now a restaurant.

Concert Hall and Evening Hall

The Concert Hall (1782/86), an early design by Giacomo Quarenghi, and the Evening Hall (1796/1809) by P. Neyelov, are both neo-Classical buildings.

Grande Caprice and Creaking Summerhouse

In 18th-century Russia as elsewhere in Europe it was fashionable to imitate Chinese art. Grande Caprice, a pavilion above an archway, built in the 1770s, and the Creaking Summerhouse, built in 1778/86, are both examples of the Chinese style. The Summerhouse owes its name to its deliberately creaky floor.

Turkish Bath

The Turkish Bath was the last of the pavilions to be erected in the park; it is a mosque-like building designed in the middle of the 19th century by the Italian architect Monighetti.

The Upper Bath

Pyramid

Catherine the Great had the Pyramid built in 1789 as a burial place for her favourite dog.

Victory Monuments

A series of monuments in the Catherine Park commemorate the First Russo-Turkish War of 1768–1774. Among the more noteworthy are: the Rostra or Chesma Column (20 m/65 ft high) in the middle of the Great Pond, atop which the Russian eagle tears at the Turkish half moon; the Morea Column erected in 1771; the Tower Ruin, symbolising the power forfeited by the Ottoman Empire as a result of the war. Catherine the Great wrote to Voltaire: "If this war continues my park in Tsarkoye Selo will soon look like a skittle alley, because for every brilliant stroke a monument is put up."
Near the Hermitage there is a gate dedicated to "My Dear Comrades in Arms", erected in 1817 to commemorate the victory over Napoleon in 1812.

Lyceum

Opening times
Mon.–Wed., Fri.–Sun.
11 a.m.–5 p.m.

In 1789/91 the North or Church wing of the Catherine Palace was extended and in 1810 the new building was made available for use by the Lyceum, a school for the children of the nobility. Alexander Pushkin (see Notable Personalities) attended the school from 1811 to 1817.
A Pushkin Museum was opened in the Lyceum in 1945. Some of the classrooms, the assembly hall, the library and Pushkin's bedroom are furnished as they were during the poet's life. Personal effects, books and papers belonging to Pushkin as well as some early 19th-century objets d'art are on display in the north wing of the Catherine Palace.

Pushkin Monument

In the garden of the Lyceum there is a monument to Alexander Pushkin, shown seated on a bench in meditative pose. The sculpture was made by Rudolph Bach in 1900 and the monument has become the symbol of the town of Pushkin in which it stands.

Pushkin Museum in Kitayev House

During 1831 Pushkin lived for a time in Kitayev House, built in 1828. Some of the rooms are open to visitors, furnished as they were in Pushkin's day. (Open: Wed.–Sun., 11 a.m.–5 p.m.)

Alexander Palace and Alexander Park

The Alexander Palace (not open to the public) was built by Catherine the Great in 1792/95 for her favourite grandson, the future Tsar Alexander I. It was a present to him on his marriage. Designed by Giacomo Quarenghi the restrained decoration on the neo-Classical façade is limited to Corinthian colonnades joining the side wings to the main building. It was the favourite residence of Nicholas II, the last Tsar of Russia.
The palace stands in Alexander Park, a garden landscaped in the English style. Among the buildings in the park are the Chinese Village, the Chinese Theatre and a neo-Gothic chapel.

Pushkin Theatre

see Ostrovskiy Square

Razumovsky Palace H7

Dvorets Razumovskovo

Location
Naberezhnaya Reki Moyki 48

Metro
Nevsky Prospekt

Bus
2, 3, 6, 7, 14, 22, 27, 44, 45

Razumovsky Palace, on the east bank of the Moyka just off Nevsky Prospekt, was built between 1762 and 1766 by Korinov and Vallin de la Mothe. The building, which houses the directorate and library of the Institute of Education, can best be described as Classical with Late Baroque features. The general design, a three-storey main block with wings forming a large entrance court, is typically Classical, as is the portico with its six Corinthian columns. The abundance of ornamentation adorning the main façade, on the other hand, is very definitely Baroque.

Ushinsky Monument

A monument to Konstantin Ushinsky (1824–1871), a founding father of Russian education, stands in the centre of the entrance court.

*Rossi Street J7

Ulitsa Rossi

Location
between Ploshchad Ostrovskovo and Ploshchad Lomonosova

Metro
Gostinyy Dvor

Bus
14, 25, 70

Rossi Street (see picture on page 127), leading from the Pushkin Theatre (see Ostrovskiy Square) to Lomonosov Square, is perfectly proportioned, being 220 m/720 ft long by 22 m/72 ft wide and the buildings on either side of it 22 m/72 ft high.
Formerly known as Theatre Street it was constructed in 1828/34 by the architect Carlo Rossi (see Notable Personalities) after whom it was renamed in 1923. Rossi designed two identical buildings confronting each other along the length of the street, their façades embellished with Ionic columns arranged in pairs. The uniform, unassuming character of the façades is reinforced by their colouring, off-white columns against an unobtrusive yellow. The two buildings now house the Vaganova Ballet School, one of the most famous in the world (founded in 1738), a theatre museum (see Information, Museums), a specialist theatre library and the Institute of Architecture and Town Planning.

Rostral Columns

see Strelka

Rumyantsev House

see History of Leningrad Museum

Razumovsky Palace

Rossi Street

Russian Museum (Mikhail Palace) J8

Russkiy Musey (Mikhaylovskiy Dvorets)

The Russian Museum occupies two buildings, the Mikhail Palace and an adjacent purpose-built block, the two being linked by a passageway. The basis of the present museum was a collection formed by Alexander III in the Anichkov Palace. When in 1895 Nicholas II acquired the Mikhail Palace for the Crown, items were added from the Hermitage (see entry), the Academy of Arts (see entry) and the Alexander Palace (see Pushkin). The enlarged collection became the Russian Museum, opened in 1898. Following the October Revolution the museum was expanded further and today has over 315,000 exhibits, making it the second most comprehensive collection of Russian art after the Tretyakov Gallery in Moscow. All aspects of Russian art are represented, from painting, sculpture and graphics to handicrafts and folk art. For the time being a large part of the museum is closed owing to extensive restoration work.

Location
Inzhernaya Ulitsa 2–4

Metro
Nevsky Prospekt/Gostinyy Dvor

Bus
2, 14, 25, 26, 100

Tram
2, 3, 5, 12, 14, 34

Opening times
Mon., Wed.–Sun. 10 a.m.–6 p.m.

The Museum Buildings

Exterior

The neo-Classical Mikhail Palace was built by Carlo Rossi between 1819 and 1825 for the Grand Duke Mikhail Pavlovich, younger brother of Czar Alexander I. The main façade, fronting onto the Square of the Arts (see entry), has a central section graced by an 8-column Corinthian portico

Russian Museum

and flanked by two projecting side wings. The resulting large entrance court is enclosed behind an ornamental wrought-iron railing. The façade at the rear overlooking the garden, considered by many to be even more splendid than the front of the building, has a 12-column loggia running almost the full width of the central section and even grander ends to the two wings.
Because the Mikhail Palace soon proved too small to house the museum, a new building designed by Benois and Ovsiannikov was erected to the west of the palace in 1912/16.

Interior

As with the exterior, every detail of the interior was designed by Rossi himself. When at the end of the 19th century the rooms were adapted for museum use, however, only part of the interior survived intact, the appearance of the White Hall and the Great Vestibule with its magnificent staircase remaining closest to Rossi's original plans.
The White Hall (Hall 11) was formerly one of the three reception rooms of the palace. The ceiling is painted with various figures and garlands, including goddesses carried in chariots of war. Recessed windows extend almost the full length on one side of the room while on the facing wall are four paintings of scenes from the "Iliad" and "Odyssey". The floor is laid in geometric figures and leaf patterns created from a variety of woods. The chandeliers, though not part of the original furnishings, were nevertheless designed by Rossi.

Russian Museum Collection

A tour of the museum begins on the upper floor of the main building with the section devoted to Early Russian Art. The departments of late 19th- and early 20th-century Soviet art are housed in the adjacent, newer building, which at present is being extensively renovated and will probably remain closed to the public until the mid 1990s.

Early Russian Art (Rooms 1–4)

The term "Early Russian Art" refers to art in Russia from the introduction of Christianity (A.D. 988) to the 17th century (the beginning of Peter the Great's reign). One of the most important art forms of this period is iconography, represented in the Russian Museum by such notable examples as "The Angel with the Golden Hair", an unusually expressive, small painted icon from the 12th century, and the icon "Boris and Gleb" (*c.* 1300) which depicts the sons of the Grand Duke Vladimir of Kiev, murdered by their brother and subsequently sanctified. Human emotions are represented in a highly individual way in the work of Andrey Rublyov (*c.* 1370–*c.* 1430), one of the most celebrated artists of the Moscow School. The icons of the Novgorod School, "The Trinity" (*c.* 1550) and "Georgi's Miracle" (15th century) for example, are distinguished by a more realistic technique and their use of bright colours. A later icon by Simon Ushakov (1626–1686), also "The Trinity", reveals a new direction in icon painting with the realism of its treatment of people and landscape elements.

White Room, Russian Museum

Icons in Russian Museum

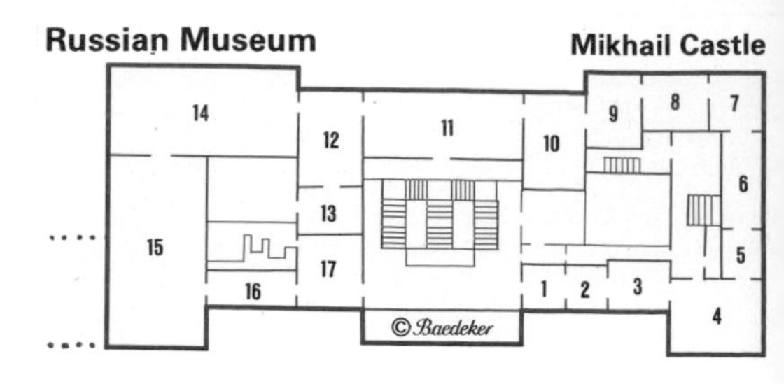

UPPER FLOOR

1–3 Icons
4 at present closed
5 Nikitin, Matveyev
6 Antropov, Lomonosov
7 C. B. Rastrelli, Golelins
8 Rokotov, F. Shchedrin
9 Losenko
10 Levitsky, Shubin
11 White Hall
12 Borovikovsky, Martos
13 at present closed
14 Andrey Ivanov, Sokolov Ugriumov Bruni, Sazonov
15 Alexander Ivanov, Ayvazovsky, B
16 S. Shchedrin, Lebedev
17 Kiprensky, Vitali

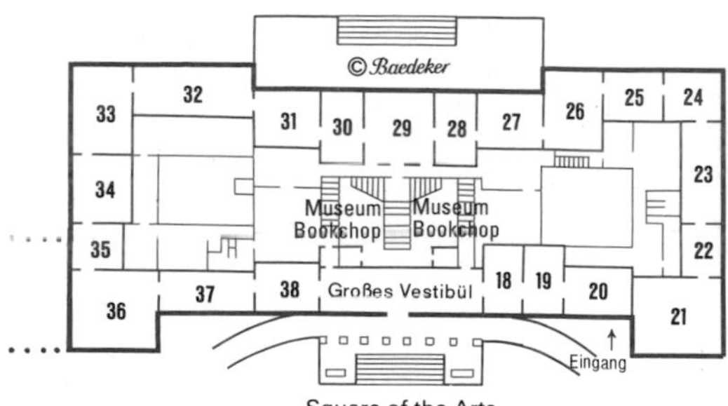

GROUND FLOOR

18–29 Temporary Exhibitions from the Museum Collection
30 Perov, Makovsky
31 Gay
32 Levitan, Shishkin, Polenov
33 Repin
34 Repin
35 Serov
36 Surikov, S. Ivanov
37 Nesteror, Korovin
38 Kustodiyev, Petrov-Vodkin Kuznetsov

18th century (Rooms 5–13)

In the 18th century the effects of Peter the Great's reforms became evident in the arts and, freed from the constraints of the Church, portraiture in particular developed into a major art form. Among the most important representatives of the period are Ivan Nikitin (*c.* 1688–1741) who did several portraits of Peter the Great, Andrey Matveyev (1701–1739), one of whose best works is "Self-portrait of the Artist with his Wife", and Aleksey Antropov (1716–1795), who was not afraid to paint his subjects as he saw them. While portrait painting was flourishing, historical painting also became important following the foundation of the Academy of Arts in 1757. While borrowing heavily from western European art, Russian painters soon developed their own "Academy Style", the work of Anton Losenko (1737–1773) being typical of the new movement.

As in painting, Russian sculpture also began to take a new direction. "Venus at her Toilet" by Fedossy Shchedrin (1751–1825) portrays Venus in a realistic pose rather than relying on Greek canons of beauty. The further development of Russian sculpture is well illustrated in the work of Ivan Martos (1754–1835), in his "The Tomb of Kurakina", for example.

First half of the 19th century (Rooms 14–17)

During the first half of the 19th century Russian painting continued to be dominated by the Academy Style, although not completely unchallenged. In one of his masterpieces "The Appearance of Christ to the People", for example, Aleksandr Ivanov (1806–1858) made a tentative effort to break free of the principles of the Academy and replace them with the "ideals of free art". Also reflected in the art of the period was the developing ideological struggle between the different social groups on the one hand, and the surge of nationalism created by Russia's success in the Napoleonic War on the other. Both are present in "Valiant deed of a young man from Kiev" by Andrey Ivanov (1776–1848), which pays tribute to the spirit of sacrifice on the part of a young man of simple origins. When the Academy financed a visit to Italy by some of its members an Italian influence was also introduced, evident in paintings like "Italian Day" and "The Last Days of Pompeii" by Karl Bryullov (1799–1852), products of the artist's stay in Rome, and also in the works of Fyodor Bruni (1799–1875). Landscape painting was another important art form during this period. Sil'vestr Schedrin (1791–1830) and Ivan Ayvazovsky (1817–1900) produced paintings in which the time of day, weather conditions and light effects are important elements.

Second half of 19th century (Rooms 30–34)

Of major importance in this period are the artists who broke away in protest from the Academy in 1863, forming a group called the Peredvizniki (the Itinerants). Although not constituting a unified movement in painting the group had in common their primary concern of drawing attention to social evils. Their aim, "to transform life through art", is reflected in the works by Nickolay Gay (1831–1894), Ivan Shishkin (1832–1898), Vasily Perov (1834–1882), Konstantin Mayakovsky (1839–1915) and of course Ilya Repin (1844–1930), one of Russia's most distinguished painters (see Notable Personalities).

End of the 19th/beginning of the 20th century (Rooms 35–38)

At the turn of the century many Russian painters were influenced by Impressionism, Valentine Serov (1865–1911) and Konstantin Korovin (1861–1939) among them. Some, Pavel Kuznetsov (1878–1968) for example, turned completely to Symbolism, while others such as Mikhail Nesterov (1862–1942) and Boris Kustodiyev (1878–1927) produced relatively traditional work. The paintings of Kusma Petrov-Vodkin (1878–1939) on the other hand represent a transition to Soviet art.

St. Andrew's Cathedral

see Bolshoy Prospekt

0099 ЛЕА

**St. Isaac's Cathedral — G7/8

Isaakievskiy Sobor

Location
Isaakievskaya Ploshchad

Bus
2, 3 10, 22, 27, 60, 100

Opening times
Mon., Thur.–Sun.
11 a.m.–7 p.m. (dome: 11 a.m.–4 p.m.); Tues. 11 a.m.–5 p.m. (dome: 11 a.m.–3 p.m.)

St. Isaac's Cathedral on the north side of Isaac Square (see entry) is one of Leningrad's largest and finest churches. Its enormous proportions, (111 m/360 ft in length, 97 m/315 ft in width and 101 m/328 ft in height), make it the world's third largest domed church after St. Peter's in Rome and St. Paul's in London. Services ceased to be celebrated here following the October Revolution and in 1928 it was decided to make the building into a museum, opened in 1931. Visitors to the Cathedral should be sure not to miss the climb up to the dome which offers an excellent view over the city (a special ticket is needed).

History

Shortly after the founding of St. Petersburg, a church was built on the site of the present Cathedral dedicated to St. Isaac of Dalmatia, on whose saint's day Peter the Great was born. Between 1768 and 1802 the existing church was replaced by another, but as soon as it was completed the new building was deemed insufficiently imposing and, following the victory against Napoleon, it was decided to erect something more appropriate in its place. A competition was arranged to find a suitable design, 24 different plans in a variety of styles being submitted by a completely unknown French architect Auguste Ricard de Montferrand. Alexander I was impressed by Montferrand's designs and decided on his neo-Classical version, work on the project beginning in 1818. The architect and his assistants faced major problems in the course of erecting the huge edifice, 20,000 tree-trunks having to be used for example before the ground was made firm enough for building to begin. Even so the foundations were considered to be insufficiently stable and between 1822 and 1825 work was suspended. Montferrand revised his design, construction went ahead, and the church was eventually consecrated in 1858. Work on the interior ornamentation continued for a further ten years, and it was not until 1858 that all was complete. During the blockade of the city in the Second World War St. Isaac's Cathedral suffered frequently in the bombardment. The interior and exterior were restored as soon as the war was over, though some signs of damage from the shelling can still be seen, especially on the south façade.

Exterior

The magnificent red-granite and grey-marble cathedral is actually rectangular in plan, but four huge porticos, those on either side of the transept being especially prominent, create the impression of a Greek cross. Granite steps lead up through the porticos on three sides to the entrances. The porticos of the main entrances on the longer north and south sides are modelled on the Pantheon in Rome, 16 monolithic columns of polished red Finnish granite with bronze bases and capitals, arranged in rows 3 deep. The porticos on the shorter east and west sides each have 8 columns. On all four sides the pediments above the columns are decorated with large bronze reliefs, "The Adoration of the Magi" by Vitali on the south side, "St. Isaac

◀ *View of St. Isaac's Cathedral from Isaac Square*

St Isaac's Cathedral

1 Steps leading to dome
2 Stained-glass window
3 Construction model of the portico columns
4 Display on the history and restoration of the Cathedral
5 Bust of Montferrand
6 Iron cast of Montferrand's sculpture on the pediment
7 Galvano-plastic dove (1850)
8 Construction model of the central dome
9 Steps leading from dome

predicting the impending death of the Emperor Valentinian" by Lemaire on the east, "Christ's Resurrection" also by Lemaire on the north side, and "St. Isaac blessing the Emperor Theodosius", again by Vitali, on the west. This latter also depicts the architect Montferrand with a small model of the cathedral (there is a bronze cast of it in the cathedral itself). Crowning the pediments are statues of the Evangelists and Apostles, while groups of angels with torches stand at the corners of the main building. Rising above a colonnaded drum the great gilded dome (26 m/85 ft in diameter) is surmounted by an octagonal lantern about 12 m/39 ft tall, on top of which is a cross. Four bell-towers with cupolas form a square round the dome.

Interior

Three entrances with colossal bronze entrance doors richly sculptured by Vitali lead into the 4000 sq m/42,000 sq ft interior of the cathedral, lit from above by the subdued light from 12 windows in the drum beneath the dome. Enclosing a space large enough to hold some 14,000 people, the walls are so heavily ornamented with the greatest conceivable variety of marble and precious and semi-precious stones, as well as 200 mosaics and paintings, that individual detail is almost lost. In all, 43 different kinds of mineral were used in the interior decoration leading to the cathedral becoming known as "the museum of Russian geology". All the minerals used were incorporated in the bust of Montferrand which can also be seen inside. The ceiling in the main dome is covered by a huge painting of the Virgin Mary surrounded by saints, Apostles and Evangelists, the work of Bryullov and Bassin.
The three-tiered iconostasis is decorated with mosaics of the saints, while to each side of its central doorway stand six half columns, one of lazurite and five of malachite. When

the doors are open the stained-glass window of the sanctuary comes into view. It depicts the Resurrection and was made in Munich. There are numerous museum exhibits connected with the history of the cathedral, including photos, drawings and some construction models.

St. Nicholas's Cathedral G6

Nikolskiy Morskoy Sobor

Location
Ploshchad Kommunarov

Bus
43, 49, 50

Tram
1, 3, 5, 11, 13, 14, 15

To the south of Theatre Square (see entry) beside the Kryukov Canal, the blue and white St. Nicholas's Cathedral with its distinctive campanile can be seen from a great distance. Also known as St. Nicholas's Maritime Cathedral it is one of 15 Russian Orthodox churches in Leningrad still open for worship.
The cathedral is dedicated to St. Nicholas, patron saint of seafarers, being located in a district where mainly sailors and dockyard workers from the Admiralty used to live. Built by Chevakinsky between 1753 and 1762, the basically simple ground-plan in the shape of a Greek cross is elaborated in a fashion typical of Russian Baroque by projections and recesses on the façades, and by clusters of columns at the corners. The façades are also relieved by windows of different shapes with stucco surrounds. True to Old Russian tradition the church has five gilded domes, the regilding of which is paid for by the parishioners themselves, obviously prepared to go without in order to pay for it.

St. Nicholas's Cathedral

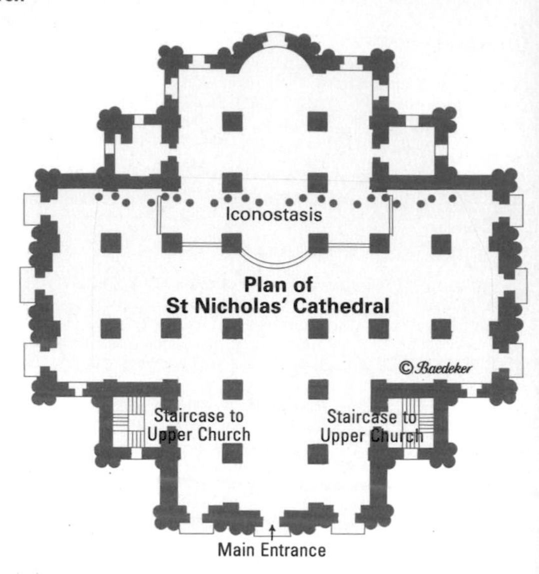

The interior of the cathedral is on two storeys, a "winter church" which can be heated on the ground floor, and a "summer church" in the rather brighter surroundings of the upper floor. The show-piece of the interior is the gilded iconostasis in the upper church, with its mid-18th-century icons.

Campanile

Standing about 100 m/325 ft distant, the graceful four-storeyed campanile (see picture page 135) contrasts sharply with the somewhat heavy structure of the cathedral itself. The uppermost storey of the tower consists of a small dome with a spire.

St. Peter's Lutheran Church

see Nevsky Prospekt

Saltykov-Shchedrin Library

see Ostrovskiy Square

Senate and Synod

see Square of the Decembrists

Sheremetyev Palace — K8

Sheremetyevskiy Dvorets

Location
Naberezhnaya Reki Fontanki 34

Metro
Gostinyy Dvor

Bus
3, 6, 7, 22, 27, 43, 44, 45, 70

Tram
5, 12, 14, 34

Built on a site beside the Fontanka river, the Sheremetyev family home was called "Fontanki Dom". The first single-storey house was erected in 1712 by Boris Sheremetyev (1659–1719), a general who distinguished himself in the war against Sweden. His sons commissioned major alterations in the 1730s and 1740s, and in 1750 they also added a second storey. The central section of the building is embellished with pilasters and crowned with a pediment bearing the Sheremetyev coat of arms (two lions holding palm branches in their mouths). The windows have white stucco surrounds.

Summerhouse

Following restoration the summerhouse is to be turned into a museum commemorating the poet Anna Akhmatova who was persecuted during the Stalin era.

Catherine Institute

No. 36, the neo-Classical building next door to the Sheremetyev Palace, was built by Quarenghi in 1804/06. It used to be the Catherine Institute, a school for the daughters of the well-to-do middle classes.

Smolny Convent — N10

Smolnyy Monastyr

Location
Ploshchad Rastrelli

Bus
1, 6, 14, 43, 65, 74, 134, 136, 137

Opening times
Exhibition in the Cathedral of the Resurrection: Mon Thur.–Sun 11 a.m.–6 p.m., Tues. 11 a.m.–4 p.m

The bright blue painted Smolny Convent (also called Smolny Monastery), one of Rastrelli's many fine Baroque buildings, stands on the west bank of the Neva to the east of the city centre. At the heart of the convent is the Cathedral of the Resurrection, visible for some considerable distance all around. It now houses the exhibition "Leningrad Today and Tomorrow".
The convent was originally founded in 1748 by Elizabeth I, who intended to spend her old age there. It took its name from the yard which occupied the site in the time of Peter the Great, where pitch for the Russian navy was boiled and stored ("smolna" meaning pitch or tar). Elizabeth I died however before the convent was completed, and three years later in 1764 the cathedral was still little more than a shell. That same year Elizabeth's successor Catherine the Great founded a school for the daughters of the nobility in part of the convent, but other buildings remained unfinished until finally completed by the architect Stasov in the 1830s. At the beginning of the 19th century the school was moved into the newly built Smolny Institute (see entry).

Convent complex

The cathedral is enclosed by four two-storeyed cell wings, laid out so as to give the whole complex the shape of a Greek cross. In the corner at one end of each wing there is a church with a tall cupola.
Three of the four convent buildings were largely complete in 1764, built to Rastrelli's Baroque design. The fourth, on the west side, was constructed between 1832 and 1835 in

the neo-Classical style, but was altered to match the others in the 1860s. Only part of the stone wall which used to completely surround the convent is still standing. It, too, has corner towers.

**Cathedral of the Resurrection

The magnificent five-domed Cathedral of the Resurrection was completed in phases. The first, from 1748 to 1764, saw only the construction of the building itself under the direction of Rastrelli. Decoration was carried out much later by Stasov in 1832/35.
The main façade is separated from Rastrelli Square by an attractive iron railing designed by Stasov. The cathedral is crowned with five onion domes, the central dome rising on a two-storeyed drum between four dome-topped towers. As is usual in Baroque buildings Rastrelli's exterior decoration is extremely elaborate. Clusters of columns and pilasters articulate the façades, and the windows have very ornate stucco surrounds. Stasov on the other hand designed a strictly neo-Classical interior, the effect of which is now largely lost. "Leningrad Today and Tomorrow", the exhibition housed in the whitewashed rooms, is in stark contrast to the cathedral's original purpose. Video films and other exhibits feature, among other things, the material and technical achievements of the USSR today.

Smolny Institute N9

Smolnyy Institut

Location
Ploshchad Proletarskoy Diktatury

Bus
1, 14, 26, 65, 74, 134, 136, 137

The Smolny Institute, a school for the daughters of the nobility, was originally established in the Smolny Convent (see entry). In 1806/08 however, Giacomo Quarenghi erected a new building for the school in the style of a large country house, on a site some 300 m/975 ft south of the convent. Quarenghi, a master of the neo-Classical style, designed a rectangular building with two side wings, the main façade being embellished with an eight columned Ionic portico.
For the Soviet people, however, the Smolny Institute is inseparably linked with the events of the October Revolution. In August 1917 the Petrograd Soviet of the Workers' and Soldiers' Deputies moved into the building from the Tauride Palace (see entry). It was here that the overthrow of the Kerensky government was planned, and it was from here that the victory of the socialist revolution was announced on the night of 25/26 October 1917. The first Soviet government, the Council of People's Commissars, met here under Lenin's leadership until it was transferred to Moscow. Lenin lived and worked in the Smolny Institute for 124 days in all. Naturally the rooms he used have been turned into a museum, although visits are only possible in groups and by appointment.
Other rooms in the Institute are now occupied by various local and regional departments of the Communist Party.
In 1927 a monument to Lenin was unveiled in front of the Smolny Institute. There are also busts of Karl Marx and

◀ *Cathedral of the Resurrection – Smolny Monastery*

Friedrich Engels in the park between the Institute and the Square of the Dictatorship of the Proleteriat.
An avenue leads from the Institute through the park, passing between two propylaea, or gatehouses, each with five columns. The neo-Classical-style gatehouses were erected by the Soviets in 1923/24. One bears the inscription "Workers of the world, unite!"

*Square of the Arts J8

Ploshchad Iskusstv

Location
between the Field of Mars and Nevsky Prospekt

Metro
Nevsky Prospekt/Gostinyy Dvor

Bus
2, 14, 25, 26, 100

Tram
2, 3, 5, 12, 14, 34

From the south side of the Square of the Arts the broad Ulitsa Brodskogo runs through to Nevsky Prospekt (see entry). The north side of the Square is dominated by the Mikhail Palace (see Russian Museum). Following completion of the palace in 1825, Carlo Rossi began to work on plans for the surrounding area. He created a large open space to heighten the impact of the palace and also designed the façades of the buildings round the square.
Originally the square and its attractive garden were called Mikhail Square, but in 1940 it was given its present name derived from its many theatres and museums.
In the middle of the square is a monument to Pushkin, unveiled on the 250th anniversary of the founding of Leningrad in 1957.
Next to the Russian Museum on the north side of the Square is the Ethnographic Museum of the Peoples of the USSR (see entry). On the west side is the Maly Opera and Ballet Theatre (Ploshchad Iskusstv 1), the former Mikhail Theatre. Bryllov erected the building in 1831/33, though he used Rossi's design for the façade. Next to the theatre, in the house where the painter Brodsky had an apartment from 1924 to 1939 (Ploshchad Iskusstv 3), there is now a commemorative museum (see Practical Information, Museums).
After the death of Dmitry Shostakovich (see Notable Personalities) the Leningrad Philharmonia took the composer's name. The Large Shostakovich Philharmonia Concert Hall stands opposite the Russian Museum, at Ulitsa Brodskovo 2 (the Small Shostakovich Philharmonia Concert Hall is on Nevsky Prospekt). The building, erected in 1834/39, was originally a gentlemen's club. It was taken over in 1921 by the Philharmonia Society, who had used its rooms on previous occasions on account of their fine acoustics. Shostakovich's Leningrad Symphony was performed here for the first time in 1942.

Pushkin Monument on the Square of the Arts

Square of the Decembrists G8

Ploshchad Dekabristov

Location
on the Neva, to the west of the Admiralty

On its north side the Square of the Decembrists is open to the Neva. The Admiralty (see entry) is to the east, St. Isaac's Cathedral to the south and the Senate and Synod to the

The "Bronze Horseman" on the Square of the Decembrists

west. The Square acquired its present appearance in the 1870s when the gardens were laid.
Like its appearance the name of the square has also been changed more than once over the years. It was first called Senate Square, then Peter Square, and in 1925 became the Square of the Decembrists. The name recalls the group of young officer aristocrats who attempted the overthrow of the Tsar here in December 1825 (see History of Leningrad).

Bus
6

Tram
31, 63

**The Bronze Horseman / Peter the Great Monument

The focal point of the Square of the Decembrists is the Peter the Great Monument, often called "the Bronze Horseman" after the poem of that title by Pushkin. The people of Leningrad are particularly attached to this sculpture of Peter the Great; it is one of the favourite settings for wedding photos and there are nearly always flowers at its base.
The bronze figure on the rearing horse was created by Etienne Maurice Falconet between 1766 and 1778, though the Tsar's head encircled by a laurel wreath was cast by Falconet's pupil Marie Collet in a single night. All the power of Peter the Great's personality is captured as he sits on horseback looking out over the Neva. The snake being trampled beneath the hooves of his horse symbolises treachery overcome.
Horse and rider stand on a single great block of stone. Originally weighing 1600 tonnes/1600 tons it was found at least 10 km/6 miles from St. Petersburg and brought with great difficulty to the city, partly overland and partly by

water (a special vessel being constructed for the purpose). Catherine the Great spared neither expense nor time in her determination to erect a monument worthy of Peter the Great, and hence of herself, too. The inscription chosen by the Empress, probably on Falconet's recommendation, is a dedication in Russian and Latin: "Peter the First, from Catherine the Second 1782". The monument was unveiled on 7 August 1782, the centenary of Peter the Great's accession to the throne.

Senate and Synod

Connected by a triumphal arch the Senate and Synod occupy the whole length of the west side of the Square of the Decembrists. Erected between 1829 and 1834 the ochre and white buildings were Carlo Rossi's last assignment, housing the Empire's two most powerful bodies of State and Church founded by Peter the Great. Each of the rectangular three-storeyed buildings is embellished with a loggia of eight Corinthian columns, while four pairs of columns flank the triumphal arches. "Justice and Piety", the group of figures decorating the attic above the arch, symbolise the unity of spiritual and worldly strength. The Central History Archives took over the two buildings in 1955.

State Bank

see Assignatsionnyy Bank

Strelka G9

Strelka

Location
eastern point of Vasil'yevskiy Island

Bus
10, 45

Tram
31, 63

*Rostral Columns

The eastern point of Vasil'yevskiy Island is called Strelka (meaning an arrow or a spit of land). At its most easterly tip is Pushkin Square (Pushkinskaya Ploshchad) with its pleasant parks and two Rostral Columns. To the north, east and south the spit is bordered by branches of the Neva, while to the west stands the Exchange (see entry) and two former warehouses. Next to the more northerly of the two warehouses is the old Custom House.
The Strelka is a wonderful vantage point for viewing the Peter and Paul Fortress (see entry) and the south embankment of the Neva.
Between 1733 and 1855 the eastern end of Vasil'yevskiy Island was the port of Leningrad. The city's commercial centre grew up right next to the harbour, with all that that entails in the way of buildings. Nowadays the Strelka is often also called the "Museum Quarter" because of the many museums to be found there.

The two 34 m/110 ft high Rostral Columns stand one at either end of the gardens in Pushkin Square. Erected in 1810 in honour of the Russian navy, the columns are decorated with the prows of ships like the Roman originals on which they were based (Latin *rostrum* means "prow").

The four allegorical figures on the two plinths represent the Russian rivers Volga, Dnieper, Neva and Volkhov. At one time the Rostral Columns were lighthouses. Now the gas-lights atop the columns are lit only for special occasions.

Warehouses

Between 1826 and 1832 two almost identical warehouses were built north and south of the Exchange. The central section of each neo-Classical building is embellished with a flat-topped loggia with three-quarter columns. The more southerly of the two warehouses is now the Zoological Museum, the main attraction in which is the mammoth room where a stuffed mammoth – the only one in the world – is on display (open: Mon.–Thur., Sun. 11 a.m.–6 p.m). The building to the north houses the Museum of Soil Sciences (currently closed for renovation), where there is an exhibition of different types of soils and different techniques for improving fertility, etc.

Custom-House

The Custom-House, erected between 1829 and 1832 near the more northerly of the two warehouses, has an eight-columned Ionic portico. Statues of Mercury, Neptune and Ceres decorate the pediment. It is now the Institute for Russian Literature (Pushkin House) and also home to the Literary Museum (currently closed for restoration). The museum contains manuscripts, first editions, pictures and personal effects belonging to famous Russian writers including Pushkin, Tolstoy, Dostoievsky, Turgenev and Gogol.

*Stroganov Palace H8

Stroganovskiy Dvorets

Location
Nevsky Prospekt 17

Metro
Nevsky Prospekt

Bus
2, 3, 6, 7, 14, 22, 27, 44, 45, 100

Built by Rastrelli in 1752/54 the main façade of the Stroganov Palace overlooks Nevsky Prospekt (see entry), while the Moyka river runs along one side. From the 15th century right up until the October Revolution, the Stroganovs were one of Russia's most important families, holding positions of influence and distinguishing themselves as collectors and patrons of the arts. In the Stroganov Palace, which remained in the family's ownership until the Revolution, the architect of the Winter Palace (see Hermitage) and the Catherine Palace at Pushkin (see entry) created one of the city's most beautiful Baroque buildings. Except for the colouring the green and white palace exterior still appears largely as it did when Rastrelli designed it, he having chosen a bright orange to combine with the white. The central section of each façade is emphasised with a row of Corinthian columns, while stucco surrounds frame the windows in many different shapes. The pediments are decorated with the family coat of arms.
Very little of the interior, now used as government offices, has survived in its original form. After a fire in the 1790s Voronikhen redesigned most of the rooms in the neo-Classical style.
Only the palace courtyard, with sculptures and sphinxes under old trees, is open to the public, the main entrance from Nevsky Prospek being through a simple arched gateway.

Stroganov Palace on the Moyka

Summer Palace

Summer Garden – pophyry vase

Garden Gateway

Summer Garden J8

Letniy Sad

The Summer Garden, on the left bank of the Neva opposite the Peter and Paul Fortress (see entry), was laid out on Peter the Great's instructions shortly after the founding of the city. A summer palace and some smaller pavilions were built within the extensive grounds.

Originally the park was much bigger than it is today, stretching as far as Nevsky Prospekt (see entry). Dances were held there on summer evenings, and military victories and other ceremonial occasions were celebrated with firework displays. Peter the Great's successors however preferred the summer palaces outside St. Petersburg, and parts of the garden soon fell victim to the demands of the fast-growing imperial metropolis.

The Summer Garden started life as a formal Baroque garden with countless ornamental fountains. Following a flood in 1777 the fountains were never replaced and the trees were left unpruned, so today the park has the appearance of an English landscaped garden with old trees, a small lake and lawns. There are also numerous benches from which to enjoy the surroundings.

Much of the statuary, the work of Italian sculptors in the 17th and 18th centuries, has been preserved intact, some pieces having adorned the main pathways from the time the garden was first laid. Among them are statues of Queen

Location
on the northern edge of the city centre

Bus
1, 2, 14, 25, 26, 46, 47, 65, 100, 134

Tram
2, 3, 12, 34, 51, 53

Opening times
Daily 8 a.m.–10 p.m. (in winter till 8 p.m.)

Christine of Sweden, Alexander the Great, the Roman Emperor Marcus Aurelius and many allegorical figures. A monument to the Russian writer Ivan Krylov (1768–1844) was unveiled in 1855, reliefs on the base depicting scenes from his fables. The 5 m/16 ft tall porphyry vase which stands at the south entrance was a gift from King Carl XIV of Sweden in 1839.

In the early 18th century the park was open to a certain section of society, "the respectably dressed" as they were described at the time; but since the October Revolution it has been open free of charge to everyone.

Garden railing

In 1784 the Summer Garden where it runs along the Neva embankment was enclosed by a wrought-iron railing designed by Velten. Supported by pink granite pillars it is an unusually fine piece of workmanship, with gilded rosettes and spikes.

After the October Revolution various Western industrialists offered to accept the railing in exchange for locomotives but, desperately needed as these were, the fledgeling Soviet government refused to part with it.

Summer Palace

Opening times
Mon., Wed.–Sun. 11 a.m.–7 p.m. (closed from 11 Nov. to 30 Apr.)

The Summer Palace, beside the Neva in the north-east corner of the Summer Garden, is one of the few buildings in Leningrad to survive intact since the time of Peter the Great. The city's founder spurned ostentation, the palace being a modest rectangular building, designed for the Tsar between 1710 and 1714 by Domenico Trezzini and Andreas Schülter. Ornamentation on the façade of the two-storeyed palace is limited to a series of reliefs running round the building above each of the ground-floor windows.

Interior

Peter the Great's rooms were on the ground floor, those of Catherine I his wife on the floor above. Furnished in the Petrine style some of the original fittings and furnishings have survived, including the wall panelling, the tiled stove, and some of the furniture in the dining-room, study and audience chamber.

Coffee-house and tea-house

Opening times
Mon., Wed.–Sun. 11 a.m.–6 p.m.

When the Summer Garden was opened to the public at the beginning of the 19th century, a coffee-house and a tea-house were erected to the south of the Summer Palace. Both are now used for exhibitions.

The tea-house was for many years the only remaining timber building in the Summer Garden, but in 1981 it was destroyed by fire. Since then it has been rebuilt in its original form.

*Tauride Palace — M9

Tavricheskiy Dvorets

Location
Ulitsa Voinova 47

The Tauride Palace is now the Communist Party's Leningrad regional high school, as well as providing accommo-

dation for meetings and congresses. It is not open to the public.
The palace was designed by I. J. Stasov and built between 1783 and 1789, the first owner being Grigoriy Potemkin (1739–1791) one of Catherine the Great's lovers. In 1783 Russia annexed the Crimea, at that time in Turkish possession, the region reverting to its old name of Tauris. Potemkin was appointed governor-general, later receiving the title of Prince of Tauride by which title his palace also became known. After Potemkin's death the property passed to Catherine the Great, who lived there for some months each year during the latter years of her life. Her son Paul I had the splendid palace converted into a barracks for the Horseguards' Regiment, turning some of the colonnaded halls into stables, but after Paul's death Alexander I restored it for use by members of the imperial family. The interior, which was renowned throughout Europe, was again completely altered when the State Duma moved into it in 1906. Lenin delivered his "April Theses" there following his return to Russia in 1917, and after the October Revolution it was also the scene of many of his speeches and addresses.
Today the exterior of the yellow and white palace still appears as it did shortly after it was completed. The central section of the neo-Classical building is graced by a six-columned portico, wings on either side ending in two-storeyed pavilions. Above the main building rises a flattened dome, modelled on the Pantheon in Rome.

Metro
Chernyshevskaya

Bus
6, 14, 26, 43, 136, 137

Kikin Palace

The Kikin Palace (in Russian Kikina Palata, "palata" meaning chambers) stands a few hundred metres east of the Tauride Palace. It was built in 1714 by the architect Andreas Schülter for A. V. Kikin. Kikin was from a modest back-

Location
Stavropolskaya Ulitsa 9

Tauride Palace

ground but had risen quickly in the official hierarchy and had become friendly with Peter the Great's son Alexey. When it became known that he had advised the Tsarevich to leave Russia Kikin was beheaded and his property confiscated. The palace was partly destroyed during the Second World War and has been rebuilt in its original form.

Theatre Square F6

Location
south-west of Isaac Square

Bus
3, 27, 43, 49, 50

Tram
1, 5, 11, 15, 31, 33, 42

Teatralnaya Ploshchad

In the 18th century what is now Theatre Square was the venue for fairs and other popular festivities, being known at that time as Carousel Square. It acquired its present appearance at the end of the 19th century.
The Kirov Opera and Ballet Theatre which dominates the square was built in 1859/60, being called originally the Maria Theatre after the wife of Alexander II. In honour of the Soviet politician Sergey Kirov (b. 1886) the theatre was renamed shortly after his murder in 1934. All the great Russian operas and ballets were premièred here, and today, as in the past, the Kirov Theatre Ballet Company is renowned the world over. The theatre holds 2000 people and is almost always sold out.
Ever since the early 19th century the building opposite the theatre has been the home of the former St. Petersburg conservatoire, now called the Rimsky-Korsakov Conservatoire. Regular concert evenings are still held in the well-known music school founded by Anton Rubenstein in 1862. There is a monument to the composer Mikhail Glinka (1804–1857) on the south side of the Conservatoire, while on the north side there is a monument to Nikolay Rimsky-Korsakov (1844–1908).

Trinity Cathedral G5

Location
Ismaylovskiy Prospekt 7a

Metro
Teknologicheskiy Institut

Bus
10, 60

Tram
2, 11, 15, 28, 34

Troitskiy Sobor

With its bright blue painted domes the Trinity Cathedral (not to be confused with the cathedral of the same name in the Alexander Nevsky Monastery) is a prominent feature in the city centre. Built between 1827 and 1835 in the form of a Greek cross, Stasov's design skilfully combines the Old Russian tradition in church architecture with neo-Classical elements. The four small domes together with the large dome and the portico create a pleasing pyramidal effect. A frieze runs round the otherwise simple white façade.
The church – where Dostoievsky was married – is not open to the public.

Trinity Cathedral ▷

Part of the Twelve Colleges

Twelve Colleges (University) F/G8/9

Dvenadtsat Kollegii (Universitet)

Location
Universitetskaya Naberezhnaya 7

Bus
7, 30, 44, 47, 60

Although the Twelve Colleges form part of Leningrad's university, only the narrow end façade of the building overlooks the Neva from University Quay. The long main façade is set at right angles to the river, facing north-east.
The terrace of twelve identical buildings was designed by a number of architects, including Domenico Trezzini and Theodor Schwertfeger. It was erected between 1722 and 1742. Each building has a central projecting bay on the east façade, while a two-storeyed gallery runs along the entire length of the terrace on the west. As is usual for the early 18th century, ornamentation on the exterior is relatively restrained, just simple white pilasters connecting the two top storeys and windows surrounded by plain white frames.
The buildings, originally commissioned by Peter the Great, were not at all as he had intended them to be. Prince Menshikov, the Tsar's close confidant and friend who himself owned land on Vasil'yevskiy Island (see Menshikov Palace), insisted on the space-saving design in Peter's absence in order not to reduce the size of his own property. This inevitably brought the Tsar's wrath down upon his head and Menshikov had his ears boxed!
The need for the buildings arose when Peter the Great established the "Colleges" – for foreign affairs, warfare,

finance, etc. – as part of his new apparatus of State administration. In 1802 Alexander I replaced the colleges with ministries which were housed elsewhere, and in 1819 the twelve buildings were handed over to the University of St. Petersburg following its foundation in the same year.
Many famous people have lectured at the University, including the chemist Dimitriy Mendeleyev (1834–1907) who devised the periodic table of the elements. His rooms (entrance: Mendeleyevskaya Liniya 2) are open to the public. Following the Second World War the university was renamed the Zhdanov State University after Andrey Zhdanov (1896–1948) who led the defence of Leningrad and who was considered a possible successor to Stalin. Only some of the 15 faculties of the university are still housed in the Twelve Colleges and adjacent buildings. The courses for which the great majority of the 22,000 students register are now taught at the new university complex near Petrodvorets (see entry).

Lomonosov Monument

In the small square between the Twelve Colleges and the Academy of Science (see entry) there is a monument to the outstandingly versatile Russian scholar Mikhail Lomonosov (see Notable Personalities).

Vorontsov Palace J7

Vorontsovskiy Dvorets

Victory Square – Monument to the Defenders of Leningrad

The Vorontsov Palace on Sadovaya Ulitsa is opposite the long south-east façade of the Large Department Store (see entry), at the end furthest from Nevsky Prospekt. It was built between 1749 and 1757 by Rastrelli for Mikhail Vorontsov, vice-chancellor under the Empress Elizabeth I, and later belonged for a time to the Knights of Malta. Today it is a military academy.
The three-storeyed central section is flanked on either side by lower wings projecting to form a wide entrance court. Separating the palace garden from the street is a finely worked wrought-iron railing designed by Rastrelli himself. The Chapel of the Knights of Malta, its pediment supported by four Corinthian columns, was added to the east wing of the palace by Quarenghi in 1798/1800.

Location
Sadovaya Ulitsa 26

Metro
Gostinyy Dvor

Bus
14, 25, 43

Tram
2, 3, 5, 13, 14

Victory Square

Ploshchad Pobedy

The modern Victory Square, laid out on a grand scale at the southern end of Moscow Prospekt, is bordered by apartment blocks and the Finnish-designed Hotel Pulkovskaya.
The Monument to the Heroic Defenders of Leningrad, unveiled on 9 May 1975, is the centrepiece of the square, being located close to the former front line where the German advance on the city was halted (see map on page 29). Standing within an incomplete circle of reddish granite symbolising the broken blockade, a 48 m/156 ft high obelisk rises in front of the sculptured group "Blockade". Other groups of sculptures complete the monument. Life in the beleaguered city is re-created by the numerous items on display in an underground exhibition hall (open: Mon., Thur.–Sun. 10 a.m.–6 p.m.; Tues. 10 a.m.–5 p.m.).

Location
south of the city centre

Metro
Moskovskaya

Yelagin Island (Kirov Park of Culture and Rest) B–E13/14

Ostrov Yelagin

Following the October Revolution the Kirov Park of Culture and Rest was established on Yelagin Island, catering for a wide range of leisure activities. While there are tranquil places to walk and take one's ease there are also sports facilities, bathing beaches, an open-air theatre, concert pavilions and a variety of other amenities including a fair ground and hire-boats. Many Leningrad people go, as Leningrad people have gone since the city's earliest days, to watch the sunset or look out to sea from the Strelka, the most westerly point of the island (not to be confused with the Strelka on Vasil'yevskiy Island).
In 1770 the island was presented by Catherine the Great to Ivan Yelagin, marshal of the imperial court, before passing into Count Orlov's possession in 1794. In 1817 Alexander I bought it back for the Crown, ownership later being transferred to his mother Maria Fyodorovna, widow of Paul I. An extensive landscaped park was laid out on the island by the landscape architect Joseph Bush, and Carlo Rossi was commissioned to alter and extend the existing palace built by Yelagin, as well as to erect several new pavilions.

Location
in the north-eastern part of the Neva delta

Bus
45, 71

Tram
12, 17, 26

Opening times
Daily 8 a.m.–10 p.m.

Yelagin Palace

Between 1818 and 1822 Rossi completely altered Yelagin Palace. His rectangular neo-Classical building stands on a raised base, stone steps flanked by a pair of sculptured lions leading up to a six-columned Corinthian entrance portico. The rear façade overlooking the river (a branch of the Nevka) has a semicircular bay in the centre, from which a terrace and steps lead down into the garden.
After Maria Fyodorovna's death the palace was used to accommodate distinguished guests. It was destroyed during the Second World War but following extensive and careful rebuilding between 1952 and 1960, the former elegance of the interior has once more been restored. The Oval Hall, where Pushkin and his much-admired wife Natalya were entertained at balls, is exceptionally beautiful.
The palace now houses a permanent exhibition of furnishings and other items from nineteenth-century interiors, besides which some of the rooms are used for temporary art exhibitions.

Kitchen

The kitchen, a separate building directly adjacent to the palace, is semicircular in plan. The outer walls are relieved only by niches decorated with statues of Greek gods, all the windows opening on to the inner courtyard.

Yusupov Palace G7

Yusupovskiy Dvorets

Location
Naberezhnaya Reki Moyki 94

Bus
3, 27

Tram
1, 5, 11, 15, 31, 33, 42

The Yusupov Palace is one of four palaces in St. Petersburg owned by the Yusupov family in the 18th and 19th century. Today the building is a cultural centre for teachers, the interior having been elaborately restored.
After the Yusupov family acquired the site on the Moyka in the 1760s Vallin de la Mothe was commissioned to enlarge the existing stone house. The façade facing the river was further extended in the 1830s, and late in the 19th century a narrow, unusually elongated wing was also added. At the end of the wing was a private theatre (where today concerts are regularly held), sumptuously decorated in the Baroque style.
The Yusupov Palace has gone down in history as the place where the infamous Rasputin was murdered by members of the court in December 1916 on account of his influence over the Tsarina. He proved a difficult man to kill. At first he was given a piece of poisoned cake which he ate and supposedly enjoyed. This, however, failed to produce the desired effect (the sugar in the cake apparently neutralising the poison). The conspirators then lost their nerve and fired wildly at him. When he still did not succumb, they threw him into a hole in the ice in a small channel off the Moyka.

A trip on the Neva ▶

НЕВА

Practical Information A–Z

Airport

Pulkovo II, the international airport, is 17 km/11 miles south of Leningrad. British Airways, Pan Am, KLM, Lufthansa and Finnair are among the international airlines which use the airport as well as Aeroflot, the Russian State airline. There is a separate, relatively small terminal for foreign flights.

Arrival

After leaving the aircraft, the first check is passport control. Passports and visas must be shown, a section of the visa being retained by the immigration officer. Unless a traveller's identity is questioned there should be little delay.
Once through passport control, luggage is collected from the conveyor belt and passengers proceed to Customs. Passports, visas and Customs declaration forms are needed (see Customs Regulations). Passengers may be asked to open their luggage. It is forbidden to take politically sensitive or even mildly pornographic literature into the Soviet Union, so be prepared to have magazines and books scrutinised and perhaps confiscated. For duty-free allowances see Customs regulations.

Transfer to hotel

Beyond Customs is a reception area where Intourist representatives and tour guides wait to meet their groups. Here things may not go entirely to plan. If you are expecting to be met but have difficulty in making contact, ask for help at the Intourist desk. People travelling independently should also go to the Intourist desk, to find out the name of their hotel (see Hotels).
For the 30-minute drive into the city there are plenty of taxis available, parked in front of the airport building.

Departure

Before the return flight a customs declaration form must again be filled in. Forms are available in several languages at the airport terminal.
Note that the only facilities for converting rubles back into hard currency are at the airport bank in the main airport building, not in the terminal for foreign flights.

Antiques

As a general rule the export of antiques from the Soviet Union is prohibited. This applies to antiques and works of art such as pictures, drawings, sculpture, carpets, icons, ecclesiastical items, furniture and household articles, weapons, clothing, manuscripts, books, musical instruments and objects of archaeological interest.
The Soviet Union has a cultural policy of making works of art accessible to everyone and discouraging private ownership. Consequently no antiques are offered for sale in shops. Antiques obtained elsewhere may only be exported with special permission from the Ministry of Culture and are subject to 100% export duty.

Banks

see Currency

Beriozka Shops

Beriozka shops ("beryosha" means "little birch") are specifically for use by foreigners and payment must be made in foreign currency. Be sure to keep receipts for all purchases, in case they are required by Customs when leaving the country.

Choice of goods

Beriozka shops offer a selection of goods from Western countries as well as Soviet products. Among the items available are some foods, especially sweets and caviar (see Caviar), spirits, beer and lemonade, cigarettes, books, records, sets of slides and, of course, souvenirs (see entry). The larger Beriozka shops also stock furs and leather goods, china, cameras, radios, jewellery and other items. Some of these can also be bought for rubles in other department stores and shops, but in Beriozka shops tiresome queueing is avoided and there is a self-service system that makes shopping easier.
Apart from souvenirs and things needed for your stay in Leningrad, it is pointless to buy much in the Beriozka shops. Even the caviar and vodka can usually be bought more cheaply at home

The largest Beriozka shop in Leningrad

. . . near the Hotel Pribaltiskaya

Opening times

Beriozka shops are open daily from 9 or 10 a.m. to 8 p.m., though most close for one hour at lunchtime (usually from 1 to 2 p.m.)

Shops

There are Beriozka shops in all the hotels catering for foreigners but the shops at Ulitsa Gertsena (No 22) and the Nevsky Prospekt (Nos. 7/9, next to Aeroflot) offer a better selection. The shop opposite the Hotel Pribaltiyskaya (Morskaya Naberezhnaya 15) is almost comparable to a department store in the West in the range of its stock.

Black Market

In and around the international hotels, and especially on Nevsky Prospekt, tourists can expect to be approached with illegal offers to exchange rubles for hard currency or to buy articles made in the West. Jeans are no longer in such great demand but clothes such as printed sweat shirts that proclaim their place of origin are very much sought after. There are always eager buyers for pocket calculators, cosmetics and magazines. Think twice before engaging in such transactions; even foreigners can expect heavy penalties if caught.

Boat Trips

On Leningrad's rivers and canals

From the pier by the Anichkov Bridge (Nevsky Prospekt).
Daily every 15 to 30 minutes from mid May to the end of August.
The round trip on the rivers Fontanka and Moyka and the Kryukov Canal lasts about 75 minutes. As a rule the commentaries are in Russian only.
Tickets are sold at the pier. An excursion with an English-speaking guide can be booked at considerably greater cost through Intourist (see Information).

Evening trip on the Neva

From the pier at the Square of the Decembrists.
Daily at 9 p.m. from 15 June to 15 July. There is a band on board that plays Russian folk music.
Reservations through Intourist.

Round trips on the Neva

From the pier by the Hermitage and other piers.
Daily from mid May to the beginning of September, leaving approximately every 15 minutes.

Hydrofoil to Petrodvorets

From the piers at the Square of the Decembrists and Hermitage.
Daily from the end of May to the end of August, leaving approximately every 15 minutes. Each trip lasts about 30 minutes. The first boat leaves at 11 a.m. the last at 5 p.m.

Book Shops

See Shopping

Street cafés – relatively new to Leningrad

Cafés

Cafeterias

A Russian "kafe" is not a café in our sense of the word, but rather a type of caféteria or snack-bar. No alcohol is served. There are a number of such "kafes" on the Nevsky Prospekt, at Nos. 15 and 06 for example (open daily, 9 a.m.–3 p.m. and 4–9 p.m.)
The Literaturnoye Kafe (Nevsky Prospekt 18) is somewhat special, being furnished in the style of the early 19th century, where Pushkin whiled away his time.

Pavement (sidewalk) cafés

Pavement (sidewalk) cafés have recently made an appearance in Leningrad, serving refreshments during the summer months.

Ice-cream parlours

The numerous cafés selling ice-cream (moróshenoye) are crowded in winter as well as in summer. They are usually much more formal than their Western counterparts, many have a doorman and a cloakroom. (In Russia it is considered bad manners to eat wearing outdoor clothes.) Ice-creams cost between 10 Kopecks to 1.50 rubles Sever on Nevsky Prospekt is well known.

Camping

Booking

Camping holidays, using your own tent or a rented one, can be booked from 1 June to 30 Sept. Tents for three or four persons are available, and renting is only slightly more expensive than taking your own. Like all travel in the Soviet Union, camping trips must follow a prearranged itinerary approved by Intourist (see Information), and must be paid for in advance.

Camping sites

The Leningrad camping site is at the Hotel Olgino (see Hotels). There is another site about 45 km/28 miles north-west of Leningrad in the small town of Repino. Sites have leisure and shopping facilities, restaurants, and areas for maintaining and washing cars.

Car Rental

Cars can be rented in Leningrad, either self-drive or with a driver. To guarantee availability it is advisable to make arrangements through Intourist (see Information) before departure for the Soviet Union. On the spot car hire can be arranged at any Intourist service desk. Normally foreigners are required to pay in hard currency.

Caviar

The Soviet Union is the World's main supplier of caviar. The Caspian Sea the lower reaches of the Volga and the Danbue delta (part of which lies in the USSR) are home to the sturgeon, a species of fish that lives in the sea and swims up river to spawn, and whose eggs, caviar, are the world's most expensive food. Although there are over 20 types of sturgeon. Caviar is obtained from only three, the *beluga,* the *osyotr* and the *sevruga*. To achieve an annual production of 500 tonnes/492 tons some 250,000 sturgeon are caught and killed each year. Stocks are maintained by rearing about 70 million fry in breeding ponds.

Types of sturgeon

The female beluga, weighing up to 500 kg/1100 lbs, yields 15 to 20 kg/33 to 44 lbs of large-grained caviar. The female osyotr averages between 25 and 40 kg/55 and 88 lbs in weight and yields about 4 to 10 kg/9 to 22 lbs of slighty smaller grained caviar. The dearest caviar is beluga. More osyotr are caught than beluga and consequently osyotr caviar is somewhat cheaper. There is little agreement among gourmets about which of the two is better. There is agreement, however, that both are better -- and hence correspondingly dearer – than caviar from the sevruga. The 9 to 10 kg/20 to 22 lbs sevruga female yields about 2 kg/4.4 lbs of fine-grained caviar.

Shopping tips

Caviar should always be bought in a tin, not a glass jar. It is best only slightly salted (look for *malosol* on the label).
Most caviar is black (red caviar is from salmon) but very occasionally is lighter in colour. Silver-grey, light brown and especially golden-brown caviar are rare and command high prices. In former times white caviar (mostly obtained from albino sturgeon) was reserved for the Tsar.
In Leningrad it is best to buy caviar in one of the Beriozka shops (see entry), although the prices are no lower than typical prices in Western Europe.

Caviar is eaten with blinis (small buckwheat pancakes), potato fritters or potato pancakes, but never with lemon. Connoisseurs eat it with a small mother-of-pearl, tortoiseshell or horn spoon, straight from the iced tin.

Serving suggestions

Cemeteries

Lazarus Cemetery
See A to Z, Alexander Nevsky Monastery: Lazarus and Tikhvin Cemetery

Nicholas Cemetery
See A to Z, Alexander Nevsky Monastery: Nicholas Cemetery

Novodevich Cemetery
Nernigovskaya Ulitsa
Metro: Moskovskiye Vorota
The poet Nekrasov is buried here.

Piskarov Memorial Cemetery
See A to Z, Piskarov Memorial Cemetery

Serafimov Cemetery
Torfyanaya Doroga
Metro: Pionerskaya

Smolensk Cemetery
Malyy Prospekt
Metro: Primorskaya

Tikhvin Cemetery
See A to Z, Alexander Nevsky Monastery: Lazarus and Tikhvin Cemetery

Volkov Cemetery
Rasstannaya Ulitsa
Metro: Elektrosila, then No. 29 or 36 bus
Lenin's mother and sister are buried in this cemetery. The graves of Plekhanov, Saltykov-Shchedrin, Leskov and Blok are on the Literatorskiye Mostki (Poets' Pathway).

Concerts

See Theatres and Concerts

Consulates

See Diplomatic and Consular Representation

Currency

The unit of currency in the Soviet Union is the ruble (Rbl) equivalent to 100 copecks (cop). There are banknotes of 1, 3,

Currency

Soviet currency

5, 10, 25, 50 and 100 ruble denominations, and coins of 1, 2, 3, 5, 10, 15, 20 and 50 copecks. There is also a 1 ruble coin.

Exchange rates (variable)

1 ruble = £0.87	£1 = 1.15 rubles
1 ruble = $1.55	$1 = 2.03 rubles

Foreign currency regulations

The Soviet Union and other eastern bloc states forbid the import and export of notes and coins of their own currencies. In the Soviet Union there is no restriction on the import of Western currencies or travellers cheques in foreign currencies, nor on the import of precious metals or articles made from them (with the exception of gold coins). However, all must be declared on entry and the currency declaration should be retained. Foreign currency and valuables up to the amount declared on entry may be taken out of the country on departure.

Changing money

Cash and other forms of currency can be exchanged for roubles at branches of the State Bank and in hotels (see Hotels). Passport, visa and, as a rule, currency declaration must be produced. Money is changed at the official rate published monthly in the Press. On departure unused roubles can be converted back at the airport bank (see Airport), but note that this is located in the main airport building, not in the terminal for foreign flights! There will, of course, be a loss on the double exchange. Travellers leaving by rail can change money back at the Customs station on the border. It is best to change only a small amount into rubles on entry, since many payments, for items from Beriozka shops, for theatre tickets from Intourist, and in some restaurants, must be made in foreign currency. This makes it advisable to carry a good supply of small notes and coins in your own currency. The black market exchange rate, repeatedly offered to foreigners (see Black Market), is considerably higher than the official rate. You should bear in mind that not only is it strictly forbidden to change money other than in the official exchange bureaux, but there is also a risk of being swindled on the black market.

Eurocheques

Eurocheques can be cashed in rubles at all exchange bureaux on presentation of the currency declaration and passport. Eurocheques cannot be cashed in foreign currency.

Credit cards

Intourist, Aeroflot and a number of restaurants accept major credit cards such as American Express, Diners Club, Eurocard and Visa.

Customs Regulations

Arrival

Articles for personal use may be imported duty free into the Soviet Union including in addition to personal effects: two still cameras with accessories, portable video recorder, video camera, transistor radio, portable musical instrument, tape recorder, portable typewriter and two watches; also 6 kg of tinned food, 250 grams of coffee and 100 grams of tea (for the journey), and presents to the value of 30 rubles. Persons over 16 years are entitled to a duty free allowance of 250 cigarettes or 250 grams of tobacco, and those over 21 years to 0.5 litres of spirits and 1 litre of wine. It is forbidden to import: Soviet currency, gold coins, weapons or ammunition, narcotics of all kinds, pornographic material including photographs or films, records or written materials that are politically or economically prejudicial to the Soviet Union. Publications such as "The Spectator" or "Time Magazine" might on occasion fall under this latter heading, but on other occasions cause no problems when passing through Customs.
A customs declaration form (available in several languages) must be completed on arrival. Enter "no" or "none" in any columns that do not apply, rather than drawing a line through them. To ensure a trouble-free passage through Customs on departure it is advisable to declare not only currency and articles of precious metal but also any other items of value.

Departure

It is forbidden to export rubles or the currencies of other eastern bloc states. An export permit from the Ministry of Culture is required for antiques and *objets d'art* and these incur export duty of 100% of the value shown in the permit. Up to 250 grams of black or red caviar may be exported duty free. Tobacco and spirits are subject to the same restrictions on export as on import.
On departure another customs declaration must be completed before proceeding through Customs, and this should be presented together with the declaration form stamped on arrival.

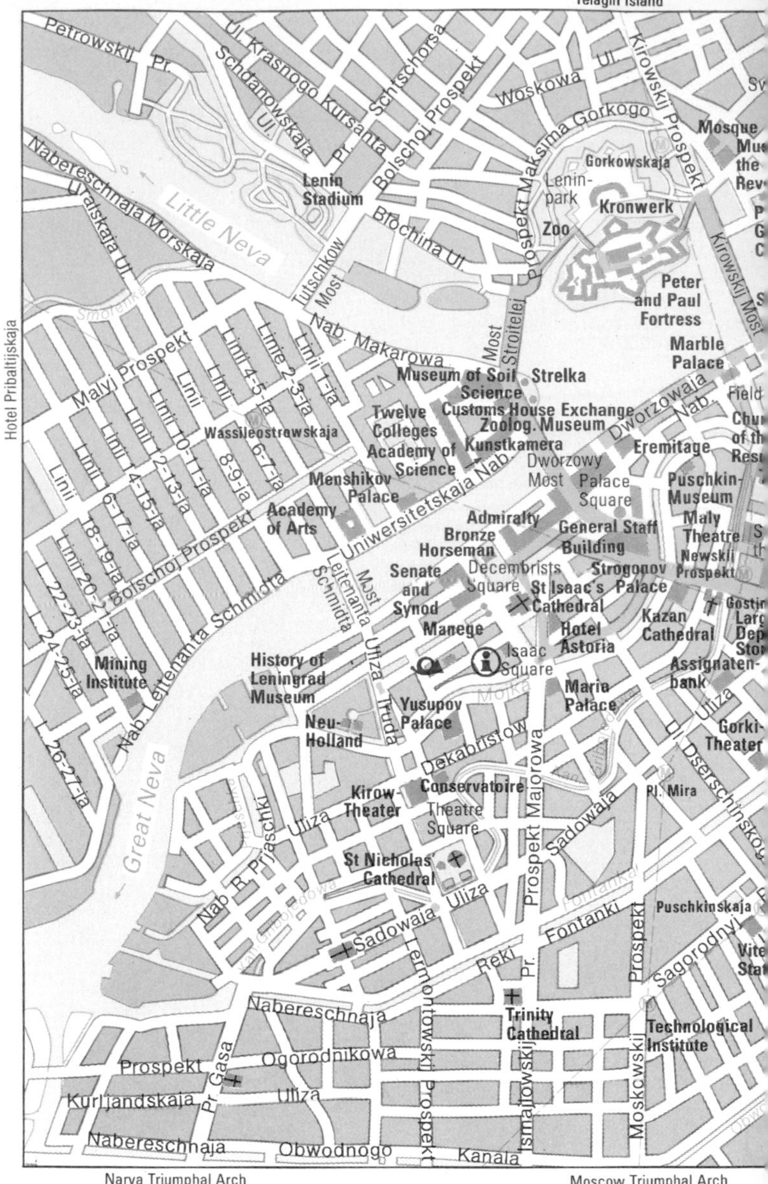
Vyborg
Yelagin Island
Petrowskij Pr.
Ul. Krasnogo Kursanta
Schdanowskaja Ul.
Pr. Schtschorsa
Bolschoj Prospekt
Woskowa Ul.
Kirowskij Prospekt
Prospekt Maksima Gorkogo
Mosque
Gorkowskaja
Lenin-park
Kronwerk
Zoo
Naberesсhnaja Morskaja
Uralskaja Ul.
Little Neva
Lenin Stadium
Blochina Ul.
Tutschkow Most
Most Stroitelej
Peter and Paul Fortress
Kirowskij Most
Smolenka
Malyj Prospekt
Linii
Linii 4-5-ja
Linie 2-3-ja
Linii 1-ja
Nab. Makarowa
Marble Palace
Museum of Soil Science
Strelka
Twelve Colleges
Customs House Exchange
Zoolog. Museum
Dworzowaja Nab.
Wassileostrowskaja
Linii 10-11-ja
Linii 12-13-ja
Linii 14-15-ja
Linii 6-7-ja
Linii 8-9-ja
Linii 16-17-ja
Linii 18-19-ja
Linii 20-21-ja
L. 22-23-ja
L. 24-25-ja
L. 26-27-ja
Academy of Science
Kunstkamera
Eremitage
Menshikov Palace
Dworzowy Most
Palace Square
Puschkin-Museum
Academy of Arts
Uniwersitetskaja Nab.
Admiralty
General Staff Building
Maly Theatre
Bolschoj Prospekt
Bronze Horseman
Newskij Prospekt
Senate and Synod
Decembrists Square
Strogonov Palace
St Isaac's Cathedral
Most Lejtenanta Schmidta
Nab. Lejtenanta Schmidta
Manege
Hotel Astoria
Kazan Cathedral
Mining Institute
History of Leningrad Museum
Isaac Square
Assignaten-bank
Uliza Truda
Moika
Marie Palace
Yusupov Palace
Neu-Holland
Dekabristow
Gorki-Theater
Great Neva
Kirow-Theater
Conservatoire
Theatre Square
Ul. Dserschinskogo
Pl. Mira
Prospekt Majorowa
Sadowaja
Nab. R. Prjaschki
Uliza
St Nicholas' Cathedral
Fontanka
Puschkinskaja
Sadowaja
Reki Fontanki
Sagorodnyj
Lermontowskij Prospekt
Pr. Ismajlowskij
Moskowskij Prospekt
Naberesсhnaja
Trinity Cathedral
Technological Institute
Prospekt Ogorodnikowa
Pr. Gasa
Kurljandskaja Uliza
Nabereschnaja Obwodnogo Kanala
Hotel Pribaltijskaja
Narva Triumphal Arch
Petrodvoretz, Lomonosov,
Riga
Moscow Triumphal Arch
Victory Square, Airport
Pushkin, Pavlovsk,
Moscow

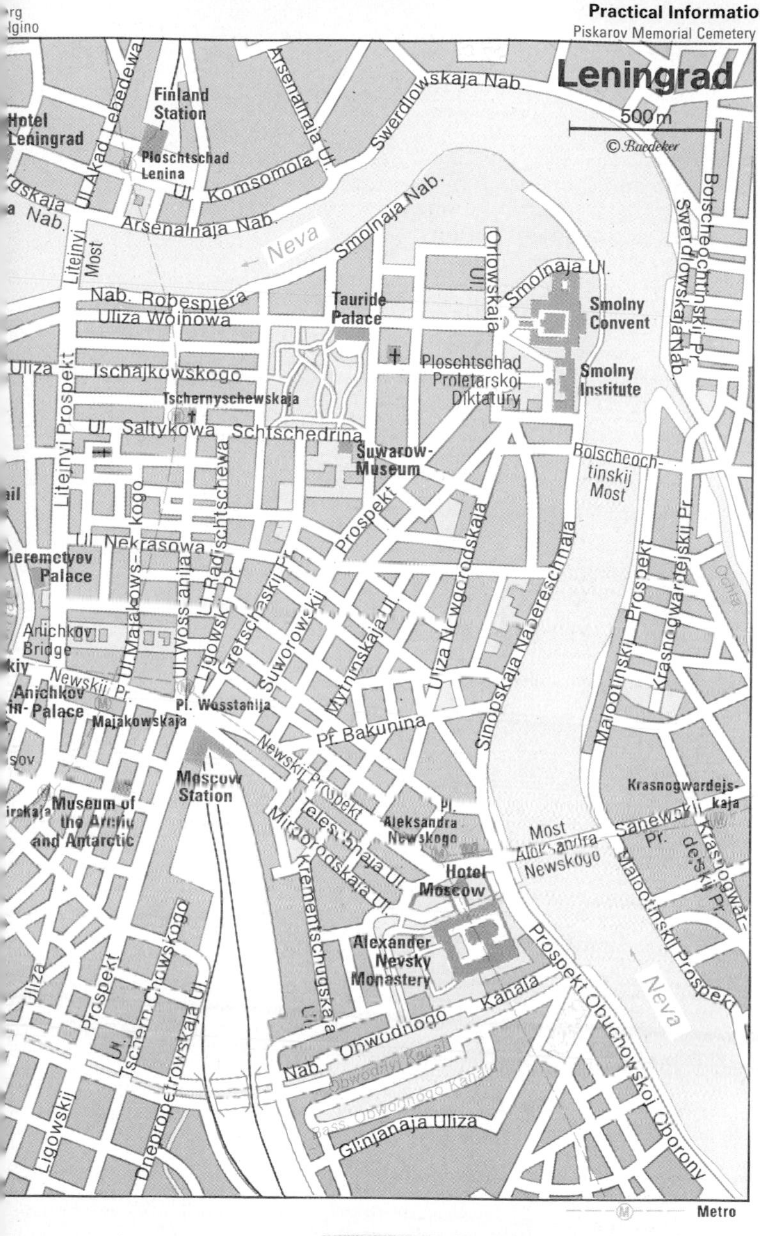

Leningrad
500 m
© Baedeker
Finland Station
Hotel Leningrad
Ploschtschad Lenina
Swerdlowskaja Nab.
Arsenalnaja Ul.
Ul. Komsomola
Arsenalnaja Nab.
Neva
Smolnaja Nab.
Litejnyj Most
Nab. Robespjera
Uliza Woinowa
Tauride Palace
Orlowskaja Ul.
Smolnaja Ul.
Smolny Convent
Ploschtschad Proletarskoj Diktatury
Smolny Institute
Bolscheochtinskij Pr.
Swerdlowskaja Nab.
Uliza Tschajkowskogo
Tschernyschewskaja
Litejnyj Prospekt
Ul. Saltykowa Schtschedrina
Suwarow-Museum
Bolscheochtinskij Most
Ul. Nekrasowa
Sheremetyev Palace
Prospekt
Ulitza Nowgorodskaja
Sinopskaja Nabereschnaja
Maloochtinskij Prospekt
Krasnogwardejskij Pr.
Anichkov Bridge
Newskij Pr.
Anichkov Palace
Majakowskaja
Pl. Wosstanija
Ul. Majakowskogo
Ul. Wosstanija
Ligowskij Pr.
Gretscheskij Pr.
Suworowskij Pr.
Mytninskaja Ul.
Pr. Bakunina
Newskij Prospekt
Moscow Station
Museum of the Arctic and Antarctic
Aleksandra Newskogo
Telesskaja Ul.
Mirgorodskaja Ul.
Most Aleksandra Newskogo
Sanewskij Pr.
Krasnogwardejskaja
Hotel Moscow
Krementschugskaja Ul.
Alexander Nevsky Monastery
Prospekt Obuchowskoi Oborony
Maloochtinskij Prospekt
Nab. Obwodnogo Kanala
Obwodnyj Kanal
Glinjanaja Uliza
Tschernjachowskogo
Dnepropetrowskaja Ul.
Ligowskij Prospekt
Metro
Suggested tour of the City

Return to the U.K

Returning direct to the United Kingdom, the normal Customs regulations for arrival from a non-EEC country apply. Note that the import of fur skins from protected species is prohibited.

Diplomatic and Consular Representation

Addresses in the Soviet Union

United Kingdom

Embassy of the United Kingdom
Naberezhnaya Morisa Toreza 14
Moscow
tel. 2 31 85 11

United States of America

Embassy of the United States of America
Ulitsa Chaykovskovo 19-23
Moscow
tel. 2 52 24 51-59

US Consulate General
15 Petr Lavrov Street
Leningrad
tel. 774-9235

Soviet Embassies

United Kingdom

Embassy of the USSR
13 Kensington Palace Gardens
London W8 4QX
tel. 01 229 3628

United States of America

Embassy of the USSR
1125 16 Street NW
Washington DC 20036
tel. 202 628 7551

Electricity

The standard voltage in the Soviet Union is 220 volts. Continental-type plugs or adaptors are required for use with power sockets.

Events

White Nights

In mid-summer, night scarcely falls in Leningrad and "White Nights", a festival of arts, is staged every year from 21 June to 29 June. Appropriately the programme includes numerous ballet productions as well as concerts, folk dancing and folk music.

Russian Winter

The second major cultural event of the year in Leningrad is the festival called "Russian Winter", which takes place from 25 Dec. to 5 Jan. Theatres stage their best productions, and there are outstanding folk-dance groups and choral concerts. In addition to the cultural programme there are troika (horse-drawn sled) rides and sports events.

Farewell to the Russian Winter

From 19 Feb. to 5 March the city celebrates its "Farewell to the Russian Winter" with folk music, dancing, and troika rides.

A useful tip

For the "Russian Winter" and "White Nights" festivals Intourist offers special holidays which include many of the major cultural events.

Excursions

Petrodvorets, Pavlovsk, Pushkin, Lomonosov

A number of delightful excursions can be made from Leningrad, especially to the former Imperial summer residences in Petrodvorets (Peterhof), Pavlovsk, Pushkin (Tsarskoye Selo) and Lomonosov (Oranienbaum). These are described in the A to Z section under their respective names. All may be visited without special permission, and are easily accessible by rail (see Railway Stations) or taxi (see entry). Intourist (see Information) arranges visits lasting about 4 hours, but this is scarcely sufficient considering the wealth of things to be seen. It is worth devoting a full day to any one of the Imperial palaces, especially if the weather is good, since all are set in extensive parks and surrounded by many smaller buildings.
Those wanting to include more in their day can combine visits to Petrodvorets and Lomonosov, or to Pavlovsk and Pushkin.

Gatchina

The Gatchina Palace complex is not open to visitors.

Rasliv

In July and August of 1917, Lenin, in danger of arrest by the Provisional Government, took refuge in the village of Rasliv (35 km/22 miles north-west of Leningrad), hiding at first in a barn and later in a hut made from hay. The barn is now a museum. A replica of the hay hut, rebuilt from year to year, forms the centre-piece of a second museum, where there is also a granite monument.
Open: Mon., Tues., Fri.–Sun. 10 a.m.–6 p.m.

Repino

Near the small town of Repino on the Gulf of Finland, about 45 km/28 miles north-west of Leningrad, is "Penaty", once the country estate of the painter Ilya Repin. The house is kept as it was during his lifetime, and his studio and personal belongings are on view.
Open: Mon., Wed.–Sun. 10.30 a.m.–5.30 p.m. (6.30 p.m. in summer).

Food and Drink

General

In the Soviet Union meals are quite substantial. At breakfast, in addition to bread, butter, jam, cold sausage and cheese, there is usually a small cooked dish, sausage, ome-

lette, fried eggs, or blinis (buckwheat pancakes) with sour cream. Lunch and supper consist of three or four courses, followed by tea or coffee.
Breakfast in hotels is generally served between 8 and 10 a.m., and lunch between 12 noon and 2 p.m. When eating out in a restaurant (see entry) the Russians allow ample time for their meal, especially since there is often musical entertainment as well. Restaurants tend to be busy from 7 p.m. onwards, and with most closing at 11, orders for a meal are unlikely to be accepted much after 10 p.m.

Ordering

Russian food terms are listed in the section on language (see entry).

Dishes

Although Russia has a tradition of good, nourishing cooking, culinary expectations should not be too high on a visit to the Soviet Union at the present time. Even in the best restaurants food is often prepared rather unimaginatively. Problems of food distribution mean that fresh vegetables and salad are served only rarely.
Some of Leningrad's restaurants (see entry) offer specialities from other Soviet republics as well as from Russia.

Starters

Lunch and supper almost always begin with an appetiser (in Russian *zakuska*), with which the Russians generally drink vodka.
Typical zakuski are vegetable salad, smoked salmon or sturgeon, herring with onion, or bits of fish or meat in aspic. A special delicacy is blinis (buckwheat pancakes) with caviar (see entry). Often the caviar will be red salmon roe, but black sturgeon roe is also commonly served.
Piroshki, pasties with savoury fillings, are another starter. They are also eaten as a snack between meals and are sold at many street stalls.

Soups

The Russians are renowned for their tasty soups. The best known is borshch made from beetroot, white cabbage, potatoes and beef, and often served with a dash of sour cream. Okroshka is a cold soup of potatoes, horse radish, cucumber, small pieces of meat, chives and kvas. Rassolnik is a beef broth with vegetables and kidneys. Solyanka is made either from boiled or roast meat to which cucumber, onions, tomato purée and olives are added, or from white fish and vegetables. Shchi is a fresh cabbage soup, with carrots, tomato purée and sour cream.

Meat dishes

The selection of meat dishes is fairly limited and rather tough steak will often have to suffice. When 'bef stroganoff' is on the menu, thin strips of beef with mushrooms and onions can be expected. There is usually a relatively wide choice of mince dishes.

Fish dishes

Fish is a mainstay of Russian cooking. Sturgeon in particular appears in a variety of dishes, while salmon, perch-pike and trout are regularly served. The menu will sometimes include zrazy, fish fillets stuffed with mushrooms, onions and parsley.

Desserts

The choice of dessert tends to be limited to ice cream or a variety of cakes, pastries or tarts.

Drinks

Travellers are advised to use only bottled water for drinking.

Kvas

The most popular cold drink is kvas, which is sold from large tanks and vending machines all over the city. It is made from fermented rye, buckwheat, malt, fruit and sugar, and is slightly alcoholic.

Lemonade, mineral water

Russian lemonade is usually very sweet, and the mineral water has a high mineral content. Pepsi-Cola is now available almost everywhere, and other cold drinks imported from the West can be bought with foreign currency.

Coffee, tea

Coffee or tea usually round off a meal. Whereas the visitor may not always enjoy the coffee, Russian tea is excellent. People are left to serve themselves from a samovar: half fill a glass or cup with the concentrated tea warming in the pot on top of the samovar, and then top it with boiling water from the samovar itself.

Beer

Russian beer (pivo) is very light and has an excellent flavour. Beer from Western countries is sold in Beriozka shops (see entry) and hard currency bars (see Night Life).

Wine, champagne

Foreigners frequently find Russian wine rather too sweet. Better tasting are the drier red and white wines from the Moldavian and Ukrainian republics. Russian champagne, "shampanskoye", is available in almost all restaurants, but a dry champagne is a rarity.

Vodka

Like all alcoholic drinks in the USSR, vodka, is sold by the gram rather than the litre. With company Russians always empty their glass in one gulp, often followed by mineral water to ameliorate the effect.

Getting to Leningrad

By plane

British Airways and Aeroflot have weekly air services to Leningrad from London Heathrow, on Saturdays and Sundays respectively. In addition there are direct flights from major European cities at least once a week. Lufthansa and Aeroflot for example have twice weekly flights from Frankfurt am Main, and weekly flights from Düsseldorf and Hamburg. Flights from London take just over 3¼ hours. There are 2 flights a week on Wednesday and Saturday from New York to Leningrad via Frankfurt – journey time approximately 17 hours. PanAm and Aeroflot fly non stop from New York to Moscow (then by train to Leningrad). Leningrad can be reached via Finnair from Helsinki.

By rail

There are several different possible routes for travel by rail, including a daily departure from Paris for Leningrad via Cologne, Hanover, Berlin (Friedrichstrasse) and Warsaw. However, few tourists choose to make the long and arduous trip by train. The journey from Berlin alone takes about 35 hours.

By car

Although touring by car (see entry) is possible in the Soviet Union throughout the year, visitors driving their own vehicles are restricted to the approved tourist routes on which suitable tourist services are available. The usual approach to Leningrad is via Warsaw, Minsk, and Tallinn or Pskov, or alternatively via Helsinki, Torfyanovka and Vyborg.
The frontier crossing points are open in summer from 7 a.m. to 9 p.m. (M.E.T.), and in winter until 6 p.m.
The precise route to be taken, any planned stopovers, and overnight accommodation, must be specified and booked in advance. It is not permitted to drive beyond a 30 km/18 mile radius of the stopping places given in the travel documents (see entry).

By boat

Going to Leningrad by boat can be quite delightful. The ferry "Finnjet", owned by the Finnish Silja Line, has sailings two or three times a week, year round, between Travemünde – reached by train from Hamburg – and Helsinki. From Helsinki the journey to Leningrad can be completed by coach, or in summer aboard the Baltic Shipping Company's "Konstantin Simonov" or the Oy Sally Line's "Sally Albatros". A ferry also sails to Leningrad from Stockholm.

By coach

When arranged by a coach tour company, coach travel to Leningrad often includes a ferry passage, sailing from Travemünde to Helsinki in the "Finnjet", for example, then continuing by coach to the frontier at Torfyanovka or Brusnichnoye, and on to Leningrad by way of Vyborg.

Group travel

Package tours to Leningrad are arranged by several British and US travel companies as well as by Intourist (see Information). As a rule there is little difference between the packages and prices offered by the various companies. Most trips are for three to eight days, and a stay in Leningrad is often combined with a short visit to Moscow and/or Kiev. Regardless of which company arranges the booking, visitors are looked after by Intourist guides during their stay in the Soviet Union.
Without question group travel is the cheapest way of visiting Leningrad. In addition to the flight, excursions, tours and other events are included at reduced prices. There are other advantages, too. In the USSR groups tend to be given priority over individuals, when waiting to be served in restaurants especially, or for admission to museums. Even those who would otherwise prefer to travel independently are, therefore, well advised to join a group package tour. Once in Leningrad it is quite possible to stay with the group for the most attractive items on the programme, such as the city tour, or for a museum visit that might otherwise involve a long wait, but to go your own way on other occasions when it suits.

Hotels

General

Whether travelling in a group or independently, visitors to Leningrad should not expect to learn the name of their hotel until arrival at the airport. Only the category of room can be specified when booking.

Intourist Hotels: Yevropeyskaya *. . . and Moskva*

Visitors from the West are usually allocated rooms with a bath or shower, toilet, telephone, refrigerator and television. Those travelling independently can expect to pay £38–£75 for a single room with breakfast and £45–£85 for a double room, again with breakfast. Requests for single rooms almost always meet with difficulties. As a rule, when travelling in a group, two men or two women travelling alone must expect to share a room. Any single room supplement paid in advance will be reimbursed by the travel agent on returning home.
Passports and visas must be surrendered on arrival at the hotel and a registration form completed. Passports and visas will normally be returned within two days.

Hotel cards

In Soviet hotels cards, are issued to guests on registration and record the room number and dates of arrival and departure. The card must be shown to the floor attendant whenever the room key is collected, and sometimes must also be shown at the hotel entrance.

Floor attendants

The system of floor attendants is another distinctive feature of hotels in the USSR. The floor attendant is in charge of the keys on each floor, keeps a supply of drinks and medicines, and puts through any telephone calls. Any complaints should also be addressed to this person.
It is only in the newest, most modern hotels that the duties of the floor attendants have been taken over by reception, as in other countries.

Hotel Pribaltiskaya

Intourist hotels

All the hotels listed below have several restaurants most of which will accept rubles as well as foreign currency (check at reception). In bars which serve spirits from Western countries however, payment must be made in hard currency. Each hotel has a Beriozka shop (see entry), a newspaper stand, an Intourist service desk (see Information), a postal desk and an exchange bureau.

Astoriya (Astoria)
Ulitsa Gertsena 39
Bus: nos. 2, 3, 10, 22, 27, 60, 100
343 rooms in two buildings. Opened in 1913, the hotel is being completely renovated at present. It has a sauna.

Yevropeyskaya (Europa)
Ulitsa Brodskovo 1/7
Metro: Nevsky Prospekt
225 rooms. The Europa was opened in 1824 and is a traditional Russian hotel. While some of the rooms still radiate a little of the splendour of bygone days, the interior is in urgent need of renovation. Negotiations are in progress for a Swedish company to carry out the work.

Kareliya
Ulitsa Tukhachevskovo 27/2
Metro: Ploshchad Mushestva (then bus nos. 40 or 101)
430 rooms. This hotel has been used by Intourist for foreign visitors since 1979.

Leningrad
Vyborgskaya Naberezhnaya 5/2
Metro: Ploshchad Lenina
743 rooms. The hotel was established in 1970 on the banks of the Neva with many beautiful views from its rooms and restaurant.

Moskva (Moscow)
Ploshchad Alexandra Nevskovo 2
Metro: Ploshchad Alexandra Nevskogo
770 rooms. This hotel, which is rather unattractive from the outside, was opened in 1975.

Olgino
Primorskoye Schosse 59
306 rooms. Opened in 1980 the Olgino is situated about 20 km/12 miles north-west of the city centre and accommodates visitors who come to Leningrad by car. There are tennis courts and a sauna, and in winter skating and cross-country skiing.

Pribaltiyskaya
Ulitsa Korablestroiteley 14
Metro: Primorskaya
Bus: no. 7 (from Nevsky Prospekt)
1200 rooms. This seaside hotel on the Gulf of Finland was opened in 1979 and has every comfort. There are a number of exclusive restaurants as well as sauna, swimming pool, massage parlour, hairdresser and beauty salon, and a bowling alley.

Pulkovskaya
Ploshchad Pobedy 1
Metro: Moskovskaya (then bus nos. 3 or 39)
840 rooms. The Pulkovskaya is the newest Intourist hotel in Leningrad, having opened its doors only in 1981. It was designed by Finnish architects and is of a standard comparable to modern hotels in the West.

Information

Intourist, the State tourist organisation, is virtually the only source of information about travel in the USSR. It has a network of information bureaux in the Soviet Union and abroad, and within the USSR it has its own hotels, camping sites and motels. It employs some 3000 guides who have on-the-spot responsibility for visitors.
Intourist also acts as an agency through which to book excursions, reserve theatre, concert or circus tickets, reserve restaurant tables, and order taxis.

In the United Kingdom

Intourist
Intourist House
219 Marsh Wall
Isle of Dogs
London E14 9PJ (no personal callers)
tel. 01–538 3202

Intourist
71 Deansgate
Manchester M3 2BW
tel. 061 834 0230

In the United States

Intourist
Rockefeller Center
630 Fifth Avenue, Suite 868
New York, NY 10111
tel. (212) 757 3884

In Leningrad

Intourist Head Office
Isaakievskaya Ploshchad 11
Intourist also has service desks in all hotels. They are open daily from 9 a.m. to 9 p.m. As a rule the staff speak fluent English.

Kolkhoz Markets

General

In the Kolkhoz markets, which have the backing of the State, kolkhozes (collective farms) and sovkhozes (State farms) sell produce surplus to their production targets, and the workers from collective farms sell the produce from their private plots, all at open market prices. The kolkhozes are agricultural co-operatives in which the workers permanently hold the land, equipment and capital in common. They are given an annual output target to fulfill. The sovkhozes on the other hand are large State-owned farms with a work force of anything up to 600. Unlike the collective farmers, the workers on a sovkhoz are employees, the land, equipment and capital belonging to the State. The sovkhozes are mainly engaged in cereal production and livestock farming.
Each kolkhoz worker is allowed a private plot of up to 1 hectare/2.5 acres and may keep a cow, one or two pigs, smaller livestock and two calves. Although these holdings amount to less than 1 per cent of the total area under agriculture, this "private sector" supplies 35 per cent of the Soviet Union's total consumption of meat and milk, 65 per

Kolkhoz markets on the Moyka

cent of potatoes, 40 per cent of vegetables and more than half the eggs. The survival to this extent of private enterprise is obviously in the interest of the State, and the kolkhoz markets are encouraged by the Soviet government with the object of improving the supply of foodstuffs.

Produce

The kolkhoz markets supply most of the foodstuffs not to be found in other shops, for example meat of a quality about which the Soviet city-dweller can otherwise only dream. Depending on the season there is a wide selection of fruit and vegetables. Herbs and spices are carefully laid out in rows and for the Western visitor it is salutory to see a tiny bunch of parsley or small bunch of radishes displayed as something of a rarity. Flowers, too, are available and in demand.

Prices

Prices in the Kolkhoz markets are regulated, and must not exceed twice the price of similar products in State shops. Often, however, there are no similar products to be found in the State shops, and kolkhoz prices, are determined by supply and demand. Meat costs something like four times as much as in the State shops, and in winter a kilogram of tomatoes or cucumbers costs up to 15 rubles. Given the average Soviet wage of 200 rubles a month it is not difficult to work out how often the average worker can afford to go shopping in a kolkhoz markets.

Kolkhoz markets in Leningrad

There are Kolkhoz markets in every district of Leningrad. For example:
Kolkhoznyy Rynok
Kuznechnyy Pereulok 3

Metro: Vladimirskaya
Kolkhoznyy Rynok
Moskovskiy Prospekt 4
Metro: Ploshchad Mira

Opening times

Mon.–Sat. 7.30 a.m.–9 p.m. (in winter 7 p.m.); Sun. 8 a.m.–4 p.m.

Language

Russian is the mother tongue of some 150 million people within the Soviet Union and 3·5 million outside, and the second language of another 50 million.
Visitors to Leningrad will find it useful at least to know the Russian (Cyrillic) alphabet as an aid to finding their way about.

The following table gives the approximate pronunciation of the letters, which is also the method of transcription used in this Guide. The last column shows the official Soviet transcription, which is closer to the German than to the normal English system.

Alphabet		*Pronunciation*	*Soviet transcription*
А	а	a as in "father"	a
Б	б	b	b
В	в	v	v

Г	г	g as in "gag" (pronounced v in the genitive ending -ogo, -ego)	g
Д	д	d	d
Е	е	e, ye	e (after consonant) je (after vowel and at beginning of word)
Ё	ё	o, yo	o (after consonant) je (after vowel and at beginning of word)
Ж	ж	zh as in "treasure"	ž
З	з	z	z
И	и	ee (transliterated i)	i, ji
Й	й	i, y	j
К	к	k	k
Л	л	l (a "dark" l)	l
М	м	m	m
Н	н	n	n
О	о	o	o
П	п	p	p
Р	р	r	r
С	с	s	s
Т	т	t	t
У	у	oo (transliterated u)	u
Ф	ф	f	f
Х	х	kh as in "loch"	ch
Ц	ц	ts	c
Ч	ч	ch	č
Ш	ш	sh	š
Щ	щ	shch	šč
Ъ	ъ	(hard sign; not pronounced)	–
Ы	ы	y (vocalic)	y
Ь	ь	(soft sign; adds slight y sound to preceding consonant)	–
Э	э	e	e
Ю	ю	yu	u (after consonant) ju (after vowel and at beginning of word)
Я	я	ya	ja

Development of the alphabet

At some time before 862 Cyril, one of the two "Apostles of the Slavs", developed out of the Greek minuscule letters an alphabet for writing the Slavonic language, the so-called Glagolitic alphabet, in which the first Biblical texts were translated from Greek.

Some decades later a pupil of his fellow Apostle Methodius devised a simplified alphabet based on the Greek majuscule letters, which was also attributed to Cyril and named Cyrillic after him. From the 10th c. onwards this displaced the older Glagolitic, and it is still the alphabet used by the Russian Orthodox Church, marking the distinction between the Orthodox and the "Latins", the Roman Catholics and Protestants who use the Latin Alphabet.

In 1710 Peter the Great decreed that this form of Cyrillic should be replaced in secular books by a simplified Cyrillic known as the "civil alphabet" (*grazhdansky shrift*) approximating more

closely to the Latin alphabet. With some further simplification in 1918, after the October Revolution, this is the alphabet still in use today.
The use of two different scripts – the older Cyrillic used by the Church and the modernised version introduced by Peter the Great – reflected the distinction between the literary language, Church Slavonic, and the non-literary language of the people. The dichotomy was not really resolved until the 19th c., when, largely thanks to Pushkin, Russia's greatest poet, a truly national language came into being.

Language Courses

Language courses in Leningrad can be booked through Intourist (see Information).
The courses last 14 or 28 days, and include a number of excursions and leisure activities. Students are accommodated in Dyuny, a small town 40 km/25 miles from the city. Lecturers from the University of Leningrad provide 4 hours tuition daily.

Medical Attention

Medical treatment

In case of illness or accident contact the hotel floor attendant, hotel reception or any Intourist service desk in the first instance. Medical treatment is free, even if a doctor is called to the hotel.

Medicines

There is normally a small charge for medicines. Western brands are seldom available, and visitors who need particular drugs should take a supply with them. Aspirin, flu remedies and the like are usually available from the floor attendant

Monuments

Leningrad is so well endowed with monuments that no summary can hope to be complete.
In the list that follows, the designer's names and year of construction are given only for monuments not described in the A to Z. section.

Monuments to artists and scientists

Glinka
See A to Z, Theatre Square

Gorky
Prospekt Maksima Gorkovo 21
Isayev, Gabe, Levinson (1968)

Krylov
See A to Z, Summer Garden

Lermontov
Lermontovskiy Prospekt 54
Mikeshin (1916)

Lomonosov
Ploshchad Lomonosova
Benois, Lytkin (1892)
also see A to Z, Twelve Colleges: Lomonosov Monument

Nekrasov
Ulitsa Nekrasova
Eydlin, Vasilkovsky (1971)

Popov
Kirovskiy Prospekt between Nos. 39 and 41
Bogolyubov, Baranov (1959)

Pushkin
See A to Z, Square of the Arts
Obelisk on the site of the duel
Kolomyashskiy Prospekt
Maniser, Lapirov (1937)

Rimsky-Korsakov
See A to Z, Theatre Square

Ushinsky
See A to Z, Razumovsky Palace: Ushinsky Monument

Monuments to historical figures

Barclay de Tolly
See A to Z, Kazan Cathedral: Kazan Square

Engels
See A to Z, Smolny Institute

Kalinin
Ploshchad Kalinina
Maniser, Baruchev (1955)

Catherine the Great
See A to Z, Ostrovskiy Square: Catherine the Great Monument

Krupskaya
Prospekt Obukhovskoy Oborony 105
Kholina, Shretter (1960)

Kutuzov
See A to Z, Kazan Cathedral: Kazan Square

Lenin
Ploshchad Lenina 3
Yevseyev, Shchuko, Helfreich (1926)
Prospekt Obukhovskoy Oborony 51
Charlamov (1926)
Bolshoy Prospekt Vassilevskovo Ostrova 55
Koslov, Kryzhanovskaya (1930)
Naberezhnaya Obvodnovo Kanala 118
Muravov, Khomutetskiy, Tomskiy (1949)
Moskovskaya Ploshchad
Anikushin, Kamenskiy (1970)

Marx
Prospekt Karla Marksa 86
Kremer, Vassilkovskiy (1968)
also see A to Z, Smolny Institute

Nicholas I
See A to Z, Isaac Square: Nicholas I Monument

Peter the Great
See A to Z, Square of the Decembrists: Bronze Horseman
also see A to Z, Mikhail Palace: Peter the Great Monument

Suvorov
See A to Z, Field of Mars: Suvorov Square

Monuments on the "Green Line of Glory"

The "Green Line of Glory" follows the line of the defences where the German advance was halted in the Second World War (see map p. 29). Monuments, stone memorials, commemorative exhibitions and trees planted in remembrance are to be found in many places along the former military front, and also along the "Lifeline", the only route connecting Leningrad with its hinterland to remain open during the blockade.

Motoring

See Touring by Car

Museums

N.B.

As well as being closed on certain days of the week, most museums also close on either the first or last day of the month, or the first or last Monday or Tuesday of each month. Admission prices range from 20 copecks to 1 rouble, though joining one of the guided tours organised by Intourist (see Information) adds considerably to the cost. In this latter case the museum visit must be booked in advance with Intourist and paid for in foreign currency.
Long queues frequently form outside the well-known museums. Local people wait patiently for admission, sometimes for hours. Travel groups normally take priority.

Museums of Art

Brodsky Museum
Ploshchad Iskusstv 3
Open: Wed.–Sun. 11 a.m.–7 p.m.
The painter Brodsky had an apartment here from 1924 to 1939 (see A to Z, Square of the Arts). On display are late 19th- and early 20th-century paintings by Russian artists.

Hermitage
See A to Z, Hermitage

Museum of Urban Sculpture
See A to Z, Alexander Nevsky Monastery: Church of the Annunciation

Museum of Mosaic Art
The Museum is to be housed in the Church of the Resurrection (see A to Z, Church of the Resurrection) once it has been restored.

Russian Museum
See A to Z, Russian Museum

Central Exhibition Hall
See A to Z, Manège

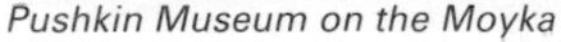

Pushkin Museum on the Moyka

Mining Institute

Literary Museums

Blok Museum
Ulitsa Dekabristov 57
Open: Mon., Thur.–Sun. 11 a.m.–6 p.m.; Tues 11 a.m.–5 p.m.
The house in which Alexander A. Blok lived and died was turned into a commemorative museum in 1980, the centenary of his birth.

Dostoyevsky Museum
Kuznechnyy Pereulok 5/2
Open: Tues.–Sun. 10.30 a.m.–6.30 p.m.
The writer lived in this house in 1846 and then from 1878 until his death in 1881.

Literary Museum
(Pushkin House)
See A to Z, Strelka: Custom House

Nekrasov Museum
Liteynyy Prospekt 36
On view are furniture and personal belongings of the politically committed writer Nicholas Nekrasov.

Pushkin House
See Literary Museum
Pushkin Museum
Naberezhnaya Reki Moyki 12
Open: Mon., Wed., Fri.–Sun. 10.30 a.m.–6.30 p.m.; Thur. noon–8 p.m.
Pushkin lived in Princess Volkonsky's house in the months before his death. The museum contains part of Pushkin's

extensive library, many pieces of his furniture, and personal effects.

Pushkin Museum in Pushkin
See A to Z, Lyceum

Museums of music and theatre

Theatre and Music Museum
Ploshchad Ostrovskovo 6
Open: Mon.–Fri. 11 a.m.–7 p.m.; Sat. 11 a.m.–4 p.m.
The history of Russian opera, ballet and drama are brought to life through theatre models, costume sketches and many other exhibits.

Rimsky-Korsakov Museum
Zagorodnyy Prospekt 28
The composer Rimsky-Korsakov taught at the conservatory in St. Petersburg in the late 19th century. His apartment has been turned into a museum.

History Museums

Museum of Anthropology and Ethnography
See A to Z, Kunstkamera

Ethnographic Museum of the Peoples of the USSR
See A to Z.

Memorial Hall of the Heroic Defenders of Leningrad
See A to Z, Victory Square

Peter the Great's Cottage
See A to Z.

Menshikov Palace
(A branch of the Hermitage)
Russian culture in the first thirty years of the 18th century. see A to Z.

Military Museum of Artillery, Engineers, and Signals
See A to Z, Peter and Paul Fortress: Kronverk

History of Leningrad Museum
See A to Z.

Branches:
The history of St. Petersburg and Petrograd 1703-1917
See A to Z, Peter and Paul Fortress: Commandant's House

The architecture of St. Petersburg and Petrograd from the early 18th to the early 20th century.
See A to Z, Peter and Paul Fortress: Engineer's House

Leningrad Today and Tomorrow
See A to Z, Smolny Convent: Cathedral of the Resurrection

Museum of Religion and Atheism
See A to Z, Kazan Cathedral

Popov Museum of Communications
Pereulok Podbelskovo 4
Open: Tues.–Fri. noon–6 p.m.; Sat.–Sun. 11 a.m.–6 p.m.
Among the exhibits are early Russian telegraph and telephone equipment, mail coaches, post-boxes and a collection of over three million stamps from all over the world.

Suvorov Museum
Ulitsa Saltykova-Shchedrina 43
Open: Mon., Thur.–Sun. 11 a.m.–6 p.m.; Tues. 11 a.m.–5 p.m.

This museum was opened in 1904 as a memorial to the 18th-century Russian Field Marshal Alexander Suvorov. On the façade are reliefs depicting Suvorov setting off for the War of the Second Coalition (War of the French Revolution) and his spectacular crossing of the St. Gotthard Pass in winter.

Chesma Museum
See A to Z, Chesma Church

Central Maritime Museum
See A to Z, Exchange

Museums of the Revolution

Kirov Museum
Kirovskiy Prospekt 26/28
Open: Mon., Tues., Fri.–Sat. 11 a.m.–7 p.m.; Thur. 2 – 7 p.m.; Sun. 10 a.m.–5 p.m.
The apartment of Central Committee Secretary Sergey Kirov who was murdered in 1934, became a museum in 1954.

Lenin Museum in the Smolny Institute
See A to Z, Smolny Institute

Museum of the October Revolution
Ulitsa Kuybysheva 4
Open: Mon., Fri. noon.–8 p.m.; Tues., Wed., Sat.–Sun. 11 a.m.–7 p.m.
Completed in 1905, this building, was taken over by the Bolsheviks during the October Revolution. It was turned into a museum in 1957.

"Cruiser Aurora" Museum
See A to Z, Aurora

Central Lenin Museum
See A to Z, Marble Palace

Science Museums

Mining Museum
See A to Z, Mining Institute

Museum of Soil Sciences
See A to Z, Strelka: Warehouses

Lomonosov Museum
See A to Z, Kunstkammer

Mendeleyev Museum
See A to Z, Twelve Colleges

Museum of the Arctic and Antarctic
Ulitsa Marata 24a
(in St. Nicholas's Church)
Open: Wed.–Sun. 10 a.m.–6 p.m.

Zoological Museum
See A to Z, Strelka: Warehouses

Night Life

Dancing and cabaret

Leningrad does not have the kind of night life that is found in the cities of the West. Travelers in search of evening entertainment must look to the restaurants (see entry) in the larger hotels, where there is dancing and cabaret until 11 p.m.

Bars

There are several bars in each hotel. Spirits and beer imported from the West can be bought only in the so-called "hard-currency bars". Many of the bars are only open until early evening, but there are "night bars" that stay open later in hotels Pribaltiyskaya, Pulkovskaya and Yevropeyskaya among others. The word "bar" is to be taken literally; nothing is served but drinks. No entertainment is provided.

Opening Hours

Shops

Shops open daily, except on Sundays and public holidays, from 9 or 10 a.m. until 8 or 9 p.m. Most close for an hour at lunchtime from 1 to 2 p.m. or 2 to 3 p.m. Larger food shops are open daily from 9 a.m. to 9 p.m. (Spirits are sold only in the afternoon.)
Almost all shops close on either the first or the last day of the month.

Department stores

Department stores are open Monday to Saturday from 8 a.m. to 9 p.m.

Beriozka shops

Beriozka shops are open daily from 9 or 10 a.m. until 8 p.m., closing for an hour at lunchtime, usually from 1 to 2 p.m.

Post offices

Post offices are open Monday to Saturday from 9 a.m. until 8 p.m. The main post office (see Post, Telegraph and Telephones) is open from 9 a.m. to 9 a.m. and on Sundays from 10 a.m. to 8 p.m.

Museums

The opening times of particular museums are given under their respective entries in the A to Z Section or Practical Information, Museums. In addition to being closed on certain days each week, most museums are also closed either on the first or last day of the month, or the first or last Monday or Tuesday of the month (see Museums). Before visiting a museum it is best to check the precise hours with Intourist (see Information).

Restaurants, Cafés

Restaurants are generally open from 12 noon to 3 p.m. and from 6 or 7 p.m. to 11 p.m. Cafés are open from 9 a.m. to 3 p.m. and from 4 p.m. to 9 p.m.

Parks and Gardens

Leningrad is not particularly rich in leisure facilities, so parks and gardens have an important part to play in the life of the city. They are popular meeting-places and offer various possibilities for recreation.

Botanical Garden
Ulitsa Professora Popova 2
Metro: Petrogradskaya
The Botanical Garden began as a small medicinal herb garden planted by Peter the Great. Today the Garden takes great pride in its palm house.

Kirov Park of Culture and Rest
See A to Z, Yelagin Island

Moscow Victory Park
Moskovskiy Prospekt
Metro: Park Pobedy

Seaside Victory Park
Morskoy Prospekt
Metro: Chornaya Rechka, then bus no. 21

Summer Garden
See A to Z

Zoological Garden
Lenin Park
Metro: Gorkovskaya

The former Imperial summer palaces at Petrodvorets, Pavlovsk, Pushkin and Lomonosov (see entries in the A to Z section) also have exceptionally beautiful gardens.

Photography and Film

Prohibited

Photographing and filming military and industrial installations, airports, railway stations, bridges and radio stations is prohibited. There is a total ban on photography in border areas and from aeroplanes flying in Soviet air space. Taking photographs inside shops and inside certain churches and museums is also forbidden.

Permitted

Those prohibitions previously mentioned aside, amateur photographers are free to take photographs and to film. Permission from the director or manager should however be obtained before using a camera in any agricultural, administrative or industrial establishment, and when taking pictures of people make sure that they have no objections.

Film, etc.

In general films and other photographic materials produced in the West are not available even in Beriozka shops (see entry). Travelers with cameras should be sure to take adequate supplies with them.

Colour slides

Sets of colour slides are sold in all Beriozka shops and Intourist hotels, as well as at many kiosks in the city. They are not always of very good quality.

Post, Telegraph and Telephone

Postage

There are both surface and airmail services for letters and postcards from Leningrad to Western Europe. Delivery takes four to six days.
Stamps can be bought at hotel postal desks and at newspaper kiosks, as well as in post offices.
Post-boxes for destinations outside Leningrad are blue.

Rates to countries in Western Europe

Postcards	20 copecks
Letters (20 grams)	30 copecks
Postcards by air	35 copecks
Letters by air	45 copecks

Post-box

Post offices

Main post office
Ulitsa Soyuza Svyazi 9
Open: Mon.–Sat. 9 a.m.–9 p.m.; Sun. 10 a.m.–8 p.m.
There are postal desks in all hotels catering for foreign visitors.

Poste Restante

Mail from outside the Soviet Union should be addressed c/o Intourist, Leningrad C-400. It must be collected at the Hotel Oktyabrskaya, Ligovskiy Prospekt 10. (Don't forget to take your passport!)

Telephone

Local calls made from a hotel room are free of charge. From a coin-operated telephone a local call costs 2 copecks. Telephone directories are practically impossible to find. The telephone enquiry service is reached by dialling 09, but the operators speak only Russian.
Calls to foreign destinations must be arranged in advance through hotel reception and in order to avoid a long wait it is advisable to book a particular time for the call to come through. A 3-minute call to the U.K. costs about £9, and to the USA about $25. Each extra minute costs about £1/$2.
Long distance telephone calls can also be made at the main telephone exchange, Ulitsa Gertsena 3/5. Open: Mon.–Fri. 9 a.m.–8 p.m.; Sat. 10 a.m.–5 p.m.

Telephone calls to Leningrad

From the United Kingdom the dialling code for Leningrad is 010 7812, which should be followed by the Leningrad number. At present dialling direct is seldom successful and it is usually necessary to go through the operator.

Telegrams

It is best to send telegrams through hotel reception, or from the main telegraph office (Ulitsa Soyuza Svyazi 14).

Public Holidays

1 January

New Year. Homes and city squares are decorated with fir trees. Gifts are exchanged. New Year's Eve is usually celebrated with a festive meal and the New Year welcomed in with toasting and fireworks.

8 March

International Women's Day. It is customary for women to receive a small present.

1 and 2 May

International Labour Day. Is a two-day holiday in the USSR. The city is decorated with huge posters and there are parades.

9 May

Victory in Europe Day. Rallies, particularly of war veterans, are held in the city to commemorate the end of the Second World War.

7 October

Constitution Day. Marks the inauguration in 1977 of the new Soviet Constitution.

7 and 8 November

Anniversary of the October Revolution. Even for the people of Leningrad the day is dominated by the great military parade in Moscow's Red Square.

Public Transport

Metro, Buses, Trolleybuses, Trams

Public transport in Leningrad consists of the Metro (Underground), buses, trolleybuses, trams and railways (see Railway Stations). During the summer there are also regular boat and hovercraft services (see Boat Trips) on the Neva. The Metro is quickest and most convenient, with 45 stations serving the city. The network is continually being extended but because the land Leningrad stands on is very marshy, the scope for building below ground is limited. Consequently a city journey often involve taking a bus or tram as well as the Metro.

Operating times

Public transport operates from 6 a.m. to 1 a.m. the following morning. Rush hour is between 7 and 9 in the morning and 4 and 6 in the evening. At peak periods there are trains about every 40 seconds and at normal times about every 1½ to 2 minutes. On each platform there are two illuminated clocks, one showing the time of day, the other indicating the time since the last train. Trams and buses run less frequently and may require a wait of ten minutes or so.

Paying the fare

A journey by Metro, bus, trolleybus or tram, costs 5 copecks whatever the distance. All forms of transport are driver-only, there are no conductors. On buses, trolleybuses and trams the same tickets are valid. They can be bought in books of ten at newspaper kiosks, metro stations, and in hotels, or from the driver, if he has none try to buy tickets from fellow passengers. Books of 10 tickets (50 copecks) can be bought in advance from metro stations, and should be punched in the cancelling machine on boarding the vehicle.
To ride the Metro you put a 5-copeck piece in the slot at the barrier and then pass through. There is no further payment when changing trains; only if you have passed through an exit barrier will you be required to pay again. At the entrance to every Metro station there are machines that will give change for larger coins.

Finding your way

When travelling on the Metro or other public transport it is essential to be able to decipher the Cyrillic alphabet. A general idea of the Metro system can be gained from the plan at the end of this guide. The colours on the plan are the same as those on the master map displayed in every Metro station. Their usefulness is limited, however, because neither the information boards nor the platform signs are in colour. These boards and signs only show the names of stations at which the train in question stops. Anyone unfamiliar with the Cyrillic alphabet should identify the stations using the transcriptions on the plan at the end of this guide. In the case of trams and buses, the main stops are shown on panels on the outside of the vehicle. People intending to make frequent use of trams and buses should obtain a copy of the special map (Schema Passazhirskogo Transporta) on which all city tram and bus routes are shown. It is available in hotels and from kiosks.

Transferring

Although on all forms of public transport the driver calls out the names of the respective stops, visitors unfamiliar with the language may well have difficulty in knowing when to get off buses and trams. This is less of a problem on the Metro where stops can be followed on the numerous plans always in view.
Changing trains on the Metro, however, can be troublesome. It is important to realise that stations at which passengers change from one line to another may be referred to by more than one name. In fact the different names refer to different stations, one on each line, connected by underground passageways. Transferring from one to the other may involve a considerable walk. To give an example (see Plan): having travelled on the green line to Ploshchad Vosstaniya Station and wanting to go on to Baltiyskaya on the red line, it will be necessary to walk some distance underground to Mayakovskaya Station to get the Baltiyskaya train. The same applies to Nevsky Prospekt and Gostinyy Dvor Stations.

Railway Stations

Lines from all parts of the USSR converge on Leningrad's five-rail termini. There are also local rail services.It is possible to get about fairly quickly and cheaply by train in the Leningrad area, to visit the summer palaces (see Excursions) for example (trains leave every 20 to 40 minutes). Special permits from Intourist (see Information) are only required if travelling to more distant destinations.

Baltic Station

Baltiyskiy Voksal
Naberezhnaya Obvodnovo Kanala 120
Metro: Baltiyskaya
Trains for Petrodvorets and Lomonosov.

Finland Station

Finlyandskiy Voksal
Ploshchad Lenina 6
Metro: Ploshchad Lenina
Trains for Repino and Finland.

Moscow Station

Moskovskiy Voksal
Ploshchad Vosstaniya 2
Metro: Ploshchad Vosstaniya/Mayakovskaya
Trains for Moscow.
This is Leningrad's oldest railway station built in 1851 for the first rail link between Moscow and St. Petersburg. The architect, Konstantin A. Thon, designed identical termini at each end of the line.
The "Aurora Express" which runs between the two cities takes a mere five hours for the 650 km/404 mile journey.

Warsaw Station
Varshavskiy Voksal

Naberezhnaya Obvodnovo Kanala 118
Metro: Baltiskaya
Trains for Warsaw and Berlin.

Vitebsk Station

Vitebskiy Voksal
Zagorodnyy Prospekt 52
Metro: Pushkinskaya
Trains for Pushkin and Pavlovsk
Tickets for short journeys (e.g. Pushkin, Petrodvorets) are bought at a ticket machine. First work out the zone in which your destination lies, then get the appropriate single or return ticket. A return to Pavlovsk, for example, costs 50 copecks.

Restaurants

General

Many Leningrad restaurants are in hotels. As a rule it is advisable elsewhere to book a table through Intourist (see Information), except in restaurants reserved for foreign tourists.
In most hotel restaurants payment can be made in either rubles or foreign currency, but other restaurants generally accept only rubles.
Ample time should be allowed for eating in a restaurant. It is not unusual for a meal to take two or three hours from ordering at the beginning – in Russia it is customary to order everything at the same time – to tea or coffee at the end. In many restaurants there is entertainment in the form of a dance band or folk music.

Opening times

Restaurants are usually open from noon to 3 p.m. and from 6 or 7 in the evening until 11 p.m. In many restaurants orders are not taken after 10 p.m.

Choice of restaurants

See Practical Information, Hotels, for the addresses of restaurants in hotels.

Baku
Sadovaya Ulitsa 12
Azerbaijani food

Daugava
in the Hotel Pribaltiyskaya
Baltic food

Kavkasskiy
Nevsky Prospekt 25
Caucasian food

Neva
in the Hotel Pribaltiyskaya
Russian food

Petrovskiy Room
in the hotel Leningrad
Russian food
Russian Room
in the Hotel Moscow
Russian food

Sadko
Ulitsa Brodskovo 1
(next to the Hotel Yevropeyskaya)
Russian food

Troika
Zagorodnyy Prospekt 27
Russian food

Chalka
Naberezhnaya Kanala Griboyedova 14
(near the Nevsky Prospekt)
Hamburg specialities and draught beer
(Payment in foreign currency)

Turku
in the Hotel Pulkovskaya
Russian and Scandinavian food

Visla
Ulitsa Dzerzhinskovo 17
Russian and Polish food

Food and Drink

See entry

Cafés

See entry

Bars

See Night Life

Shopping and Souvenirs

It would be quite pointless to think of spending time just wandering round the shops in Leningrad in the way that people do in Western countries. A walk along the Nevsky Prospekt and a glance at the food shops and department stores shows that there is less available here than in Moscow.
A little patience is needed by anyone setting out to buy articles for use or souvenirs. Having decided to buy a particular item the shopper must first find out the price, then go to the cashier (kassa) to pay, and finally return to the sales counter where the receipt must be presented before the purchase is obtained.
In contrast Beriozka shops (see entry) are self-service and shopping in them does not usually involve having to wait in long queues.

Department stores

Gostinyy Dvor (the Large Department Store)
See A to Z, Large Department Store

Shopping arcade

"House of Books"

Kirovskiy
Ploshchad Stachek 9

Moskovskiy
Moskovskiy Prospekt 205/207 and 220

Passazh (Passage)
See A to Z, Nevsky Prospekt: Passage

Books

Dom Knigi
Nevsky Prospekt 28
There is only a limited selection of English books in Leningrad's largest bookshop. Maps can be found here too.

Mir
Nevsky Prospekt 13 and 16
Books published in Soviet countries
This shop also has the best selection of foreign language books in Leningrad. Fiction and reference books are sold at No. 13, illustrated travel books and guides to many different countries at No 16.

Gifts

Podarki
Nevsky Prospekt 54

Podarki
Bolshoy Prospekt 51

Suveniry
Nevsky Prospekt 92

Arts and crafts

Isdeliya Khudozhestvennykh Promyslov
Nevsky Prospekt 51

Food shops

Gastronom No. 1
Nevsky Prospekt 56
The interior of Leningrad's oldest food shop still retains something of the air of past splendours.

Paintings

Magasin-Salon "Lavka Khudozhnika"
Nevsky Prospekt 8

China and glass

Farfor, Chrystal
Nevsky Prospekt 64
(Second-hand china, sometimes quite valuable, is sold at Podarki, Nevsky Prospekt 54)

Records

Melodiya
Nevsky Prospekt 32/34

Jewellery

Yachont
Ulitsa Gertsena 24

Shoes

Salon Modelniy Obuvi
Nevsky Prospekt 11

Toys and children's clothes

Dom Leningradskoy Torgovli
Ulitsa Zhelyabova 21/23

Beriozka shops

See entry

Kolkhoz markets

See entry

Opening times

See entry

Souvenirs

Art and craft work is particularly suitable for souvenirs of the USSR. The plump "Matryoshka" wooden dolls, with about five or six smaller dolls inside, are always popular. Attractive also are the miniature paintings from Palekh, the brooches, trays and caskets from Fedoskino with their vividly coloured decoration on fairy-tale themes, and the bowls, jugs and spoons from Khokhloma. There are pieces of elaborate filigree, work lacquered boxes and embroidery, as well as some ceramics, and carpets. The amber jewellery, too, is likely to tempt the souvenir-hunter.
For a different kind of souvenir it is worth looking at the water-colours, oil paintings and sketches sold on the street, sometimes on the Nevsky Prospekt but usually by the Kazan Cathedral and St. Catherine's Church, where one or two portrait painters are often to be found looking for customers.
Books, records and stamps, of which there are some fine examples, also make suitable souvenirs. Recently Intourist (see Information) has produced some video cassettes of Leningrad, in particular of opera, ballet and circus performances.
Many people may consider caviar (see entry) an appropriate souvenir. Beriozka shops (see entry) stock various different qualities but prices are not significantly below those to be found in Western Europe. Much the same is true of vodka.
The souvenirs mentioned are available in Beriozka shops and in the shops listed above.

Sightseeing

These suggestions for sightseeing are intended to help independent travellers to make the most of a short visit to Leningrad.
Unless otherwise indicated, references in the text are to the A to Z Section.

One day

In view of the considerable distances involved anyone with only a day to spend in Leningrad would do best to join one of the city coach tours organised by Intourist (see Practical Information, Information). A morning tour of the city would leave the afternoon free for a visit to the Hermitage (see entry).
For those who prefer to explore the city for themselves on foot despite the distances involved here is a suggested route (see also Map pp 36–37). Except for a fairly long lunch break, the whole day will be needed.
Start at the Admiralty (see entry). Its "golden needle", on which all the main thoroughfares converge, is the city's emblem. Then walk through the lawned gardens to the Square of the Decembrists (see entry), where the Bronze Horseman stands, the famous monument to Peter the Great. Across the Neva, on University Quay, some of the city's finest buildings will be in view (see Academy of Arts, Twelve Colleges, Academy of Sciences and the Kunstkamera). Going south from the Square of the Decembrists it is only a few hundred metres to St. Isaac's Cathedral (see entry) and a climb up to the gallery under the dome will be rewarded by a magnificent view of old St. Petersburg. Following a brief stop in Isaac Square (see entry) to see Nicholas I's monument and the Mariya Palace, either walk or take the bus (nos. 2, 3, 10, 22, 27, 60, or 100) along the Moyka to the Nevsky Prospekt (see entry).
Nevsky Prospekt, Leningrad's main traffic artery and principal shopping street, is almost always bustling with activity. Follow the crowds thronging eastwards and a succession of splendid houses, palaces and churches will unfold, including the Kazan Cathedral (see entry). Those who would like an insight into Soviet shopping habits should next make a quick sortie into the Gostinyy Dvor (see Practical Information, Shopping); otherwise, continue along the Nevsky Prospekt, passing Ostrovskiy Square (see entry) dominated by the imposing Pushkin Theatre with Rossi Street (see entry) leading off behind, and on to another outstanding landmark, the Anichkov Bridge (see entry) which once lay on the St. Petersburg boundary. Leave the Nevsky Prospekt at this point and walk northwards, along the west bank of the Fontanka, for a sight of the Sheremetyev Palace (see entry) soon in view on the opposite bank; then turn back a short way to Ulitsa Rakova, which leads to the Square of the Arts (see entry). The Square takes its name from the theatres and museums built round it, the Russian Museum (see entry) in particular deserving notice.
Since places to eat are rare in Leningrad it is wise to interrupt the sightseeing here to look for a restaurant in the nearby Hotel Yevropeyskaya (see Practical Information, Hotels, Restaurants).

Gothic Chapel . . .

. . . and the Cottage, Petrodvorets

After lunch follow the Griboyedov Canal northwards to the Church of the Resurrection (see entry), and through the park to the south entrance of the Summer Garden (see entry), on to which faces the once fortress-like Mikhail Castle (see entry). Go past a pond, under old trees and finally to Peter the Great's modest Summer Palace on the bank of the Neva.

If preferred the walk can now be shortened by turning left along the south bank of the Neva, past the Marble Palace (see entry) to the Hermitage palaces (see entry), rejoining the route described below at the Winter Palace.

Otherwise, cross the Neva by the Kirov Bridge (see entry) and enter the Peter and Paul Fortress (see entry) by the Peter Gate, going as far as the inner precinct (no admittance from here). There is no time to see more of the Fortress, so leave this hub of the old city by the north exit, walk westwards alongside a tributary of the Neva, and cross the "Little Neva" to the point of land known as Strelka (see entry) on Vasil'yevskiy Island. Here, built beside what was then the harbour of St. Petersburg, stands the Exchange (see entry). Glancing back from the Palace Bridge re-crossing the "Great Neva", there is a superb view of the impressive Kunstkamera (see entry), but already the former Winter Palace (see Hermitage) on the other side of the river captures attention. In front of the south façade of the turquoise and white palace extends Palace Square (see entry) with the Alexander Column and the General Staff Building. After pausing to admire the gigantic proportions and stunning architectural effect of the traffic-free square, a short cut through the great arch of the General Staff Building leads

back to the Nevsky Prospekt, along which a short walk in a northwest direction brings the tour back to where it began, at the Admiralty.
After the day's sightseeing there is no more pleasant way to spend the evening than at a Leningrad restaurant (see Practical Information, Restaurants) enjoying the folk music and dancing, or at the theatre, a concert or the circus (reservations through Intourist, see Practical Information, Information).

Two days

With two days to spend in Leningrad visitors can do no better on the first day than to follow the shortened version of the city walk just described, leaving the visit to the Peter and Paul Fortress and the Strelka for the second morning. In the afternoon a visit to the Hermitage is not to be missed, and an early evening boat trip on the Neva or the Fontanka (see Practical Information, Boat Trips) rounds off the day's sightseeing in more leisurely fashion.

Three days

Having seen most of Leningrad on the first two days, the third day should include a visit to one of the former Imperial summer residences. The palaces and parks of Petrodvorets (see entry) are considered by many to be the most worthwhile. In summer Petrodvorets is easily reached by hydrofoil (see Practical Information, Boat Trips) or by train (see Practical Information, Railway Stations). The afternoon might be spent visiting the Alexander Nevsky Monastery (see entry) or the Russian Museum (see entry) or even both. In the summer months the long hours of daylight also allow some sightseeing in the late evening, perhaps a trip to the Smolny Convent (see entry) or to St. Nicholas's Cathedral (see entry), where the liturgy and other Orthodox services are still celebrated. On the other hand many visitors are drawn simply to spend time absorbing the atmosphere of a city that is often compared to Amsterdam; this is best achieved by a stroll along one of the many rivers or canals.

Taxis

Official taxis

Taxis are usually yellow with a narrow chequered band round the body or a chequered sign on the roof. A green light behind the windscreen indicates that it is available. Taxi ranks are marked with a board bearing the letter "T". People either wait at a stand – there is generally a small queue – or hail an empty taxi. Sometimes taxis wait in front of the tourist hotels. Taxis can be ordered through Intourist (see Information), but expect some considerable delay.
Prices are still relatively reasonable: the cost is 20 copecks with an additional charge of 20 copecks for every kilometre travelled.

Private taxis

Car owners are allowed to earn extra money by using their cars for private hire, but are required to pay a relatively high State licence fee. Many of them evade this requirement and operate as unlicensed taxi-drivers. It is quite safe to make use of these private taxis, but essential to agree the fare in advance. This will usually be higher than that charged by an official taxi.

Theatres and Concerts

Tickets

Tickets are booked through Intourist (see Information). Since there is always a quota allocated for foreigners, there is usually no problem obtaining tickets for a particular performance providing the reservation is made in good time. Payment to Intourist must generally be in foreign currency. The price of a ticket is normally between £10/$17 and £20/$34.
Any attempt to get tickets with rubles at the box-office, will almost certainly be unsuccessful.

Times of performances

Theatre and circus performances normally begin at 7.30 p.m., concerts a little later at about 8 p.m.

Opera and ballet

Kirov Theatre
Teatralnaya Ploshchad 1
See A to Z, Theatre Square

Maly (Small) Opera and Ballet Theatre
Ploshchad Iskusstv 1
See A to Z, Square of the Arts

Drama

Pushkin Theatre
Ploshchad Ostrovskovo 2
See A to Z, Ostrovskovo Square

Gorky Theatre
Naberezhnaya Reki Fontanki 65

Comedy Theatre
Nevsky Prospekt 56
See A to Z, Nevsky Prospekt

Musical Comedy Theatre
Ulitsa Rakova 13

Puppet theatres

Large Puppet Theatre
Ulitsa Nekrasova 10

Puppet Theatre
Nevsky Prospekt 52

Concert Halls

Large Shostakovich Philharmonia Concert Hall
Ulitsa Brodskovo 2
See A to Z, Square of the Arts

Small Shostakovich Philharmonia Concert Hall
Nevsky Prospekt 30
See A to Z, Nevsky Prospekt

Glinka Kapella (Choral Hall)
Naberezhnaya Reki Moyki 20

Circus

Leningrad Circus
Naberezhnaya Reki Fontanki 3

Time

Leningrad is in the East European Time Zone, 3 hours ahead of Greenwich Mean Time and 8 hours ahead of New York. Clocks are put forward 1 hour between 1 April and 30 September.

Tipping and Gifts

Tipping was officially abolished in the Soviet Union at the time of the Revolution. All prices are inclusive of service, and there is no charge for the obligatory cloakroom service in museums, theatres and restaurants.
However, it has now become customary to give waiters, porters, floor attendants and other staff, a little token of appreciation for good service.
A gift of some kind will almost certainly bring greater pleasure than money. Ideally it should be something from the West, and cigarettes, cigarette lighters, ballpoint pens, cosmetics, T-shirts, tights, fashion magazines and chocolates are especially well received. The Intourist guides are not allowed to accept money, but they are almost invariably happy to receive foreign books and magazines. Children occasionally ask tourists for chewing-gum. It is best to come equipped with a small assortment of suitable presents, but a limited selection of goods from Western countries is also available in Beriozka shops.

Touring by car

Road conditions

The condition of the roads in the USSR varies. Pot-holes are commonplace, especially in the small towns but also in the side-streets in Leningrad. Tram rails often stick up above the asphalt surface, while man-hole covers are often set below it. Outside the towns there are no lane markings, and verges can be extremely soft!

Traffic regulations

In general the traffic regulations in the Soviet Union are much the same as those in western European countries and the United States. Vehicles travel on the right, with passing on the left.
The speed limit in built-up areas is 60 km p.h./37 m.p.h. Outside built-up areas the speed limit for vehicles up to 3.5 tonnes/3.5 tons is 90 km p.h./56 m.p.h., and for vehicles over 3.5 tonnes/3.5 tons it is 70 km p.h./44 m.p.h. Drivers who have held a licence for less than two years are not allowed to exceed 70 km p.h./44 m.p.h.

Right of way

Traffic on major roads, indicated by the standard yellow diamond priority sign with a black and white border, has right of way over traffic on a minor road. Otherwise the rule is "right before left" even at roundabouts. This is important. It means that when you are in a roundabout you must give way to all vehicles joining, and if you are joining you must take priority. If filter lights permit a right or left turn you

must proceed only if the way is clear of other traffic. Left filter lights permit a u-turn if the road is clear. Where no special right of way applies trams and buses have priority over other vehicles.
Vehicles and convoys with flashing lights or sirens must be allowed to overtake. You must remain stationary till the last vehicle flashing a green light has passed you.

Safety

Seat belts must be worn at all times, and there are heavy fines for not doing so.
All cars must carry a fire extinguisher, a warning triangle and a first-aid kit.

Lighting

In built-up areas with street lighting, side-lights should be used rather than dipped headlights.

Alcohol prohibition

It is strictly forbidden in the USSR to drive after drinking even the smallest quantity of alcohol.

Instructions for foreign motorists

Foreign tourists travelling in their own cars must adhere to the official 'Instructions for Foreign Motorists'. These require visitors to keep to the route specified in their travel documents, any changes to which must be approved in advance by Intourist and recorded on the documents. The Instructions also stipulate that visitors drive only during the day, and not more than 500 km/310 miles in any one day. Giving lifts to strangers is forbidden. More generally, motorists are required to observe the traffic regulations in force in the USSR, as well as the rules and regulations relating to public order. Expect a lot of attention from the police if driving a foreign registered car. Most of it is just curiosity, foreign vehicles are still relatively rare.

Petrol and diesel

Fuel cannot normally be bought for cash except in major cities. Coupons, to be exchanged for 10 litres of fuel, can be purchased at the frontier and also from Intourist. Unused coupons will be reimbursed on presentation of the original receipt.
At present a litre of Super grade petrol costs about 40p, or £1·82 a gallon. Diesel costs about 36p a litre, or £1·64 a gallon. Diesel and Super grade petrol are not available at all petrol stations, so it is advisable to carry a large can of spare fuel with you. Fill the can up after crossing the frontier, because customs duty must be paid on fuel in cans imported into the Soviet Union.

Insurance

Motor insurance is not obligatory in the USSR, so it is highly advisable to arrange comprehensive cover for the duration of your visit. The international Green Card is not valid but most insurance companies issue special certificates. Insurance can also be arranged at the frontier through the Soviet state insurance company, Ingosstrakh.

Accidents

Accidents must be reported to the nearest Intourist office, to the police, and Ingosstrakh, Ulitsa Pyatnitskaya 12, Moscow 113 035 (tel. 00 95/2 33 20 70). The police must also be called to the scene of any accident in which vehicles are seriously damaged or a person is injured.

Breakdown and repair	Apply to Intourist for assistance regarding breakdowns or repairs. In the case of breakdown, although there are emergency telephones on tourist routes they can be as much as 150 km/93 miles apart. Callers will be connected automatically to the police and should ask for Intourist. Any expenses will have to be met by the motorist.
Emergency telephone numbers	Emergency telephone numbers: Police 02; Fire 01; Ambulance 03.
Vehicle documents	See Travel Documents
Frontier crossing points	See Getting There

Travel Documents

Personal documents	All visitors to the Soviet Union must have a valid passport and a Soviet tourist visa. British citizens must have a full 10-year passport, a British Visitor's passport is not accepted. All passports must be valid for three months beyond the date of return from the Soviet Union. Applications for a visa must be made on the official application form, either through a travel agent or directly to Intourist (see Information). The visa itself is free but Intourist makes a small service charge. The application must be accompanied by three identical passport-type photographs and clear photostat copies of the first five pages of the applicant's passport, trimmed to size. The application must be sent to Intourist who require 7–10 days to process it. There will be no stamps or entries made in the passport itself.
Vehicle documents	Visitors driving their own car must have, in addition to passports and visas: travel documents issued by Intourist before departure, specifying the route to be taken, stopovers and overnight accommodation (see Getting to Leningrad); "Instructions for Foreign Motorists", also issued by Intourist before departure; either an International Driving Permit or their national driving licence with a translation in Russian (obtained from Intourist at the frontier crossing point); a valid vehicle registration certificate. Vehicles must display a nationality plate (GB/USA) of internationally approved shape and size.
Pets	Anyone taking a pet (cat or dog) into the USSR requires a veterinary health certificate dated no more than ten days before entry.
Insurance	See Touring by car

When to go

Leningrad is at its most beautiful at the time of "White Nights" in June and July, when the days are longest and darkness lasts for no more than 40 minutes. The arts festival "White Nights" (see Events) which takes place during this period attracts more and more visitors. August and September are also pleasant months, when the "City on the Neva" is unlikely to be found shrouded in fog (see Facts and Figures, Climate). The same is true of April and May, but as the trees are hardly in bloom until May, the beautiful Leningrad parks and the former summer palaces outside the city are still somewhat bleak

In winter when the streets and squares are snow-covered and the rivers and canals frozen, Leningrad has a rather sombre air. Many winter days never become properly light, and leaden fog often hangs over the city's golden domes. A winter visit is really only to be recommended for people who are happy to devote most of their time to the museums, concerts and theatres.

Notes

Plan of the Leningrad Metro
M
Komsomolskaya
Grazhdanskiy Prospekt
Akademicheskay
Politekhnicheskay
Pl. Muzhestva
Lesnaya
Vyborgskaya
Pl. Lenina
Chernyshevskaya
Prospekt Prosveshcheniya
Ozerki
Udelnaya
Pionerskaya
Chornaya Rechna
Petrogradskaya
Gorkovskaya
Primorskaya
Vasileostrovskaya
Nevsky Prospekt
Pl. Vosstaniya
Mayakovskaya
Gostinyy Dvor
Vladimirskaya
Pl. Mira
Ligovskiy Prospekt
Pushkinskaya
Pl. Aleksandra Nevskogo
Tekhnologi cheskiy Institut
Krasnogvardeyskay
Ladozhskaya
Prospekt Bol'shevikov
Baltiyskaya
Narvskaya
Kirovskiy Zavod
Avtovo
Leninskiy Prospekt
Prospekt Veteranov
Frunsenskaya
Moskovskiye Vorota
Elektrosila
Park Pobedy
Moskovskaya
Zvyozdnaya
Kupchino
Yelizarovskaya
Lomonosovskaya
Proletarskaya
Obukhova
Rybatskoye
© Baedeker
under construction or planned